Internet Policies and Issues

snova
New York

Internet Policies and Issues

The First Responder Network (FirstNet): Elements, Issues, Progress
Margaret Saunders (Editor)
2015. ISBN: 978-1-63483-850-4 (Hardcover)
2015. ISBN: 978-1-63483-851-1 (eBook)

Copyright and Creativity in the Digital Economy: Balancing Policy, Protection and Innovation
Matthew Newman (Editor)
Noel Oliver (Editor)
2014. ISBN: 978-1-62948-189-0 (Hardcover)
2014. ISBN: 978-1-62948-190-6 (eBook)

Online Privacy Laws: European Union and Select Foreign Countries
Ethan P. Williams (Editor)
2013. ISBN: 978-1-62808-623-2 (Hardcover)
2013. ISBN: 978-1-62808-624-9 (eBook)

Assessing the Digital Nation: Broadband Adoption, Deployment and Use
Darius L. Shea (Editor)
2013. ISBN: 978-1-62948-362-7 (Hardcover)
2013. ISBN: 978-1-62948-363-4 (eBook)

From Cyber Bullying to Cyber Safety: Issues and Approaches in Educational Contexts
Ria Hanewald (Editor)
2013. ISBN: 978-1-62618-179-3 (Hardcover)
2013. ISBN: 978-1-62618-253-0 (eBook)

More information about this series can be found at
https://novapublishers.com/product-category/series/internet-policies-and-issues/

Suzanne M. Williams
Editor

A Closer Look at Online Deception and Disinformation

snova
New York

Library of Congress Cataloging-in-Publication Data

ISBN: 979-8-88697-310-5

Published by Nova Science Publishers, Inc. † New York

Contents

Preface

In the two-plus decades since the creation of the internet, we have seen life for Americans and their families transformed in many positive ways. The internet provides new opportunities for commerce, education, information, and connecting people.

However, along with these many new opportunities, we have seen new challenges as well. Bad actors are stocking the online marketplace, using deceptive techniques to influence consumers, deceptive designs to fool them into giving away personal information, stealing their money, and engaging in other unfair practices.

Chapter 1

Americans at Risk: Manipulation and Deception in the Digital Age*

Committee on Energy and Commerce

Wednesday, January 8, 2020
House of Representatives,
Subcommittee on Consumer Protection and Commerce,
Committee on Energy and Commerce,
Washington, DC.

The subcommittee met, pursuant to call, at 10:32 a.m., in the John D. Dingell Room 2123, Rayburn House Office Building, Hon. Jan Schakowsky (chairwoman of the subcommittee) presiding.

Members present: Representatives Schakowsky, Castor, Veasey, Kelly, O'Halleran, Luján, Cárdenas, Blunt Rochester, Soto, Matsui, McNerney, Dingell, Pallone (ex officio), Rodgers (subcommittee ranking member), Burgess, Latta, Guthrie, Bucshon, Hudson, Carter, and Walden (ex officio).

Also present: Representative Clarke.

Staff present: Jeffrey C. Carroll, Staff Director; Evan Gilbert, Deputy Press Secretary; Lisa Goldman, Senior Counsel; Waverly Gordon, Deputy Chief Counsel; Tiffany Guarascio, Deputy Staff Director; Alex Hoehn-Saric, Chief Counsel, Communications and Consumer Protection; Zach Kahan, Outreach and Member Service Coordinator; Joe Orlando, Executive Assistant;

* This is an edited, reformatted and augmented version of Hearing before the Subcommittee on Consumer Protection and Commerce, of the Committee on Energy and Commerce, House of Representatives, One Hundred Sixteenth Congress, Second Session, Serial No. 116–86, dated January 8, 2020.

In: A Closer Look at Online Deception and Disinformation
Editor: Suzanne M. Williams
ISBN: 979-8-88697-310-5

Alivia Roberts, Press Assistant; Chloe Rodriguez, Policy Analyst; Sydney Terry, Policy Coordinator; Rebecca Tomilchik, Staff Assistant; Anna Yu Professional Staff Member; Mike Bloomquist, Minority Staff Director; S.K. Bowen, Minority Press Assistant; William Clutterbuck, Minority Staff Assistant; Jordan Davis, Minority Senior Advisor; Tyler Greenberg, Minority Staff Assistant; Peter Kielty, Minority General Counsel; Ryan Long, Minority Deputy Staff Director; Mary Martin, Minority Chief Counsel, Energy, and Environment and Climate Change; Brandon Mooney, Minority Deputy Chief Counsel, Energy; Brannon Rains, Minority Legislative Clerk; Zack Roday, Minority Director of Communications; and Peter Spencer, Minority Senior Professional Staff Member, Environment and Climate Change.

Ms. SCHAKOWSKY. Good morning, everyone. The Subcommittee on Consumer Protection and Commerce will now come to order. We will begin with Member statements, and I will begin by recognizing myself for 5 minutes.

Opening Statement of Hon. Jan Schakowsky, a Representative in Congress from the State of Illinois

Good morning, and thank you for joining us here today. Given what is going on in the world, it is really impressive to see the turnout that is here today, and I welcome everyone.

In the two-plus decades since the creation of the internet, we have seen life for Americans and their families transformed in many positive ways. The internet provides new opportunities for commerce, education, information, and connecting people.

However, along with these many new opportunities, we have seen new challenges as well. Bad actors are stocking the online marketplace, using deceptive techniques to influence consumers, deceptive designs to fool them into giving away personal information, stealing their money, and engaging in other unfair practices.

The Federal Trade Commission works to protect Americans from many unfair and deceptive practices, but a lack of resources, authority, and even a lack of will has left many American consumers feeling helpless in this digital world. Adding to that feeling of helplessness, new technologies are increasing the scope and scale of the problem. Deepfakes, manipulation of video, dark patterns, bots, and other technologies are hurting us in direct and indirect ways.

Congress has, unfortunately, taken a laissez faire approach to regulation of unfair and deceptive practices online over the past decade, and platforms have let them flourish. The result is Big Tech failed to respond to the grave threats posed by deepfakes, as evidenced by Facebook scrambling to announce a new policy that strikes me as wholly inadequate—we will talk about that later— since it would have done nothing to prevent the video of Speaker Pelosi that amassed millions of views and prompted no action by the online platform. Hopefully, our discussion today can change my mind about that.

Underlying all of this is Section 230 of the Communications Decency Act, which provides online platform links like Facebook a legal liability shield for third-party content. Many have argued that this liability shield results in online platforms not adequately policing their platforms, including online piracy and extremist content.

Thus, here we are, with Big Tech wholly unprepared to tackle the challenges we face today. A top-line concern for this subcommittee must be to protect consumers, regardless of whether they are online or not. For too long, Big Tech has argued that e-commerce and digital platforms deserve special treatment and a light regulatory touch.

We are finding out that consumers can be harmed as easily online as in the physical world, and in some cases that online dangers are greater. It is incumbent on us in this subcommittee to make clear that the protections that apply to in-person commerce also apply to virtual space.

[The prepared statement of Ms. Schakowsky follows:]

Prepared Statement of Hon. Jan Schakowsky

Good morning and thank you for joining us here today. In the two plus decades since the creation of the internet, we have seen life for Americans and their families transformed in many positive ways. The internet provides new opportunities for commerce, education, information, and connecting people.

However, along with these many new opportunities, we have seen new challenges. Bad actors are stalking the online marketplace using deceptive techniques to influence consumers, deceptive designs to fool them into giving away personal information, stealing their money, and engaging in other unfair practices.

The Federal Trade Commission works to protect Americans from many unfair and deceptive practices, but a lack of resources, authority, and even a lack of will has left many American consumers feeling helpless in the digital world.

Adding to that feeling of helplessness, new technologies are increasing the scope and scale of the problem. Deepfakes, manipulated video, dark patterns, bots, and other technologies are hurting us in direct and indirect ways.

Congress has unfortunately taken a laissez faire approach to regulating unfair and deceptive practices online over the past decade and platforms have let them flourish.

The result is big tech failed to respond to the grave threat posed by deep-fakes, as evidenced by Facebook scrambling to announce a new policy that strikes me as wholly inadequate, since it would have done nothing to prevent the altered video of Speaker Pelosi that amassed millions of views and prompted no action by the online platform. Hopefully our discussion today can change my mind.

Underlying all of this is Section 230 of the Communications Decency Act, which provided online platforms like Facebook a legal liability shield for 3rd party content. Many have argued that this liability shield resulted in online platforms not adequately policing their platforms, including online piracy and extremist content. Thus, here we are, with Big Tech wholly unprepared to tackle the challenges we face today.

A topline concern for this subcommittee must be to protect consumers regardless of whether they are online or not. For too long, Big Tech has argued that e-commerce and digital platforms deserved special treatment and a light regulatory touch. We are finding out that consumers can be harmed as easily online as in the physical world. And in some cases, the online dangers are greater. It's incumbent on this subcommittee to make clear that protections that apply to in-person commerce also apply in the virtual space. I thank the witnesses for their testimony, and I recognize Ranking Member Rodgers for 5 minutes.

* * *

Ms. SCHAKOWSKY. I thank the witnesses for their testimony today, and I recognize Ranking Member Rodgers for 5 minutes.

Opening Statement of Hon. Cathy Mcmorris Rodgers, a Representative in Congress from the State of Washington

Mrs. RODGERS. Thank you. Thank you, Chair Schakowsky. Happy New Year, everyone. Welcome to our witnesses. I appreciate the chair leading this effort today to highlight online deception.

I do want to note that last Congress, Chairman Walden also held several hearings on platform responsibility. Disinformation is not a new problem. It was also an issue 130 years ago when Joseph Pulitzer and the New York World and William Randolph Hearst and The New York Journal led the age of, quote, "yellow journalism." Just like clickbait on online platforms today, fake and sensational headlines sold newspapers and boosted advertising revenue. With far more limited sources of information available in the 1890s, the American people lost trust in the media. To rebuild trust, newspapers had to clean up their act. Now the Pulitzer is associated with something very different.

I believe we are at a similar inflection point today. We are losing faith in sources we can trust online. To rebuild it, this subcommittee, our witness panel and members of the media are putting the spotlight on abuses and deception.

Our committee's past leadership and constructive debates have already led to efforts by platforms to take action. Just this week, Facebook announced a new policy to combat deepfakes, in part, by utilizing artificial intelligence. I appreciate Ms. Bickert for being here to discuss this in greater detail. Deepfakes and disinformation can be handled with innovation and empowering people with more information.

On the platforms they choose and trust, it makes far more productive outcomes when people can make the best decisions for themselves, rather than relying on the government to make decisions for them. That is why we should be focusing on innovation for major breakthroughs, not more regulations or government mandates.

As we discuss ways to combat manipulation online, we must ensure that America will remain the global leader in AI development. There is no better place in the world to raise people's standard of living and make sure that this technology is used responsibly.

Software is already available to face swap, lip sync, and create facial reenactment to fabricate content. As frightening as it is, we can also be using AI to go after the bad actors and fight fire with fire. We cannot afford to shy away from it, because who would you rather lead the world in machine learning technology: America or China? China is sharing its AI surveillance technology with other authoritarian governments, like Venezuela. It is also using its technology to control and suppress ethnic minorities, including the Uighurs in Chinese concentration camps.

The New York Times has reported just last month that China is collecting DNA samples and could be using this data to create images of faces. Could China be building a tool to further track and crack down on minorities and political dissidents? Imagine the propaganda and lies it could develop with this technology behind the Great Chinese Firewall, where there is no free speech or an independent press to hold the Communist Party accountable.

That is why America must lead the world in AI development. By upholding our American values, we can use this as a force for good and save people's lives. For example, AI technology and deep learning algorithms can help us detect cancers earlier and more quickly. Clinical trials are already underway and making major breakthroughs to diagnose cancers.

The continued leadership of our innovators is crucial to make sure that we have the tools to combat online deception. To win the future in a global economy, America should be writing the rules for this technology so that real people, not an authoritarian state like China, are empowered.

I am also glad that we are putting a spotlight on dark patterns. Deceptive laws, fake reviews, and bots are the latest version of robocall scams. I am pleased that the FTC has used its Section 5 authority to target this fraud and protect people. We should get their input as to how we discuss how to handle dark patterns.

We also must be careful where we legislate so that we don't harm the practices that people enjoy. A heavy-handed regulation will make it impossible for online retailers to provide discounts. This would especially hurt lower- and middle-income families. In a digital marketplace, services people enjoy should not get swallowed up by strict definition of a dark pattern. How we make these distinctions is important, so I look forward to today's discussion.

I want to thank the panel, and I yield back.

[The prepared statement of Mrs. Rodgers follows:]

Prepared Statement of Hon. Cathy McMorris Rodgers

Thank you, Chair Schakowsky and welcome to our witnesses. I appreciate your work to highlight online deception.

Last Congress, Chairman Walden led several hearings on platform responsibility, before it became the popular cause it is today.

Disinformation is not a new problem.

It was also an issue 130 years ago when Joseph Pulitzer and the New York World and William Randolph Hearst and the New York Journal led the age of quote "yellow journalism."

Just like "clickbait" on online platforms today, fake and sensational headlines sold newspapers and boosted advertising revenue.

With far more limited sources of information available in the 1890s, the American public lost trust in the media.

To rebuild trust, newspapers had to clean up their act.

Now the name Pulitzer is associated with something very different. I believe we are at a similar inflection point today.

We are losing faith in sources we can trust online.

To rebuild it.this subcommittee, our witness panel, and members of the media are putting the spotlight on abuses and deception.

Our committee's past leadership and constructive debates have already led to efforts by platforms to take action.

Just this week Facebook announced a new policy to combat deepfakes, in part by utilizing artificial intelligence.

I appreciate Ms. Bickert for coming here to discuss this in greater detail. "Deepfakes" and disinformation can be handled with innovation and empowering people with MORE information.

On the platforms they choose and trust, it's a far more productive outcome when people can make the best decisions for themselves rather than relying on the government to make decisions for them.

That's why we should be focusing on innovation for major breakthroughs. Not more regulations or government mandates.

As we discuss ways to combat manipulation online, we must ensure America will remain the global leader in AI development.

There's no better place in the world to raise people's standard of living and make sure this technology is used responsibly.

Software is already available to face swap, lip sync, and create facial reenactment to fabricate content.

As frightening as this is, we can also be using AI to go after bad actors and fight fire with fire.

We cannot afford to shy away from it because who would you rather lead the world in machine learning technology?

America or China?

China is sharing its AI-surveillance technology with other authoritarian governments like in Venezuela.

It's also using this technology to control and suppress ethnic minorities, including the Uighurs in Chinese concentration camps.

The New York Times reported just last month that China is collecting DNA samples of Uighurs and could be using this data to create images of their faces.

Could China be building a tool to further track and crack down on minorities and political dissidents?

Imagine the propaganda and lies they could develop with this technology behind the Great Chinese Firewall, where there's no free speech or an independent press to hold the Communist Party accountable.

This is why America must lead the world in AI development.

By upholding our American values, we can use this as a force for good and save people's lives.

For example, AI technology and deep-learning algorithms can help us detect cancers earlier and more quickly.

Clinical trials are already making major breakthroughs to diagnose cancers.

The continued leadership of our innovators is crucial to make sure we have tools to combat online deception too.

I applaud the Trump administration for their forward-thinking leadership in setting a light-touch framework for encouraging continued, responsible American innovation in AI.

To win the future in a global economy, America should be writing the rules for this technology so real people—not an authoritarian state like China—are empowered.

I'm also glad we're putting a spotlight on "dark patterns."

Deceptive ads, fake reviews, and bots are the latest version of robocall scams.

I'm pleased that the FTC has used its Section 5 authority to target this fraud and protect people.

We should get their input as we discuss how to handle dark patterns.

We must be careful where we legislate so we don't harm practices that people enjoy.

A heavy-handed regulation will make it impossible for online retailers to provide discounts.

This would especially hurt lower- and middle-income families.

In the digital marketplace, services people enjoy should not get swallowed up by a strict definition of a "dark pattern."

How we make these distinctions is important.

I'm looking forward to today's discussion. Thank you again to our panel. Thank you, and I yield back.

* * *

Ms. SCHAKOWSKY. The gentlelady yields back.

And the Chair now recognizes Mr. Pallone, chair of the full committee, for 5 minutes for his opening statement.

Opening Statement of Hon. Frank Pallone, Jr., a Representative in Congress from the State of New Jersey

Mr. PALLONE. Thank you, Madam Chair.

Americans increasingly rely on the internet for fundamental aspects of their daily lives. Consumers shop online for products ranging from groceries to refrigerators. They use the internet to telecommute or to check the weather and traffic before leaving for the office, and they use social media networks to connect with family and friends, and as a major source of news and information.

When consumers go online, they understandably assume that the reviews of the products that they buy are real, that the people on the social networks are human, and that the news and information they are reading is accurate. But, unfortunately, that is not always the case. Online actors, including nation-states, companies, and individual fraudsters, are using online tools to manipulate and deceive Americans. While some methods of deception are well-known, many are new and sophisticated, fooling even the most savvy consumers.

Today, technology has made it difficult, if not impossible, for typical consumers to recognize what is real from what is fake. And why exactly are people putting so much effort into the development and misuse of technology? Because they know that trust is the key to influencing and taking advantage of people, whether for social, monetary, or political gain. If bad actors can make people believe a lie, then they can manipulate us into taking actions we wouldn't otherwise take.

In some instances, we can no longer even trust our eyes. Videos can be slowed to make someone appear intoxicated. Faces can be Photoshopped onto someone else's body. Audio can be edited in a way that a person's words are basically taken out of context. And the extent of such manipulation has become extreme. Machinelearning algorithms can now create completely fake videos, known as deepfakes, that look real. Deepfakes can show real people saying or doing things that they never said or did.

For example, face-swapping technology has been used to place actor Nicolas Cage into movies where he never was. Actor/director Jordan Peele created a deepfake supposedly showing President Obama insulting President Trump.

The most common use of deepfakes is nonconsensual pornography, which has been used to make it appear as if celebrities have been videotaped in compromising positions. And deepfake technology was also used to humiliate a journalist from India who was reporting on an 8-year-old rape victim.

Advances in algorithms are also behind the glut of social media bots, automated systems that interact on social media as if they were real people. These bots are used by companies and other entities to build popularity of brands and respond to consumer service requests. Even more alarming is the use of these bots by both state and nonstate actors to spread disinformation, which can influence the very fabric of our society and our politics.

And manipulation can be very subtle. Deceptive designs, sometimes called dark patterns, capitalize on knowledge of our senses, operate to trick us into making choices that benefit the business. Have you ever tried to unsubscribe from a mailing list and there is a button to stay subscribed that is bigger and more colorful than the unsubscribe button? And that is deceptive design. Banner ads have been designed with black spots that look like dirt or hair on the screen to trick you into tapping the "add" on your smartphone. And there are so many other examples.

And since these techniques are designed to go unnoticed, most consumers have no idea they are happening. In fact, they are almost impossible for experts in types of techniques to detect. And, while computer scientists are working on technology that can help detect each of these deceptive techniques, we are in a technological arms race. As detection technology improves, so does the deceptive technology. Regulators and platforms trying to combat deception are left playing Whac-a-mole.

Unrelenting advances in these technologies and their abuse raise significant questions for all of us. What is the prevalence of these deceptive techniques? How are these techniques actually affecting our actions and decisions? What steps are companies and regulators taking to mitigate consumer fraud and misinformation?

So I look forward to beginning to answer these questions with our expert witness panel today so we can start to provide more transparency and tools for consumers to fight misinformation and deceptive practices.

And, Madam Chair, I just want to say I think this is a very important hearing. I was just telling my colleague, Kathy Castor, this morning about a discussion that we had at our chairs meeting this morning, where the topic was brought up. And I said, "Oh, you know, we are having a hearing on this today." So this is something a lot of Members and, obviously, the public care about. So thank you for having the hearing today.

I yield back.

[The prepared statement of Mr. Pallone follows:]

Prepared Statement of Hon. Frank Pallone, Jr.

Americans increasingly rely on the internet for fundamental aspects of their daily lives. Consumers shop online for products ranging from groceries to refrigerators. They use the internet to telecommute or to check the weather and traffic before leaving for the office. And they use social media networks to connect with family and friends and as a major source of news and information.

When consumers go online they understandably assume that the reviews of the products they buy are real, that the people on their social networks are human, and that the news and information they are reading is accurate. Unfortunately, that is not always the case.

Online actors, including nation-states, companies, and individual fraudsters, are using online tools to manipulate and deceive Americans. While some methods of deception are well known, many are new and sophisticated, fooling even the most savvy consumers. Today, technology has made it difficult, if not impossible, for typical consumers to recognize what's real from what's fake.

And why exactly are people putting so much effort into the development and misuse of this technology? Because they know that trust is the key to influencing and taking advantage of people. Whether for social, monetary, or political gain, if bad actors can make people believe a lie, they can manipulate us into taking actions we wouldn't otherwise take.

In some instances, we can no longer even trust our eyes. Videos can be slowed to make someone appear intoxicated. Faces can be Photoshopped onto someone else's body. Audio can be edited in a way that takes a person's words out of context.

The extent of such manipulation has become extreme. Machine learning algorithms can now create completely fake videos, known as deepfakes, that look real. Deepfakes can show real people saying or doing things they never said or did.

For example, face-swapping technology has been used to place actor Nicolas Cage into movies he was never in. Actor-director Jordan Peele created a deepfake supposedly showing President Obama insulting President Trump. The most common use of deepfakes is nonconsensual pornography, which has been used to make it appear as if celebrities have been videotaped in compromising positions. Deepfake technology was also used to humiliate a journalist from India who was reporting on an 8-year-old rape victim.

Advances in algorithms are also behind the glut of social media bots, automated systems that interact on social media as if they were real people. These bots are used by companies and other entities to build popularity of brands and respond to customer service requests. Even more alarming is the use of these bots by both state and nonstate actors to spread disinformation, which can influence the very fabric of our societies and our politics.

And manipulation can be very subtle. Deceptive design, sometimes called "dark patterns," capitalize on knowledge of how our senses operate to trick us into making choices that benefit the business. Have you ever tried to unsubscribe from a mailing list and there's a button to stay subscribed that's bigger and more colorful than the unsubscribe button? That's deceptive design. Banner ads have been designed with black spots that look like dirt or a hair on the screen to trick you into tapping the ad on your smartphone. And there are many more examples.

Since these techniques are designed to go unnoticed, most consumers have no idea they are happening. In fact, they are almost impossible for experts in types of techniques to detect.

While computer scientists are working on technology that can help detect each of these deceptive techniques, we are in a technological arms race. As detection technology improves, so does the deceptive technology. Regulators and platforms trying to combat deception are left playing Whac-a-Mole.

Unrelenting advances in these technologies and their abuse raise significant questions for all of us. What is the prevalence of these deceptive techniques? How are these techniques actually affecting our actions and decisions? What steps are companies and regulators taking to mitigate consumer fraud and misinformation?

I look forward to beginning to answer these questions with our expert witness panel today so that we can start to provide more transparency and tools for consumers to fight misinformation and deceptive practices.

* * *

Ms. SCHAKOWSKY. The gentleman yields back.

And now the Chair recognizes Mr. Walden, the ranking member of the full committee, for 5 minutes for his opening statement.

Opening Statement of Hon. Greg Walden, a Representative in Congress from the State of Oregon

Mr. WALDEN. Good morning, Madam Chair. Thanks for having this hearing and welcome everyone in. I guess this is the second hearing of the new year. There is one that started earlier upstairs, but we welcome you all to hear this important topic and glad to hear from our witnesses today, even those who I am told have health issues this morning, but thanks for being here.

As with anything, the internet presents bad actors with those seeking to harm others some ample opportunities to manipulate the users and take advantage of consumers, which often tend to be some of the most vulnerable in the population. Arguably, the digital ecosystem is such that harmful acts are easily exacerbated, and as we all know, false information or fake videos spread at breakneck speeds.

That is why, when I was chairman of this committee, we tried to tackle this whole issue with platform responsibility head on, and we appreciate the input we got from many. Last Congress, we, as you heard, held hearings and legislated on online platforms not fulfilling their Good Samaritan obligations, especially when it comes to online human trafficking.

Companies' use of algorithms and the impact such algorithms have on influencing consumer behavior, we took a look at that. Improving/expanding the reach of broadband services so rural and urban consumers of all ages can benefit in a connected world from the positive aspects of the internet. Explaining the online advertising ecosystem, preservation and promotion across border data flows, a topic we need to continue to work on. Other related issues we face in the connected world, such as cybersecurity, Internet of Things, artificial intelligence, to name just a few.

We also invited the heads of the tech industry to come and explain their practices right in this hearing room. Two of the committee's highest-profile hearings in recent memory focused squarely on platform responsibility. The CEO of Facebook, Mark Zuckerberg, came and spent about 51⁄2 hours right at that table to answer some pretty tough questions on the Cambridge Analytica debacle as well as provide the committee with more insight into how Facebook collects consumer information and what Facebook does with that information.

We also welcomed the CEO of Twitter, Jack Dorsey, to provide the committee with more insight into how Twitter operates, decisions Twitter makes on its platform, and how such decisions impact consumers specifically, so voices don't feel silenced.

I am pleased that Chairman Pallone brought in the CEO of Reddit last year, and hope the trend will continue as we understand this ever-evolving and critically important ecosystem from those that sit on the top of it.

This hearing today helps with that, as this group of experts shine a light on questionable practices I hope can yield further fruitful results. Such efforts often lead to swifter actions than any government action can get done.

Following our series of hearings, there is proof that some companies are cleaning up their platforms, and we appreciate the work you are doing. For example, following our hearing on Cambridge Analytica, Facebook made significant changes to its privacy policies and Facebook reformatted its privacy settings, to make more accessible and user-friendly, ease the ability for its users to delete and control their information, took down malicious entities on its platform, and invested in programs to preserve and promote legitimate local news operations.

And during that hearing, Representative McKinley actually pushed Mr. Zuckerberg pretty hard on some specific ads he had seen illegally selling opioids without prescriptions on Facebook, and as a result, Facebook removed those ads. In fact, we got a call, I think as Mr. Zuckerberg was headed to the airport that afternoon, that those had already been taken down.

Also notable, through the Global Internet Forum to Counter Terrorism, platforms such as Facebook, Twitter, and YouTube have been working together to tackle terrorist content and, importantly, disrupt violent extremists' ability to promote themselves, share propaganda, and exploit digital platforms. And we thank you for that work.

Now, this is not to suggest the online ecosystem is perfect. It is far from it. Can these companies be doing more to clean up their platforms? Of course, and I expect them to, and I think you are all working on that.

So let me be very clear. This hearing should serve as an important reminder to all online platforms that we are watching them closely. We want to ensure we do not harm innovation, but, as we have demonstrated in a bipartisan fashion in the past, when we see issues or identify clear harms to consumers and we do not see online entities taking appropriate action, we are prepared to act.

So, Madam Chair, thanks for having this hearing. This is tough stuff. I have a degree in journalism. I am a big advocate of the First Amendment. And it can be messy business to, on the one hand, call on them to take down things we don't like and still stay on the right side of the First Amendment, because vigorous speech, even when it is inaccurate, is still protected under the First Amendment. And if you go too far, then we yell at you for taking things down that we liked. And if you don't take down things we don't like, then we yell at you for that. So you are kind of in a bit of a box, and yet we know 230 is an issue we need to revise and take a look at as well.

And then speaking of revise, I had to chuckle that we all get the opportunity to revise and extend our remarks throughout this process and clean up our bad grammar. So maybe some of what we have is kind of fake reporting, but anyway, we will leave that for another discussion on another day.

And, with that, I yield back, Madam Chair.

[The prepared statement of Mr. Walden follows:]

Prepared Statement of Hon. Greg Walden

Good morning, and welcome to our witnesses. I want to first thank Chair Schakowsky for organizing today's incredibly insightful hearing—which is focused on deception online.

For many years, the internet has been a force for good. It provides consumers with unbelievable access to unlimited information, goods and services, and people— no matter where they are in the world.

But, as with anything, the internet presents bad actors and those seeking to harm others ample opportunities to manipulate users and take advantage of consumers, which often tend to be some of our most vulnerable populations. Arguably, the digital ecosystem is such that harmful acts are easily exacerbated and, as we all know, false information or fake videos spread at breakneck speeds. That is why when I was chairman of this committee, we tackled platform responsibility head-on.

Last Congress, we held hearings and legislated on:

- Online platforms not fulfilling their "Good Samaritan" obligations, especially when it comes to online human sex trafficking.
- Companies' use of algorithms and the impact such algorithms have on influencing consumer behavior;
- Improving and expanding the reach of broadband services so rural and urban, consumers of all ages, can benefit in a connected world;
- Explaining the online advertising ecosystem;
- Preservation and promotion of cross-border data flows; and
- Other related issues we face in the connected world such as cybersecurity, Internet of Things, artificial intelligence, to name just a few.

We also invited the heads of tech industry to come explain their practices in this hearing room. Two of the committee's highest profile hearings in recent memory were focused squarely on platform responsibility.

I brought in the CEO of Facebook, Mark Zuckerberg, to answer tough questions on the Cambridge Analytica debacle, as well as provide the committee with more insight into how Facebook collects consumer information, and what Facebook does with that information.

I also welcomed the CEO of Twitter, Jack Dorsey, to provide the committee with more insight into how Twitter operates, decisions Twitter makes on its platform, and how such decisions impact consumers, specifically so voices don't feel silenced.

I am pleased that Chairman Pallone brought in the CEO of Reddit last year and hope the trend will continue as we understand this ever-evolving ecosystem from those that sit on top of it. This hearing today helps with that as this group of experts shine a light on questionable practices that I hope can yield further fruitful results. Such efforts often lead to swifter action than any government action can.

Following our series of hearings, there is proof that some companies are cleaning up their platforms. For example, following our hearing on the Cambridge Analytica scandal, Facebook made significant changes to its privacy policies. Facebook reformatted its privacy settings to make it more accessible and user friendly; eased the ability for its users to control and delete their information; took down malicious entities on its platform; and, invested in programs to preserve and promote legitimate local news operations. And during that hearing Rep. McKinley pushed Mr. Zuckerberg on specific ads he'd seen illegally selling opioids without prescription on Facebook. As a result, Facebook removed the ads.

Also notable—through the Global Internet Forum to Counter Terrorism—platforms such as Facebook, Twitter, and YouTube have been working together to tackle terrorist content and, importantly, disrupt violent extremists' ability to promote themselves, share propaganda, and exploit digital platforms.

Now this is not to suggest the online ecosystem is perfect—it is far from it. Can these companies be doing more to clean up their platforms? Of course, they can, and I expect them to.

So, let me be very clear: This hearing should serve as an important reminder to all online platforms that we are watching them closely. We want to ensure we do not harm innovation, but as we have demonstrated in a bipartisan fashion in the past, when we see issues or identify clear harms to consumers and we do not see online entities taking appropriate action, we are prepared to act.

Thank you. I yield back.

* * *

Ms. SCHAKOWSKY. The gentleman yields back.

And the Chair would like to remind Members that, pursuant to committee rules, all Members' opening statements shall be made part of the record.

I would now like to introduce our witnesses for today's hearing.

Ms. Monika Bickert, vice president of Global Policy Management at Facebook. I want to acknowledge and thank you, Ms. Bickert. I know that you are not feeling well today and may want to abbreviate some of your testimony, but we thank you very much for coming anyway.

I want to introduce Dr. Joan Donovan, research director of the Technology and Social Change Project at the Shorenstein Center on Media, Politics and Public Policy at Harvard Kennedy School.

Mr. Justin Hurwitz, assistant professor of law and director of NU Governance and Technology Center at the University of Nebraska College of Law, and director of law and economics programs at the International Center for Law and Economics.

And finally, Dr. Tristan Harris, who is executive director for the Center for Humane Technology.

We want to thank our witnesses for joining us today. We look forward to your testimony.

At this time, the Chair will recognize each witness for 5 minutes to provide their opening statement. Before we begin, I would just like to explain the lighting system for those who may not know it. In front of you are a series of lights. The lights will initially be green at the start of your opening statement. The light will turn to yellow when you have 1 minute remaining, and if you could please begin to wrap up your testimony at that point, and then the light will turn red when your time has expired.

So, Ms. Bickert, you are recognized for 5 minutes.

Statement of Monika Bickert, Vice President of Global Policy Management, Facebook

Ms. BICKERT. Thank you, Chairwoman Schakowsky, Ranking Member McMorris Rodgers, and other distinguished members of the subcommittee. Thank you for the opportunity to appear before you today.

My name is Monika Bickert. I am the vice president for Global Policy Management at Facebook, and I am responsible for our content policies. As the chairwoman pointed out, I am a little under the weather today so, with apologies, I am going to keep my remarks short, but will rely on the written testimony I have submitted.

We know that we have an important role to play at Facebook in addressing manipulation and deception on our platform. And we have many aspects to our approach, including our community standards, which specify what we will remove from the site, and our relationship with third-party fact checkers, through which fact-checking organizations can rate content as false. We put a label over that content saying that this is false information, and we reduce its distribution.

Under the community standards, there are some types of misinformation that we remove, such as attempts to suppress the vote or to interfere with the Census. And we announced yesterday a new prong in our policy where we will also remove videos that are edited or synthesized, using artificial intelligence, or deep learning techniques, in ways that are not apparent to the average person that would mislead the average person to believe that the subject of the video said something that he or she did not, in fact, say.

To be clear, manipulated media that doesn't fall under this new policy definition is still subject to our other policies and our third-party fact checking. That means that deepfakes are still an emerging technology. One area where internet experts have seen them is in nudity and pornography. All of that violates our policies against nudity and pornography, and we would remove it. Manipulated videos are also eligible to be fact-checked by these third-party fact-checking organizations that we work with to label and reduce the distribution of misinformation.

We are always improving our policies and our enforcement, and we will continue to do the engagement we have done outside the company with academics and experts to understand the new ways that these technologies are emerging and affecting our community. We would also welcome the opportunity to collaborate with other industry partners and interested stakeholders, including academics, civil society, and lawmakers, to help develop a consistent industry approach to these issues. Our hope is that by working together with all of these stakeholders, we can make faster progress in ways that benefit all of society.

Thank you, and I look forward to your questions.

[The prepared statement of Ms. Bickert follows:]

Prepared Statement of Monika Bickert

Introduction

Chairwoman Schakowsky, Ranking Member McMorris Rodgers, and distinguished members of the Subcommittee, thank you for the opportunity to appear before you today. My name is Monika Bickert, and I am the Vice President of Global Policy Management at Facebook. In that role, I lead our efforts related to content policy and counterterrorism. Prior to assuming my current role, I served as lead security counsel for Facebook, working on issues ranging from children's safety to cybersecurity. And before that, I was a criminal prosecutor with the Department of Justice for 11 years in Chicago and Washington, DC, where I prosecuted federal crimes, including public corruption and gang violence.

Facebook is a community of more than two billion people, spanning countries, cultures, and languages across the globe. Every day, members of our community express themselves on our platform in diverse ways, having conversations and posting content from text and links to photos and videos. We are proud of the wide array of expression on Facebook, but we also recognize the important role we play in addressing manipulation and deception on our platform.

Combating Manipulation and Deception

Community Standards

We publish Community Standards governing the types of content and behaviors that are acceptable on Facebook. For example, we prohibit hate speech, harassment, content posted by fake accounts, and—under a new policy—misleading manipulated media, including certain types of deepfakes. When we become aware of content that violates our Community Standards, through either proactive technical measures or reports, we remove it.

Some types of misinformation—such as attempts to interfere with or suppress voting or participation in the census—violate our Community Standards, and we work proactively to remove this type of harmful content. We are mindful of our responsibility to respect freedom of expression, but our Community Standards are clear that we remove content when it has the potential to contribute to offline physical harm.

We recognize the risks of manipulated media. Manipulated media can be made with simple technology like Photoshop, or with sophisticated tools that use artificial intelligence or "deep learning" techniques to create videos that distort reality—usually called "deepfakes." While these videos are still relatively rare on the internet, they present a significant challenge for our industry and society as their use increases, and we have been engaging broadly with internal and external stakeholders to better understand and address this issue. Based on these conversations, we have been considering a number of options regarding misleading manipulated media, including deepfakes. That is why we just announced a new policy that we will remove certain types of misleading manipulated media from our platform. In particular, under this policy, which is part of our Community Standards, we will remove videos that have been edited or synthesized using artificial intelligence or deep learning techniques in ways that are not apparent to an average person and that would mislead an average person to believe that a subject of the video said words that they did not say. The policy is designed to prohibit the most sophisticated attempts to mislead people.

To be clear, forms of misleading manipulated media that do not meet these criteria—such as videos that have been edited solely by splicing to omit or change the order of words, or parodies or satires—are still subject to our other Community Standards and are eligible for fact-checking. For example, a synthesized video of a celebrity in which the celebrity is nude would violate our nudity policies. Manipulated media may also be spread in a coordinated manner by fake accounts, which would violate our policies against inauthentic behavior; in such cases, the content posted by such accounts would also be removed.

Misinformation

We recognize that some types of misleading information lack quality and integrity, despite not directly violating our Community Standards. Our approach to such misinformation has several components, including working with independent, third-party fact-checkers to help reduce the spread of false news and other types of viral misinformation; investigating AI-generated content and deceptive behaviors like fake accounts; partnering with academia, government, and industry on tackling broad issues; and exposing the bad actors behind these efforts.

People share millions of photos and videos on Facebook every day. We know that this kind of sharing is particularly compelling because it is visual. That said, it also creates an opportunity for manipulation by bad actors. Manipulated photos and videos can be fact-checked by one of our independent, third-party fact-checking partners, who are certified through the non-partisan International Fact-Checking Network. We now have over 50 partners around the world fact-checking content in over 40 languages, and we are investing in ways to scale these efforts further. Fact-checkers use their own expertise to determine which stories to review; many of our third-party fact-checking partners focus on misinformation in images and videos. This includes identifying when an image or video is being presented out of context using tools such as reverse image search or utilizing video editing programs to identify when manipulation has occurred. Fact-checking partners are able to assess the truth or falsity of a photo or video by combining these skills with original reporting, including outreach to technical experts, academics, or government agencies.

Once a fact-checker rates a photo or video as false or partly false, we reduce its distribution in News Feed and reject it if it's being run as an ad. We also implement an overlaid warning screen on top of photos and videos marked as false. If people try to share the content, they will be notified of the additional reporting. They will also be notified if content they have shared in the past has since been rated false by a fact-checker.

Moreover, in order to more effectively fight false news, we also take action against Pages and domains that repeatedly share or publish content which is rated as false. Such Pages and domains will see their distribution reduced as the number of offenses increases. Their ability to monetize and advertise will be removed after repeated offenses. Over time, Pages and domains can restore their distribution and ability to monetize and advertise if they stop sharing false news.

We also use machine learning to assist in our fight against misinformation. Algorithms cannot fundamentally tell what content is true or false, but they do help in the process. For example, our machine learning models use various signals to identify content which might be false or partly false. Comments expressing disbelief are one signal that helps inform our prediction, as well as feedback from our community when people mark something as false news. And we use model predictions to prioritize the content we show third-party fact-checkers. Since there are hundreds of millions of pieces of content per week shared on Facebook, we prioritize third-party fact-checkers' time. In addition to helping us predict content for fact-checkers to review, machine learning helps us identify duplicates of debunked stories. In turn, fact-checker ratings help further train our machine learning model, so it's a cyclical process.

We are always improving our policies and enforcement practices, and we will continue to closely monitor this issue and to consult with external stakeholders to ensure we're taking the right approach. Across the world, we've been driving conversations with more than 50 global experts with technical, policy, media, legal, civic, and academic backgrounds to inform our policy development. As these partnerships and our own insights evolve, so too will our policies toward manipulated media. In the meantime, we're committed to investing within Facebook and to working with other stakeholders in this area to find solutions with real impact.

Coordinated Inauthentic Behavior

The idea behind Facebook is to help bring communities together in an authentic way. We believe that people are more accountable for their statements and actions when they use their authentic identities. Fake accounts are often behind harmful and misleading content, and we work hard to keep them off Facebook. We took down over 5 billion fake accounts in the first three quarters of 2019, and our technology stopped millions of additional attempts every day to establish fake accounts before they were created. When we take down these accounts, it's because of their deceptive behavior (like using networks of fake accounts to conceal their identity); it's not based on the actors behind them or what they say.

Our efforts to prevent coordinated inauthentic behavior focus on four areas. First, our expert investigators use their experience and skills in areas like cybersecurity research, law enforcement, and investigative reporting to find and take down the most sophisticated threats. Second, we build technology to detect and automatically remove the most common threats. Third, we provide transparency and reporting tools so users can make informed choices when they encounter borderline content or content that we miss. We publicize our takedowns of coordinated inauthentic behavior for all to see, and we also provide information about them to third parties for their review and share relevant data with researchers, academics, and others. Fourth, we work closely with civil society, researchers, governments, and industry partners, so they can flag issues and we can work to resolve them quickly. Engaging with these partners regularly helps us improve the efficacy of our techniques and learn from their experiences.

Using this combination of tools, we continually adapt our platforms to make deceptive behaviors much more difficult and costly. When we conduct a takedown, we identify the tactics the bad actors used, and we build tools into our platforms to make those tactics more difficult at scale. By continuing to develop smarter technologies, enhance our defenses, improve transparency, and build strong partnerships, we are making the constant improvements we need to stay ahead of our adversaries and to protect the integrity of our platforms.

Partnering to Improve Deepfake Detection

Deepfake techniques have significant implications for determining the legitimacy of information presented online. Yet researchers in academia, government, and industry still lack strong data sets to analyze and benchmark this challenge. We want to encourage additional research and development in this area and ensure there are better open-source tools to detect deepfakes. That's why Facebook has partnered with a cross-sector coalition of organizations including the Partnership on AI, Cornell Tech, the University of California Berkeley, MIT, WITNESS, Microsoft, the BBC, and AWS, among several others in civil society and the technology, media, and academic communities to build the Deepfake Detection Challenge.

The goal of the Challenge is to produce technology that everyone can use to better detect when AI has been used to alter a video in order to mislead the viewer. The Deepfake Detection Challenge includes a data set and leaderboard, as well as grants and awards, to spur the industry to create new ways of detecting and preventing media manipulated via AI from being used to mislead others. The governance of the Challenge will be facilitated and overseen by the Partnership on AI's new Steering Committee on AI and Media Integrity, which is comprised of members including Facebook and others in civil society and the technology, media, and academic communities.

It's important to have data that is freely available for the community to use. That is why we constructed a new training data set specifically for this Challenge, working with a third-party vendor to engage a diverse set of individuals who agreed to participate in creating the data set for the Challenge. We are also funding research collaborations and prizes for the Challenge to help encourage more participation. In total, we are dedicating significant resources to fund this industry-wide effort.

We also recently launched an e-learning course as a partnership between the Facebook Journalism Project and Reuters Institute. The course, titled "Identifying and Tackling Manipulated Media," aims to help newsrooms around the world equip themselves to identify manipulated media. It includes real-world examples, hypothetical cases, and insights into the evolving technology used to create and detect manipulated media, including deepfakes. It teaches journalists about the various types of altered media and the ways in which newsrooms can confidently verify and publish truthful content from third-party sources.

Manipulated media presents a constantly evolving challenge, and our hope is that by helping the industry and the AI community come together, we can make faster progress in a way that benefits the whole of society.

Conclusion

We recognize that both the issues and challenges in addressing manipulated media are rapidly evolving. Experts have called on the industry to come together to develop a consistent approach across platforms. As they have pointed out, consistent enforcement across platforms is important to protect consumers from such content migrating from platform to platform. We agree.

As our CEO Mark Zuckerberg has said, we need to develop consistent industry standards on issues such as manipulated media. We have encouraged the industry through our trade association to work together—specifically on manipulated media—in a more uniform way, pushing for common standards and a consistent approach across platforms. We welcome the opportunity to collaborate and partner with other industry participants and interested stakeholders, including academics, civil society, and lawmakers to help develop such an approach.

Leading up to the 2020 US election cycle, we know that combating misinformation, including deepfakes, is one of the most important things we can do. We will continue to look at how we can improve our approach and the systems we've built, including through continued engagement with academics, technical experts, and policymakers.

Thank you, and I look forward to your questions.

Ms. SCHAKOWSKY. Thank you.

And now, Dr. Donovan, you are recognized for 5 minutes.

Statement of Joan Donovan, Ph.D., Director, Technology and Social Change Project, Shorenstein Center on Media, Politics and Public Policy, Harvard Kennedy School

Dr. DONOVAN. Thank you, Chairwoman Schakowsky, Ranking Member McMorris Rodgers, Chairman Pallone, and Ranking Member Walden, for having me today. It is truly an honor to be invited.

I lead a team at Harvard Kennedy's Shorenstein Center that researches online manipulation and deception, and I have been a researcher of the internet for the last decade. So I know quite a bit about changes in policies as well as the development of platforms themselves and what they were intended to do.

One of the things that I want to discuss today is online fraud, which is a great deal more widespread than many understand. Beyond malware, spam, and phishing attacks, beyond credit card scams and product knock-offs, there is a growing threat from new forms of identity fraud enabled by technological design. Platform companies are unable to manage this alone, and Americans need governance. Deception is now a multimillion-dollar industry.

My research team tracks dangerous individuals and groups who use social media to pose as political campaigns, social movements, news organizations, charities, brands and even average people. This emerging economy of misinformation is a threat to national security. Silicon Valley corporations are largely profiting from it, while key political and social institutions are struggling to win back the public's trust.

Platforms have done more than just given users a voice online. They have effectively given them the equivalent of their own broadcast station, emboldening the most malicious among us. To wreak havoc with a media manipulation campaign, all one bad actor needs is motivation. Money also helps. But that is enough to create chaos and divert significant resources from civil society, politicians, newsrooms, healthcare providers, and even law enforcement, who are tasked with repairing the damage. We currently do not know the true cost of misinformation.

Individuals and groups can quickly weaponize social media, causing others financial and physical injury. For example, fraudsters using President Trump's image, name, logo and voice have siphoned millions from his supporters by claiming to be part of his reelection coalition. In an election year, disinformation and donation scams should be of concern to everyone. Along with my coresearchers Brian Friedberg and Brandi Collins-Dexter, I have studied malicious groups, particularly white supremacists and foreign actors, who have used social media to inflame racial divisions. Even as these imposters are quickly identified by the communities they target, it takes time for platforms to remove inciting content. A single manipulation campaign can create an incredible strain on breaking news cycles, effectively turning many journalists into unpaid content moderators and drawing law enforcement towards false leads.

Today, I argue that online communication technologies need regulatory guardrails to prevent them from being used for manipulative purposes. And in my written testimony, I have provided a longer list of ways that you could think about technology differently.

But right now, I would like to call attention to deceptively edited audio and video to drive clicks, likes, and shares. This is the AI technology commonly referred to as deepfakes. And what I would also like to point out, with my coresearcher Britt Paris, that we have argued that cheapfakes are a wider threat. Like the doctored video of Speaker Pelosi, last week's decontextualized video of Joe Biden seemingly endorsing a white supremacist talking point poses another substantial challenge. Because the Biden video was clipped from nonaugmented footage, platforms refused to take down this cheapfake. Millions have now seen it.

Platforms, like radio towers, provide amplification power and, as such, they have a public-interest obligation. And I point out here that platforms are highly centralized mechanisms of distribution, while the internet is not. So I am not trying to conflate platforms with the internet, but this is why we place the burden of moderation on platforms and not with ISPs.

The world online is the real world, and this crisis of counterfeits threatens to disrupt the way Americans live our lives. Right now, malicious actors jeopardize how we make informed decisions about who to vote for and what causes we support, while platform companies have designed systems that facilitate this manipulation.

We must expand the public understanding of technology by guarding consumer rights against technological abuse, including a cross-sector effort to curb the distribution of harmful and malicious content. As Danah Boyd and I have written, platform companies must address the power of amplification and distribution separately from content, so that media distribution is transparent and accountable. I urge Congress to do the same. Platforms and politics and regulation and technology must work in tandem, or else the future is forgery. Thank you.

[The prepared statement of Dr. Donovan follows:]

Prepared Statement of Joan Donovan, Ph.D.

Online fraud is a great deal more widespread than many understand. Beyond malware, spam, and phishing attacks, beyond credit card scams and product knock-offs, there is a growing threat from new forms of identity fraud enabled by technological design. Platform companies are unable to manage this alone and Americans need governance.[1]

Online deception is now a multimillion-dollar global industry. My research team tracks dangerous individuals and groups who use social media to pose as political campaigns, social movements, news organizations, charities, brands, and average people. This emerging *economy of misinformation* is a threat to national security. Silicon Valley corporations are largely profiting from it, while key political and social institutions are struggling to win back the public's trust.[2]

---

[1] Klonick, Kate, "The New Governors: The People, Rules, and Processes Governing Online Speech." 131 *Harv. L. Rev*. 1598. https://harvardlawreview.org/wp-content/uploads/2018/ 04/ 1598-1670_Online.pdf.

[2] Funke, Daniel, Susan Benkelman, and Cristina Tardáguila. 2019. "Factually: How Misinformation Makes Money." *American Press Institute*. https://www.americanpressi

Platforms have done more than just given users a voice online. They have effectively given them the equivalent of their own broadcast station, emboldening the most malicious among us.[3] To wreak havoc with a media manipulation campaign, all one bad actor needs is motivation. Money also helps. But that's enough to create chaos and divert significant resources from civil society, politicians, newsrooms, healthcare providers, and even law enforcement, who are tasked with repairing the damage.[4] *We currently do not know the true costs of misinformation.*

Individuals and groups can quickly weaponize social media to cause others financial and physical injury. For example,

1. Fraudsters using President Trump's image, name, logo, and voice have siphoned millions from his supporters by claiming to be part of his re-election coalition.[5] In an election year, disinformation and donation scams should be a concern for everyone.[6]
2. Along with my co-researchers, Brian Friedberg and Brandi Collins-Dexter, I have studied malicious groups, particularly white supremacists and foreign actors, who have used social media to inflame racial divisions.[7] Even as these imposters are quickly identified by the communities they target, it takes time for platforms

---

nstitute.org/fact-checking-project/factually-newsletter/factually-how-misinformation-makes-money/.

Vaidhyanathan, Siva. 2018. *Antisocial Media: How Facebook Disconnects Us and Undermines Democracy*. New York, NY, United States of America: Oxford University Press.

[3] Glaser, April. 2019. "Bring Back the Golden Age of Broadcast Regulation. Especially for YouTube and Facebook." *Slate Magazine*. https://slate.com/technology/2019/06/youtube-facebook-hate-speech-regulation-how.html.

[4] Bradshaw, Samantha, and. Howard, P. "The Global Disinformation Order: 2019 Global Inventory of Organised Social Media Manipulation." Working Paper 2019.3. *Oxford, UK: Project on Computational Propaganda*. https://comprop.oii.ox.ac.uk/research/cybertroops 2019/.

[5] Severns, Maggie. 2019. "Trump Campaign Plagued by Groups Raising Tens of Millions in His Name." *Politico*. https://www.politico.com/news/2019/12/23/trump-campaign-compete-agai nst-groups-money-089454.

[6] Benkler, Yochai, Robert Faris, and Hal Roberts. 2018. *Network Propaganda: Manipulation, Disinformation, and Radicalization in American Politics*. Oxford University Press.

[7] Friedberg, B., & Donovan, J. 2019. On the Internet, Nobody Knows You're a Bot: Pseudoanonymous Influence Operations and Networked Social Movements. *Journal of Design and Science*, (6). https://doi.org/10.21428/7808da6b.45957184.

Collins-Dexter, B. 2019. "The Dangers of Weaponized Truth." *Journal of Design and Science*, (6). https://jods.mitpress.mit.edu/pub/273294u8.

to remove inciting content.[8] A single manipulation campaign can create an incredible strain on breaking news cycles, effectively turning many journalists into unpaid content moderators and drawing law enforcement towards false leads.[9]

Specific features of online communication technologies need regulatory guardrails to prevent them from being used for manipulative purposes. These include:

1. Registering, buying, and selling fake accounts, comments, and reviews to generate artificial attention, sometimes using botnets and automated text-generators to game algorithmic systems;[10]
2. Advertising products designed to inflate engagement metrics and/or force misinformation into users' search returns, feeds and timelines;[11]
3. Networked factions (groups of loosely affiliated actors) strategically coordinating harassment, distributing hateful content, or inciting violence for profit or political ends;[12]

---

[8] Donovan, Joan. 2019. "Opinion | First They Came for the Black Feminists." *The New York Times*. https:/www.nytimes.com/interactive/2019/08/15/opinion/gamergate-twitter.html.

[9] Donovan, Joan. 2019. "How Hate Groups' Secret Sound System Works." *The Atlantic*. March 17, 2019. https://www.theatlantic.com/ideas/archive/2019/03/extremists-understand-what-tech-platforms-have-built/585136/.

[10] Caplan, Robyn, Lauren Hanson, and Joan Donovan. 2018. "Dead Reckoning: Navigating Content Moderation After 'Fake News.'" *Data & Society*. https://datasociety.net/output/dead-reckoning/.

Confessore, Nicholas, Gabriel J. X. Dance, Rich Harris, and Mark Hansen. 2018. "The Follower Factory." *The New York Times*. https://www.nytimes.com/interactive/2018/01/27/technology/social-media-bots.html, https://www.nytimes.com/interactive/2018/01/27/technology/social-media-bots.html.

Woolley, Samuel C. and Philip N. Howard. 2016. "Automation, Algorithms, and Politics| Political Communication, Computational Propaganda, and Autonomous Agents — Introduction." *International Journal of Communication* 10(0):9. https://ijoc.org/index.php/ijoc/article/view/6298.

[11] Braun, Joshua A., and Jessica L. Eklund. 2019. "Fake News, Real Money: Ad Tech Platforms, Profit-Driven Hoaxes, and the Business of Journalism." *Digital Journalism* 7 (1): 1–21. https://doi.org/10.1080/21670811.2018.1556314.

Noble, Safiya Umoja. 2018. *Algorithms of Oppression: How Search Engines Reinforce Racism*. New York: NYU Press.

[12] Donovan, Joan and Brian Friedberg. 2019. "Source Hacking: Media Manipulation in Practice." *Data & Society*. https://datasociety.net/output/source-hacking-media-manipulation-in-practice/.

Lukito, Josephine, Jiyoun Suk, Yini Zhang, Larissa Doroshenko, Sang Jung Kim, Min-Hsin Su, Yiping Xia, Deen Freelon, and Chris Wells. 2019. "The Wolves in Sheep's Clothing: How Russia's Internet Research Agency Tweets Appeared in U.S. News as Vox Populi."

4. Misusing platforms' donation features to raise funds for dangerous or imposter groups;[13]
5. Promoting misinformation about health care to sell harmful or ineffective treatments; and[14]
6. Using deceptively edited audio/video, like "deep fakes" and cheap fakes, to drive clicks, likes, and shares.[15]

Regarding the last point, the AI technology commonly called 'deep fakes' presents an immediate identity threat. Deep fakes are audio and video that realistically depict a person saying and doing things that never happened.[16] Social media companies are devising policies to prevent deep fakes from misrepresenting public figures and average citizens, but this does not mean companies will adequately enforce these terms of service and address the damage done to society.

For example, in a recent report, researchers found 96% of deep fakes are pornography mostly targeting women.[17] This poses troubling questions about harassment and consent.[18] Mary Anne Franks and Danielle Citron have advocated for laws prohibiting non-consensual images because the potential for profit, exploitation, and extortion is high.[19] Unfortunately, even the most cutting-edge detection technology can be fooled by skillful deep fakes. For that reason, we need governance.

My co-researcher Britt Paris and I argue that so-called 'cheap fakes' are a wider threat. Like the doctored video of Representative Pelosi, last week's

---

The International Journal of Press/Politics, December, 1940161219895215. https://doi.org/10.1177/1940161219895215.

[13] Koh, Yoree. 2018. "Hate Speech on Live 'Super Chats' Tests YouTube." *Wall Street Journal*. https://www.wsj.com/articles/hate-speech-on-live-super-chats-tests-youtube-1541205849.

[14] Zadrozny, Brandy. 2019. "These Are the Fake Health News That Went Viral in 2019." *NBC News*. https://www.nbcnews.com/news/us-news/social-media-hosted-lot-fake-health-news-year-here-s-n1107466.

[15] Paris, Britt, and Joan Donovan. 2019. "Deepfakes and Cheap Fakes." *Data & Society* (blog). 2019. https://datasociety.net/output/deepfakes-and-cheap-fakes/.

[16] Paris, Joan Donovan, Britt. 2019. "Deepfakes Are Troubling. But So Are the 'Cheapfakes' That Are Already Here." *Slate Magazine*. June 12, 2019. https://slate.com/technology/2019/06/drunk-pelosi-deepfakes-cheapfakes-artificial-intelligence-disinformation.html.

[17] Ajder, Henry, Giorgio Patrini, Francesco Cavalli, and Laurence Cullen 2019. "The State of Deepfakes: Landscape, Threats, and Impact." *Deep Trace Labs*. https://deeptracelabs.com/mapping-the-deepfake-landscape/.

[18] Chesney, Robert and Citron, Danielle Keats, "Deep Fakes: A Looming Challenge for Privacy, Democracy, and National Security." 2019. *California Law Review* 1753. https://ssrn.com/abstract=3213954.

[19] Danielle K. Citron & Mary Anne Franks. 2014. "Criminalizing Revenge Porn" 49 *Wake Forest Law Review* 345. https://scholarship.law.bu.edu/faculty_scholarship/643.

decontextualized video of Joe Biden seemingly endorsing a white supremacist talking-point poses a substantial challenge.[20] Because the Biden video was clipped from non-augmented footage, platforms refused to take down this cheap fake. Millions have now seen it. Platforms, like radio towers, provide amplification power and as such they have public interest obligations.

The world online is the real world, and *this crisis of counterfeits* threatens to disrupt the way Americans live our real lives. Right now, malicious actors jeopardize how we make informed decisions about who to vote for and what causes we support, while platform companies' own products facilitate this manipulation, placing our democracy and economy at significant risk.[21] What makes manipulated content so dangerous is the ease of distribution and the hidden protocols of moderation.[22]

We must expand the public understanding of technology by guarding consumer rights against technological abuse, including a cross-sector effort to curb the distribution of harmful and manipulated content. As danah boyd and I have written, platform companies must address the power of amplification—separately from content— so that media distribution is transparent and accountable.[23] I urge Congress to do the same. Platforms have politics.[24] Regulation and technology must work in tandem, or else *the future is forgery*.

Ms. SCHAKOWSKY. Thank you.

---

[20] PBS. 2020. "How 2020 Candidates Are Grappling with Online Disinformation." *PBS NewsHour*. https://www.pbs.org/newshour/show/how-2020-candidates-are-grappling-with-online-disinformation.

[21] Charlet, Katherine, and Citron, Danielle. 2019. "Campaigns Must Prepare for Deepfakes: This Is What Their Plan Should Look Like." *Carnegie Endowment for International Peace*. https://carnegieendowment.org/2019/09/05/campaigns-must-prepare-for-deepfakes-this-is-what-their-plan-should-look-like-pub-79792.

Acker, Amelia, and Donovan, Joan. 2019. "Data Craft: A Theory/Methods Package for Critical Internet Studies." *Information, Communication & Society* 22(11):1590–1609. https://doi.org/10.1080/1369118X.2019.1645194.

[22] Gillespie, Tarleton. 2018. *Custodians of the Internet: Platforms, Content Moderation, and the Hidden Decisions That Shape Social Media*. New Haven: Yale University Press.

Roberts, Sarah T. 2019. *Behind the Screen: Content Moderation in the Shadows of Social Media*. New Haven, CT: Yale University Press.

Roberts, Sarah. 2017. "Social Media's Silent Filter." The Atlantic. March 8, 2017. https://www.theatlantic.com/technology/archive/2017/03/commercial-content-moderation/518796/.

[23] Donovan, Joan, and boyd, danah. 2019. "Stop the Presses? Moving From Strategic Silence to Strategic Amplification in a Networked Media Ecosystem:" *American Behavioral Scientist*, September. https://doi.org/10.1177/0002764219878229.

[24] Gillespie, Tarleton. 2010. "The Politics of 'Platforms'." *New Media & Society* 12 (3): 347–64. https://doi.org/10.1177/1461444809342738.

And now, Mr. Hurwitz, you are recognized for 5 minutes.

Opening Statement of Justin (Gus) Hurwitz, Director of Law and Economics Programs, International Center for Law and Economics

Mr. HURWITZ. Thank you, Ms. Chairwoman, along with members of the committee, for the opportunity to speak to you today. I would also be remiss if I did not thank my colleague Kristian Stout and research assistant Justin McCully for help in drafting my written testimony.

I am a law professor, so I apologize. I will turn to discussing the short law review article I have written for you as my testimony and assigned to you to read in a moment. Before I turn to that, I want to make a couple of book recommendations. If you really want to understand what is at stake with dark patterns, you should start by reading Brett Frischmann and Evan Selinger's recent book, "Re-Engineering Humanity." In my spare time, I am a door-to-door book salesman. I have a copy here. Their book discusses how modern technology, data analytics, combined with highly programmable environments, are creating a world in which people are, to use their term, programmable. This book will scare you.

After you read that book, you should then read Cliff Kuang and Robert Fabricant's recent book, "User Friendly." This was just published in November. It discusses the importance and difficulty of designing technologies that seamlessly operate in line with user expectations as user-friendly technologies. This book will help you understand the incredible power of user-friendly design and fill you with hope for what design makes possible, along with appreciation for how difficult it is to do design well. Together, these books will show you both sides of the coin.

Dark patterns are something that this committee absolutely should be concerned about, but this committee should also approach the topic with great caution. Design is powerful, but it is incredibly difficult to do well. Efforts to regulate bad uses of design could easily harm efforts to do and use design for good.

How is that for having a professor testify? I have already assigned two books and a law review article of my own for you to read. I will do what I can to summarize some of the key ideas from that article in the next 3 minutes or so.

Dark pattern is an ominous term. It is itself a dark pattern. It is a term for a simple concept. People behave in predictable ways. These behavioral patterns can be used to program us in certain ways, and the concern is that sometimes we can be programmed to act against our own self-interest.

So I have some examples. If we can look at the first example, this is something from the internet.

[Slide shown, included in Mr. Hurwitz's prepared statement below.]

You look at this for a moment. Who here feels manipulated by this image? It is OK to say yes. I do. The designer of this image is using his knowledge of how people read text in an image to make it feel like the image is controlling us, making us control how our eyes are following it and predicting where we are going to go next. Weird stuff.

Let's look at another example. Again, you can definitely tell from the internet.

[Slide shown, included in Mr. Hurwitz's prepared statement below.]

Again, who feels like this image is manipulative? The previous image was harmless, but this one hints at the darker power of dark patterns. Most of you probably missed the typos in the first line and then the second line until the text points them out to you. What if this had been a contract and this trick was used to insert a material term or distract you from a material term in the contract that you were agreeing to? This has now gone from weird stuff to scary stuff.

On the other hand, these same tricks can be used for good. In this same example, what if this trick were used to highlight an easily missed but important concern for consumers to pay attention to? This could be beneficial to consumers.

Design is not mere aesthetics. All design influences how designs are made. It is not possible to regulate bad design without also affecting good design.

So how much of a problem are dark patterns? Recent research shows that websites absolutely are using them, sometimes subtly, sometimes overtly, to influence users. And other research shows us that these tactics can be effective, leading consumers to do things that they otherwise wouldn't do. We have already heard some examples of these, so I won't repeat what has already been discussed. Rather, I would like to leave you with a few ideas about what, if anything, we should do about them.

First, dark patterns are used both online and offline. Stores use their floor plans to influence what people buy. Advertisers make consumers feel a sense of need and urgency for products. Try canceling a subscription service or returning a product. You will likely be routed through a maddening maze of consumer service representatives. If these patterns are a problem online, they are a problem offline, too. We shouldn't focus on one to the exclusion of the other.

Second, while these tricks are annoying, it is unclear how much they actually harm consumers or how much benefit they may confer. Studies of mandatory disclosure laws, for instance, find that they have limited effectiveness. On the other hand, these tricks can also be used to benefit consumers. We should be cautious with regulations that may fail to stop bad conduct while reducing the benefits of good conduct.

Third, most of the worst examples of dark patterns very likely fall within the FTC's authority to regulate deceptive acts or practices. Before the legislature takes any action to address these concerns, the FTC should attempt to use its existing authority to address them. It is already having hearings on these issues. If this proves ineffective, the FTC should report to you, to Congress, on these practices.

Fourth, industry has been responsive to these issues and, to some extent, has been self-regulating. Web browsers and operating systems have made many bad design practices harder to use. Design professionals scorn dark patterns practices. Industry standardization and best practices and self-regulations should be encouraged.

Fifth, regulators should——

Ms. SCHAKOWSKY. Wrap it up.

Mr. HURWITZ. Yes. Last and building on all of the above, this is an area well-suited to cooperation between industry and regulators. Efforts at self-regulation should be encouraged and rewarded. Perhaps even more important, given the complexity of these systems, industry should be at the front line of combating them. Industry has greater design expertise and ability to experiment than regulators, but there is an important role for regulation to step in where industry fails to police itself.

In a true professor—thank you. I look forward to discussion.

[The statement of Mr. Hurwitz follows:]

Prepared Statement of Justin (Gus) Hurwitz[25]

Introduction

"Dark pattern" is a new term for an old practice: using design to prompt desired (if not necessarily desirable) behavior.[26] For instance, a website may present terms of service or an upgrade offer in a window that is more difficult to cancel than it is to accept. A website might, possibly falsely, report to a user that many other users have made a similar purchase recently or that only a limited number of units of a product remaining.[27] A car salesperson may present add- ons or upgrades at the end of a high-pressure negotiation, or a supermarket may stock a checkout aisle with high margin "impulse purchase" items.[28] An employer might offer on-site amenities and perks that make employees happier, but that also result in them spending more time on the job. Subscription services – online and offline – may run customers through a "maze" of customer service representatives to cancel service. A social-media platform may make it easy and rewarding to uncritically "share" posts, facilitating the widespread dissemination of false information.[29]

The basic idea of dark patterns is straightforward: humans are not perfectly rational decision-makers. Rather, we constantly use various heuristics to efficiently make decisions subject to imperfect information. These heuristics can be turned against us, however, and used, to some extent, to "program" us for specific behavior.[30]

---

[25] The author thanks the Committee for the opportunity to present this material. In addition, he thanks Kristian Stout and Justin McCully for extraordinary assistance in completing this testimony in a short period of time. All views expressed are those of the author and do not necessarily represent any other individual or organization. Any errors or omissions are the authors alone. Given the short timeframe on which this material has been prepared, errors are unfortunately likely – best efforts have been made to ensure the accuracy of this material.

[26] *Dark Patterns*, https://www.darkpatterns.org/ (last visited Jan. 2, 2020).

[27] Practices such as these are discussed in Arunesh Mathur et al., *Dark Patterns at Scale: Findings from a Crawl of 11k Shopping Websites*, discussed *infra*.

[28] *But see,* Mario Miranda, *Determinants of Shoppers' Checkout Behaviour at Supermarkst*, 16 *J. Targeting, Measurement & Analysis for Marketing* 312 (2008) (finding that "shoppers' purchases at grocery checkouts may not be spontaneous and unreflective …, but demonstrative of conscious concern with making efficient use of their shopping time. Not all purchases at checkouts can therefore be casually referred to as impulse purchase.").

[29] *See* Alex Kantrowitz, *The Man Who Built the Retweet: "We handed a Loaded Weapon to 4-Year-Olds," Buzzfeed* (JULY 23, 2019), https://www.buzzfeednews.com/article/alexka ntro witz/how-the-retweet-ruined-the-internet. *See also* Soroush Vosoughi, et al, *The spread of true and false news online,* 359(6380) *Science* 1146 (2018).

[30] *See* Brett Frischmann and Evan Selinger, *Re-Engineering Humanity* (Cambridge 2018).

There are myriad common examples of these cognitive biases. But this is a case where it may be easier to show than to tell: the images at the top of the next page demonstrate simple "dark patterns" at work.

As these images demonstrate, there are patterns in how we interact with information. Designers study these patterns and can use them to present information in ways that influence how we respond to that information. Designers may present information in a manner that follows the flow of how readers or users are likely to naturally process it; or in a way that highlights details that may be easily missed; or by "hiding" information despite it being plainly disclosed.

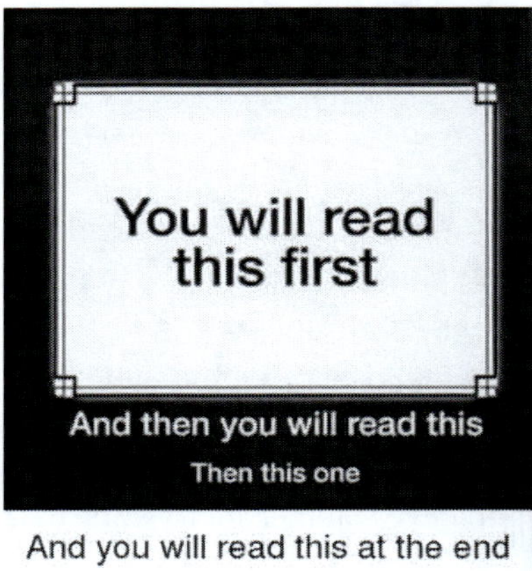

The first image[31] takes advantage of how humans scan information in an image or on a page. In this case, design is being used to make the reader feel like they are being controlled by the image. While this is presented in a somewhat jocular or didactic manner, it may nonetheless leave some readers perplexed or even feeling manipulated. The second image is somewhat more nefarious,[32] even if innocuously so: it contains errors that most readers' brains will automatically correct and skip over as they are read and plays with the reader by calling attention to these overlooked errors. Imagine if, instead of minor typos or grammar errors, this image had "tricked" the reader into accepting substantive errors, such as the inclusion or omission of the work "not," or an extra digit in the price of a product. Patterns like these could be

---

[31] Zer0Effect, *And You Will Read This at The End* (2019), https://www.reddit.com/r/dankmemes/comments/apcf4f/and_you_will_read_this_at_the_end/.

[32] MEMEPRO1, *If You Did It Great!* (2018), https://imgflip.com/i/225k37.

used to "trick" users into accepting terms or disclosing information, ostensibly knowingly.

While there is nothing terribly new about merchants shaping the customer experience to their own advantage, new attention has been paid in recent years to practices like these when used in the online environment. First given the name "dark patterns" at the beginning of last decade, concern about these practices has grown in the academic literature and popular press in recent years.[33] The phenomenon has also increasingly gained legislative attention.[34] Recently attention has been driven, in particular, by concerns in the privacy community about the effectiveness of privacy disclosures and notice-and-consent requirements and concerns about mis- and dis-information.[35]

This testimony addresses dark patterns – what they are and the extent to which we should be concerned about them. The first part contains a background discussion of the characteristics of dark patterns, paying particular attention to how the concept may differ in the online context as compared to the offline context. The second part then discusses the difficulties of design, especially of software interfaces, and argues that "patterns," dark or otherwise, are both inevitable and difficult to understand. This discussion foreshadows part three, which addresses the extent to which we should be worried about dark patterns and what, if anything, we should do to address these concerns.

I thank the Committee for the opportunity to share these thoughts. This is an important topic at the forefront of a complex and dynamic area – it is important that the Committee be considering these issues. In line with the complex and dynamic nature of this area, I submit this material with the

---

[33] *See, e.g.*, Ryan Calo, *Digital Market Manipulation*, 82 Geo.Wash. L. Rev. 995 (2014); Paul Ohm, *Forthright Code*, 56(2) *Hous. L. Rev.* 471 (2018); Ari Ezra Waldman, *Power, Process, and Automated Decision-Making*, 88(2) Fordham L. Rev. 613 (2019); Frischmann & Selinger, *supra* note 6. A WestLaw search of news sources for the term "dark patterns" yields 198 results from 2019, 114 results from 2018, and an average of about 45 results per year for from 2013-2017.

[34] *See, e.g.,* Deceptive Experiences to Online Users Reduction Act (DETOUR Act), S.1084, 116th Cong., (2019), *available* at https://www.congress.gov/bill/116th-congress/senate-bill/1084/text.

[35] *See* Ari Ezra Waldman, *Power, Process, and Automated Decision-making*, 88 Fordham L. Rev. 1 (2019); Ari Ezra Waldman, *Privacy's Law of Design*, 9 U.C. Irvine L. Rev. 1239 (2019); Lindsey Barrett, *Confiding in Con Men: U.S. Privacy Law, the GDPR, and Information Fiduciaries* 42 Seattle U. L. Rev. 1057 (2019); Neil M. Richards & Woodrow Hartzog, *The Pathologies of Digital Consent*, 96 Wash. U. L. Rev. 1461 (2019); Lior Jacob Strahilevitz & Jamie Luguri, *Consumertarian Default Rules*, 82 L. & Contemp. Probs. 139 (2019); Ohm, *supra* note 9; Lauren E. Willis, *Why not Privacy by Default*, 29 Berkeley Tech. L.J. 61 (2014); Frischmann & Selinger, *supra* note 6.

important proviso that any one perspective, set of examples, or expression of concerns or assurances can at most shine a small light on a large issue.

Dark Patterns

What They Are

First coined in 2010,[36] the term "dark patterns" was created to describe user interface design patterns that are "crafted with great attention to detail, and a solid understanding of human psychology, to trick users into do things they wouldn't otherwise have done."[37]

The term is used primarily to describe user interface design choices intended to invoke particular behavior (usually to the benefit of the designer and/or the designer's employer). Many, if not most, examples have offline analogs. But the arguably unique thing about dark patterns is that software interfaces to online platforms are infinitely and instantly malleable: there is practically no limit to design choices, and those design choices can be changed, tweaked, updated, and targeted with ease – including in real-time and in response to specific users or user actions. This is different from more traditional sales channels. For instance, a supermarket checkout aisle needs to be roughly a constant size; needs to target the average customer insofar as its impracticable to send customers to different aisles based on, e.g., their buying history; can only fit so many products on the shelves; and can't be easily changed outside of a set schedule.

Another unique aspect of dark patterns is that, sometimes, the underlying code is available. So, for instance, if a webpage is targeting different interfaces to different users using browser-side techniques, the underlying code can be inspected. Similarly, online interfaces are typically used from the relative comfort of one's home or office, or while out and about on one's mobile device. Both of these factors give users greater control over how they choose to interact with an interface than is possible in many offline settings.

Dark patterns take advantage of a few key behaviors of imperfectly rational humans. First, people are unwilling to devote a large amount of cognitive resources to relatively low value activities. As such, people skim when they read, often missing some details – particularly those that may be

---

[36] Harry Brignull, *Dark Patters: dirty tricks designers use to make people do stuff*, 90 Percent of Everything (Jul. 8, 2010), https://www.90percentofeverything.com/2010/07/08/dark-patterns-dirty-tricks-designers-use-to-make-people-do-stuff/.

[37] *Id.*

designed in a way that makes them relatively easier to miss. Our eyes follow common patters when reading text on a screen or page, based upon how we have learned salient information is likely to be presented.[38] Second, if there is a cost to correct a mistake, people may just accept the mistake if the cost in time or effort exceeds the cost of continuing on their present course. Few people will take the time to return a product for a $2.00 refund, even if that product was shipped to them (and they were charged for it) in error (or fraud). Third, people are social creatures and we frequently rely on the behavior of others to guide out their own conduct. Thus, when presented with information such as "Bonnie in New Jersey recently purchased item X" or "12 other people are looking at this deal right now," consumers will potentially feel an elevated sense of pressure to commit to a purchase. This heuristic, sometimes referred to as "social proof," can be understood as entirely rational, reflecting the wisdom of the crowd; but it can also be taken advantage of to make a decision seem more desirable than it really is.[39]

There is no doubt that firms use dark patterns, or that they may be effective. One recent study analyzed 53,000 different product pages across 11,000 different online shopping sites, and found 1,818 instances of dark pattern usage.[40] In another study, respondents presented with either a "moderate" or "aggressive" dark pattern designed to push them into purchasing credit monitoring services were 228%-371% more likely to purchase the offered services.[41]

At the same time, and as discussed below, design is, simply put, hard, and not all "dark" patterns are intentional or malicious. Some are benign or even beneficial. Design decisions are necessary to any interface and negative effects may be inadvertent or practicably unavoidable. For example, one of the studies above used screen shots from the PlayStation live service and its promotion of a 12-month subscription over the 1-month option by using larger text for the former to demonstrate a deceptive dark pattern.[42] But, considering the large volume of gamers that use that service, it may simply be the case that the

---

[38] A search on Amazon.com for books on "eye tracking," for instance, yields dozens of results.

[39] Indeed, the term "social proof," is generally traced to Robert Cialdini's 1984 book *Influence: The Psychology of Persuasion*, one of the seminal books on the psychology of persuasion and marketing.

[40] Arunesh Mathur et al., *Dark Patterns at Scale: Findings from a Crawl of 11k Shopping Websites*, Proceedings of the ACM on Human-Computer Interaction (Nov. 2019), https://arxiv.org/pdf/1907.07032.pdf.

[41] Jamie Luguri & Lior Strahievitz, *Shining a Light on Dark Patterns* 21-22 (U of Chicago, Pub, Law Working Paper No. 719, 2019), *available* at https://papers.ssrn.com/sol3/papers.cfm?abstract_id=3431205.

[42] *Id.* at 13-17.

annual savings and convenience of not having to subscribe month-to-month benefits one group of users, even though it may be annoying or undesirable to a second set of users. In other words, using larger text sizes to make the option most desired by most users easier to find, while leaving the alternate option available on the same page for users who prefer it, may be the preferred design for most users. Further, designs intended to bring about certain effects may be ineffective and intended effects may be beneficial – for example, reminding users of abandoned shopping carts and reminding users of necessary complementary products may confer a benefit on both the seller (more sales) and the buyer (purchasing desired products). It may be the case that the annoyance of being "pushed" to purchase items in a cart or to buy items related to those in a cart is relatively minor, even spread across thousands of users, to avoid a greater inconvenience for users who fail to click the final button to complete a purchase or who are about to purchase a product only to later discover that they needed to have purchased complementary goods to use it.

Dark patterns also are nothing new. Indeed most have existed in one form or another in the offline world for a long time. Stores keep candy near registers because it's easier for parents to simply placate a whining child than to discipline them in a checkout aisle, and tabloids to entertain customers and distract them from the feeling of impatience while waiting to pay. When purchasing a car at a dealership, the salesperson may "consult" with a hidden "manager" to make a customer feel he is getting a good deal; and the customer then frequently needs to go through two or three layers of personnel for finalizing the deal, each time being offered various "upgrades" to the vehicle being purchased. Homeowners needing contractors for home remodeling, fence installation, or a major repair will frequently not be able to receive a price over the phone – even if pricing is relatively standard – because such companies prefer to send a salesperson to the premises who can talk the potential customer through objections.

These are all common "tricks" of the sales trade – they are patterns of doing business that allow firms to generate more revenue from customers. In some cases these may be deceptive or harmful, or at least have no positive social value (as opposed to merely transferring wealth from customer to firm). In other cases, there may be real value to them. A company may prefer to send contractors to visit customers' homes because experience shows customers often don't understand which product best suites their needs, or have the wrong work done on their house to solve a given problem. Sending the contractor to inspect the job site before giving a quote may allow for better quotes and performance and, even more important, avoid creating unhappy (and complaining) customers. And in other cases, these "tricks" may be a mechanism for price discrimination – sorting customers by their willingness to pay for a given product. While controversial, the economics of price discrimination are widely understood and it is generally legal. The net effect of price discrimination in competitive markets generally doesn't increase firm revenues significantly. Rather, by charging some customers more and keeping the average price the same, firms are able to offer other customers lower prices, which can allow them to offer their goods or services to consumers who may otherwise be priced out of the market.

Dark Patterns: The Good, the Bad, and the Ambiguous[43]

Although the literature on dark patterns is relatively new, there are some readily identifiable patterns which deserve discussion. What follows is a discussion of some of these common patterns, and an attempt to differentiate them along other examples in terms of "good," "bad" and "ambiguous" effects.

Bad-Effect Design

Websites may use design to trick consumers into undesired action. This includes, for instance, employ things like "countdown timers"[44] indicating that a customer only has "X" amount of time remaining to complete a purchase. If fraudulent information, this may create a needless sense of urgency that compels a customer to make a purchase that they would not upon less pressured reflection. Sites also employ a "limited-time message"/"scarcity message"[45] indicating a particular deal will only exist for a short period of time, or that the item is on the verge of selling out. When fraudulent, this is used to motivate a buyer without need. Upsells are also common, a design that introduces steps meant to encourage users to purchase an additional good or service (e.g., insurance for a travel ticket). When a design "confirmshames"[46] users, it employs a choice interface ("yes" or "no") in a way that manipulates a consumer's emotions. Thus, instead of just allowing a "no" choice to decline optional insurance for a vacation, the offered choice may be "No, I don't want to protect my valuables and loved ones during my trip."

---

[43] Note, these "bad/ambiguous/good" behavior headings are approximate, meant to offer intuitive examples to demonstrate that design can be good or bad.

[44] Mathuer et al., supra note 16, at 12.

[45] *Id.* at 16-17.

[46] *Id.* at 17.

Visual interference[47] is used to put important text in obscured or otherwise difficult to see color and layout schemed.[48] One way this manifests online is to offer users upgrade options in a window that offers them an obvious way to accept, but obscures how to decline, the offer. The cognitive effect of this design is that it gives users inclined to decline the offer a few additional seconds to change their minds (and, because we have a natural predisposition to ideas that we have encountered recently, may in fact make them marginally more likely to do so). Even if the conversion rate is small, if offered immediately after a sale this mechanism only has upside revenue potential.

More traditionally, supermarkets manage the length of lines to generate a sunk-cost bias. Also, as noted above, impulse buy items are offered alongside the waiting shoppers to encourage them to add more to their order. Sites sometimes use sneaking[49] cramming, which automatically adds items to a shopper's cart. One of the most classic examples of off-line manipulative behavior is creating roadblocks or users to shape their behavior. Typically, this takes the form of making it difficult to cancel a service or return a product. For example, canceling cell phone service frequently requires transfers between multiple sales representatives and navigation of complex phone menus. Canceling cable or Internet services often requires consumers to go through a similarly circuitous experience.

Ambiguous-Effect Design

There are a host of behaviors that arguably straddle the line between benign and unsavory. Websites frequently employ automated messaging systems to periodically remind browsing customers of items they left in their carts. Technically unsolicited, messages such as these may be an annoyance, but may also serve to remind users of purchases that they want to return to or even thought that they had completed. Complementary product notices are similar. To some users, being offered complementary products may be an annoyance or even induce undesired purchases, but for others they can provide important

---

[47] *Id.*

[48] At times, this pattern goes beyond simple design choices in terms of font and color, and moves into introducing wholly out of place elements clearly meant to confuse a user. For example, one shoe retailer placed a picture of a hair over top of their otherwise legitimate ad in an effort to trick users into swiping up. Some users, thinking they were ridding their screen of a hair, actually ended up on the retailer's web site. *See* Katitlyn Tiffany, *This Instagram Story ad with a fake hair in it is sort of disturbing*, *Verge* (Dec. 11, 2017), *available* at https://www.theverge.com/tldr/2017/12/11/16763664/sneaker-ad-instagram-stories-swipe-up-trick (note, however, that deceptively obtained consent is ineffective).

[49] *Id.*

information and avoid substantial future costs. For instance, a site may suggest a customer who is buying a plumbing fixture also buy Teflon plumbing tape. If the customer is unaware that Teflon plumbing tape is needed to properly install most fixtures, this is valuable information that may save the consumer from having to make a subsequent purchase (or even from improperly installing the fixture). On the other hand, if the customer already has such tape, this may be a minor annoyance. And if the suggested product is not actually needed this suggestion may be harmful to the customer.

Grocery stores use inconsistent labeling on the price stickers placed on goods – similar items may have their unit prices calculated using different units.[50] This can be misleading (making more expensive products appear less expensive), or just irritating, as it forces consumers to do their own comparisons and makes pure price competition among venders more difficult. Some argue that this is a devious mechanism forcing consumers into buying more expensive products by making it harder for customers to identify which products have the best prices. But it can also be way of promoting non-price competition, where consumers are unlikely to compare the quality of products if their sole focus is price. Indeed, research suggests that consumers may over-rely on price comparisons as strong indictors of quality.[51]

Arguably, even familiar and widely used user interface elements such as a "like" button or a "retweet" button represent a degree of user manipulation, albeit with ambiguous effects. Social networks are today defined, to some extent, on the degree of reach that individual users can affect. Much of this reach is measured by user engagement, which is, in turn, driven by activities such as liking and retweeting.[52] These design features were explicit choices meant to encourage user interaction on the social networks, and thus represents user manipulation to a degree. The social value of these platforms is subject to important debate and scrutiny, from their ability to serve as vectors for and amplifiers of mis- and dis-information and concerns about potentially

---

[50] Melanie Pinola, *How the Unit Pricing Labels in Stores Can Trick You into Spending More*, *Lifehacker* (Oct. 03, 14), https://lifehacker.com/how-the-unit-pricing-labels-in-stores-can-trick-you-int-1641793755.

[51] Dengfeng Yan, Jaideep Sengupta, Robert S. Wyer Jr. *Package size and perceived quality; The intervening role of unit price perception*, 24(1) *J. of Consumer Psychol*. 3, 14 (2014) (finding that consumers use unit price as a proxy to determine quality when comparing similarly sized and different sized goods).

[52] Jeffrey Krans, 7 Social Media Engagement Metrics for Tracking Followers and Growing Community, *Buffer* (Sept. 21, 2015), https://buffer.com/resources/measure-social-media-engagement.

addictive behavior patterns.[53] Nonetheless, social media has unquestionably been beneficial to many in society – often most to minority and other disadvantaged voices that have historically not had access to high-profile platforms and, for which, social media has served as a significant amplifier of their messages, concerns, and ideas – and the design elements that have allowed these platforms to succeed have allowed these user groups to benefit from them.

Or, to return to an echo of the PlayStation example used above: during its regular membership drive, NPR strongly encourages listeners to become "sustaining members." That is, they want listeners to agree to small, automatic, monthly donations instead of larger, one-time donations. But why should NPR care if a listener gives $120 once in January or $10/month over a period of 12 months? The answer is that this is a dark pattern.[54] Getting listeners to sign up for the monthly subscription makes is more likely that they will continue paying long into the future – rather than hoping that each year they affirmatively choose to make a single large donation, the psychological burden is shifted to the listener to discontinue making small regular donations, which many are unlikely to do. NPR, of course, is a good, honest, hardworking news organization with pure motives, so would never be criticized for taking advantage of its listeners by tricking them into emptying their pocketbooks into public broadcasting's coffers. But when companies like Microsoft and Adobe use this same practice, it is clearly deceptive.[55]

Good-Effect Design

Design choices can also be obviously aimed at good ends. Apple and Amazon are two of the best examples of carefully considered design meant to drive positive user experiences. The so-called "Apple tax," the price premium that Apple is able to charge for its products compared to similar-quality products from other companies, is a reflection of Apple's reputation for producing well-

[53] *See* Christian Montag et al., *Addictive Features of Social Media/Messenger Platforms and Freemium Games against the Background of Psychological and Economic Theories*, 16(14) *Int'l. J. Envtl. Res. Pub. Health* 2612, 2623 (2019); Hilary Anderson, *Social media apps are 'deliberately addictive to users*, BBC News (Jul 8, 2018), https://www.bbc.com/news/technology-44640959.

[54] *See* Priscella Esser, *Getting Users' Long-Term Commitment with a Monthly Charge*, *Interaction Design Foundation* (2018), https://www.interaction-design.org/literature/article/getting-users-long-term-commitment-with-a-monthly-charge.

[55] *Id.* Lest the dripping irony be lost, the effects of these practices in the cases of both NPR and commercial entities like Microsoft and Adobe are ambiguous, with both positive and negative effects for different groups of users.

designed products.[56] Amazon, likewise, to an important degree made e-commerce accepted and trusted through the great strides it made in both creating secure environments that customers could trust, and removing as much of the friction in the shopping experience as possible. Its famous "1-click" patent, and the associated ease with which it designed its checkout experience, was an important part of that innovation.[57]

Individual apps that cater to differ user lifestyles also introduce design choices – often using the same techniques derided as manipulative in the social media context – to encourage, for example, healthier lifestyles. Apple's watch has a built-in app that reminds users to breathe deeply periodically[58], and an app that reminds users to stand up and walk around once an hour to combat the problems associated with modern work habits.[59] Other apps help dieters remember when they are allowed to eat, encourage them to make healthier choices, and to drink enough water.

Design Patterns

Design is difficult. It is also necessary. A car must have a mechanism for steering, which must be located somewhere and be articulated in a certain manner. Design choices will affect how easy it is to operate the car, how responsive the car is to the driver and to road conditions, and how safely the car can be operated. Design decisions will affect the aesthetics of the car, how comfortable the car is, and the cost of manufacturing the car. Indeed, the decision of whether to invest significantly in R&D relating to the car's steering mechanisms will affect the cost, quality, and safety of the car.

And things just get more complicated from there. If regulators want to ensure the safety of cars, they need to design systems for measuring, monitoring, and enforcing safety metrics. If, for instance, regulators use crash test dummies modelled after the typical male driver, car manufacturers will

[56] Kevin Downey, *Why are Apple products so friggin' expensive?*, Kimkomando (Mar. 9, 2019), https://www.komando.com/money-tips/why-are-apple-products-so-friggin-expensive/549472/.

[57] *Why Amazon's '1-Click' Ordering Was a Game Changer*, *Knowledge@Wharton* (Sept. 14, 2017), https://knowledge.wharton.upenn.edu/article/amazons-1-click-goes-off-patent/#.

[58] Lucy Hattersley, What is Breath for Apple Watch I How to use Apple Breathe app in watchOS3, *Macworld* (Oct. 03, 2016), https://www.macworld.co.uk/feature/iphone/what-is-breathe-for-apple-watch-how-use-apple-breathe-app-in-watchos-3-3643692/.

[59] *Close your rings*, *Apple*, https://www.apple.com/watch/close-your-rings/ (last visited Jan 5., 2020).

design cars that are safe for typical male drivers – and possibly unsafe for female drivers.[60] Design, in other words, is difficult.

... It's Complicated

In some systems, including nearly all software-based systems, design is more that just difficult, it is "complicated." Complex systems are systems with many interconnected parts, in which changes to any one of those parts can affected other parts, often in unexpected and hard to understand ways. The measure of complexity in these systems is said to grow polynomially, exponentially, or even factorially in proportion to the total number of components in the system. In other words, doubling the number of components in a system from 5 to 10 may increase the overall complexity – the possible number of interactions between those components – by a factor of over 30,000.

One of the primary goals of "design" is to reduce complexity. This is primarily done by reducing the number of possible interactions between the components of a system – and this, in turn, means reducing the overall functionality of the system. The challenge is figuring out which functionality to excise and which to retain. Sometimes reducing overall system complexity can even entail adding new components. For instance, a system can be designed with a "basic" or "default" mode in which users cannot change most settings, but can also have an additional "advanced" mode in which the user has greater control. This requires developing two separate interfaces and a way to switch between them – and to educate users on this multi-interface system.

Complexity abounds, often with tragic results. The Three Mile Island disaster is a classic example – perhaps the most famous. As described by the Washington Post following the disaster, "The [Three Mile Island] control room is a vision from science fiction. It sits under the shadow of the 190-foot-high domed reactor containment building. Inside, a horseshoe-shaped panel stretches 40 feet along three walls lined with dials, gauges and 1,200 warning lights color-coded red and green."[61] All of those dials, gauges, and warning lights were working well when the disaster occurred. But they presented too much information to be useful, and did so in a way that could not be useful, in the event of a real-time emergency. Subsequent investigation determined that the indicator light for the pump responsible for the chain of events that led to

---

[60] This is a topic that has been discussed extensively in recent years. For one example, *see* Astrid Linder & Mats Svensson, *Road Safety: The Average Male as a Norm in Vehicle Occupant Crash Safety Assessment*, 44 *Interdisciplinary Sci. Revs.* 140 (2019).

[61] *A Pump Failure and Claxon Alert*, *The Washinton Post* (1979), http://www.washingtonpost.com/wp-srv/national/longterm/tmi/stories/ch1.htm.

the eventual disaster communicated ambiguous information that misled the facility staff as they tried to figure out why the power plant was malfunctioning.[62] As Don Norman, Emeritus Professor and Director of the University of California San Diego Design Lab, explained it "the control room and computer interfaces at Three Mile Island could not have been more confusing if they had tried."[63]

The August 21, 2017, collision of the Navy destroyer John S McCain presents a more recent, and more poignantly tragic, example of the complexity and stakes of design decisions. The NTSB's report on that incident identifies "the design of the destroyer's Integrated Bridge and Navigation System" as one of the factors contributing to the collision, and finds that "The design of the John S McCain's touch-screen steering and thrust control system increased the likelihood of the operator errors that led to the collision."[64] Moreover, it focuses extensively on issues relating to operational procedures and crew training that are directly related to the design of the IBNS.[65] As documented in a subsequent ProPublica report, the IBNS design failures eerily echo the design failures at Three Mile Island: an easily-overlooked pop-up window indicated which station had steering and thrust control at any given time.[66] In a more modern twist, the use of touch-screens added additional complexity. As noted by the NTSB report, "the touch-screen throttle controls deprived the lee helmsman of tactile feedback when the throttles were unganged and mismatched," which was likely another contributing factor to the incident.[67]

Both of these tragedies are examples of "normal accidents" – a term first coined by Charles Perrow.[68] The core of Perrow's insight into "normal accidents" is that they are an inevitable part of any sufficiently complex, tightly coupled system. Perrow specifically considered the potential for these accidents in systems with a high catastrophic potential – Three Mile Island

---

[62] Pulkit Verma, *3 button designs from 3 different decades that almost results in catastrophe*, *UX Collective* (Oct. 18, 2019), https://uxdesign.cc/3-button-designs-from-3-different-decades-that-almost-results-in-catastrophe-9ac65498c9c4.

[63] *Id.*

[64] Nat'l. Transp. Safety Bd., *Marine Accident Report Ntsb/Mar-1901 Collision Between Us Navy Destroyer John S McCain and Tanker Alnic Mc Singapore Strait, 5 Miles Northeast Of Horsburgh Lighthouse* 33 (2019), https://www.ntsb.gov/investigations/AccidentReports/Reports/MAR1901.pdf. [hereinafter "NTSB"].

[65] *Id.*

[66] T. Christian Miller, Megan Rose, Robert Faturechi & Agnes Chang, *Collision Course*, *Propublica* (Dec. 20, 2019), https://features.propublica.org/navy-uss-mccain-crash/navy-installed-touch-screen-steering-ten-sailors-paid-with-their-lives/.

[67] NTSB, supra note 40, at 33.

[68] Charles Perrow, *Normal Accidents: Living with High-Risk Technologies* (1984).

was his motivating example – to make argue that, as a society, we must either accept the inevitable tragedies that accompany complex systems such as these or abandon them. But his basic insight, that complex systems will behave in unpredictable and at times undesirable ways and that we cannot design this characteristic out of them, generalizes across any complex system.

Almost all software is a complex system, subject to the analysis above. Consider, alone, the challenges that websites face in standardizing their user interface across different web browsers and operating systems. Although the problem is less severe now due to browsers relying on more standardized rendering engines, for the first decade or two of the world wide web, it was a common phenomenon for a website to only work well on one browser, and one operating system (typically Windows with Internet Explorer). This was not the result of a nefarious plan on the part of web developers, but was, rather, the result of developers making design decisions under imperfect conditions.[69] The rendering engines of different browsers often made it difficult to perfectly render the same user interface in the same manner across every browser and OS combination.[70] Thus, websites frequently would have problems with certain sections not rendering correctly, functionality missing, or scripts not executing as expected.

With the entrance of mobile phones and tablets, the problem has been made more complicated. Designers now face the challenge of designing interfaces to run on multiple browsers running on multiple classes of devices with dramatically different user interfaces – both in terms of display and input – across desktops, laptops, tablets, and phones. Sometimes, firms have the resources to customize their interfaces for many combinations of devices and browsers, but this is often not the case. Thus, designers create interfaces that attempt to average out the differences across device and browser combinations or choose to focus on certain more popular or higher-value combination to the exclusion of others.

These concerns are compounded when we add in different types of users – both in terms of soft characteristics like preferences and harder characteristics like age and disability.

---

[69] Tom Warren, *Chrome is turning into the new Internet Explorer 6*, *Verge* (Jan 4, 2018), https://www.theverge.com/2018/1/4/16805216/google-chrome-only-sites-internet-explorer-6-web-standards.

[70] Marco Tabini, *Why some websites don't work properly in your favorite browser, Macworld* (Jan 10, 2013), https://www.macworld.com/article/2023682/why-some-websites-dont-work-properly-in-your-favorite-browser.html.

It is nigh impossible to design an interface that accommodates any given set of user preferences and system requirements perfectly. And the more variables that you try to accommodate, the more complex the system becomes – with the result that the better a job a designer tries to do in delivering a satisfactory experience to all users, the more likely it becomes that the system will fail catastrophically.

Of course, the degree of catastrophe between Three Mile Island and a website recommending the wrong product to a shopper is not truly comparable. But it is nonetheless the case that the underlying causes of many seemingly "dark patterns" may be as innocent and inevitable as the Three Mile Island accident.

This, of course, is not to excuse the truly and myriad inexcusable examples of deceptive dark patterns that many firms unquestionably use. A firm that programs its system to provide false information to a user knowing that the user may act upon that information is not an example of a normal accident, or the sort of design mishap that results from the complex nature of systems. On the other hand, this is a cautionary story about inserting regulators or regulation into the design process. Such regulatory intervention increases complexity, sometimes dramatically. This is not a reason not to undertake design-related regulation – it is, however, a reason to do so cautiously and narrowly.

… It's Competitive

Product design is a key margin along which firms compete. Consumers desire products that are "user friendly" and "easy to use." Importantly, "user friendly" and "easy to use" are defined in terms of the users, not the product designers. The story of Apple's success is one tale that captures this. Apple's recent history, and the role of design in it, is reasonably well know:[71] the iPod, the iMac, and the iPhone were all as revolutionary and successful as they were largely due to their design. Apple took a streamlined and minimalist approach to design, delivering products with simplified interfaces designed to operate smoothly and intuitively. This approached served Apple, and Apple's customers, well – but it is important to note that it does not serve all customers well.

---

[71] For a recent account, focusing on the recent departure of Apple's longtime chief of design Johnny Ives, *see* Chris Welch, *Jony Ive leaving Apple after nearly 30 years to start new design firm*, *Verge* (Jun. 27, 2019), https://www.theverge.com/2019/6/27/18761736/jony-ive-apple-leave-iphone-chief-design-officer-lovefrom-company-quit.

But Apple's history goes back to far before the iPod. The introduction of the original Macintosh computer in 1984 was arguably even more revolutionary: it marked a transition in computer design, from computers that were designed for computer engineers to computers that were designed for ordinary users. It could be used by anyone without specialized training; it included basic applications that did most of the things that ordinary users wanted, in ways that most of them understood. Simple word processing, simple graphics editing, simple file management, a simple graphical interface.

But this simplicity – both from the Macintosh era and the iPod era – comes at a cost. Apple products are exceptionally good at doing what they are designed to do – but part of creating such products is "locking them down." They can be relatively difficult to customize or to configure for applications unanticipated by Apple's design. The result is that some users rather dislike Apple products. The competition for the personal computer in the 1980s was largely between locked-down architectures like Apple's and open architectures like the IBM compatible PC. The competition on mobile devices today is largely between the closed-platform iPhone and open-platform Android devices.

Neither of these approaches is necessarily better or worse than the other. To the contrary, these design elements define how the platforms compete. Apple provides a more consistent, uniform, and in some ways limited, set of product features, and affords greater integration across its ecosystem of products. Android is less consistent, but supports a wider range of hardware and applications, and generally requires more complicated tools for cross-device integration. Different users prefer differently designed systems. The fact that we have multiple, different, competing designs makes all users better off.

It is also important to consider the development process that is popular among technology producers. Given the complexity of design, the initial version of new products rarely support a full range of features, platforms, users, &c. It is prohibitively expensive to develop fully-featured software in an initial release, particularly given the high failure rate of most new products. Rather, firms develop an initial release targeting a specific cohort for entry – perhaps a hypothetical typical customer, or perhaps a specific type of customer that the firm thinks is suitable to target for the product's initial launch. Once the product has achieved a minimum successful launch, the design can be incrementally modified to support wider or more specific user bases.

This model of software design has distinct benefits: it enables rapid delivery of new goods and services to market, and it enables competition from smaller firms. Introducing requirements that a design must be "complete" before release – however that is determined – would make entry difficult or impossible for a large amount of potential entrepreneurs. Further, even the products of medium and large firms would be negatively affected by requiring completed designs. The rapid prototyping process works the same for both small and large firms.

In the context of dark patterns, these observations urge two types of caution. First, what may appear to be a "dark pattern" may merely be a design artifact. A product may have been designed for one user cohort or for one interface and may now be being used by other users or on other devices. The default settings for an initial user base may not be the same as we would expect for the expanded user base, and it may appear that the platform is designed to push users into disadvantageous decisions. Or an interface that was designed, for instance, to run on desktop or laptop computers, may be awkward to use on a mobile device in ways that, again, seem to be intentionally-designed dark patterns. On the other side of this coin, requiring firms to "completely" design systems prior to launching them is, at best, a burden that is detrimental to competition and, at worse, impossible. Such a requirement would dramatically increase the cost of developing new products and bringing them to market, disproportionately hampering smaller competitors. And it would make these firms liable for unanticipated uses of their products.

A better approach to addressing concerns like this is to rely on competition. Customers are generally keenly aware of design issues – there is little better way to drive customers away from a product than for it to have an awkward, cumbersome, of "unfriendly" interface. Where firms are able to compete, and especially where there is evidence that firms to compete, regulation over design elements or design decisions is likely undesirable except in the rarest cases of overtly intentional or exceptionally harmful design patterns.

Regulating Patterns

None of the discussion above is meant to argue that dark patters may not be used in problematic ways – or that they are, in fact, being used in problematic ways. There is, without a doubt, plenty of bad conduct happening, both online and off. Industry behavior in this regard is frequently disappointing. The question becomes what should be do about it, particularly given the sometimes-difficulties of distinguishing between good and bad design practices, the potential for competitive pressures to address some of these concerns, and the danger that regulating poorly may exacerbate already-difficult design challenges. This is made even harder in the online setting where so many parts of the ecosystem continue to change: to the extent industry standards and self-regulation presents viable solutions to these concerns, such mechanisms are yet in their infancy. Given time, such mechanisms may address many of the concerns of dark patterns – or they may not.

In other words, the point of the above is that we need to be careful in how and why we regulate these practices, including understanding when and whether we should at all. In some cases, regulatory efforts may be better focused on other areas; in some cases, it may make more sense to allow the underlying technology and markets to continue to improve before stepping in with regulatory intervention; and in other cases still beneficial regulatory intervention may simply not be possible.

Assessing the Problem

There is yet little empirical evidence about the extent of the dark patterns as a problem – meaning both the incidence of use of dark patterns, the effectiveness of those patterns, and, ultimately, the extent to which use of these patterns actually harms consumers. The literature cited above, such as recent studies showing that various dark patterns are being used on shopping web sites and that these patterns can be effective at increasing the likelihood of consumers taking actions that they otherwise would not, are compelling evidence that there is reason to be concerned.[72]

On the other hand, behavioral psychology literature studying the effects of disclosure rules in high-stakes transactions, such as home mortgages, have found that regulation of disclosures – effectively the design of how and what information is presented to consumer borrowers – have little to no effect on borrowing behavior.[73] This raises questions about whether regulation of dark patterns is justified. If their effect is only limited to low-value transactions, the impact on consumers may not be sufficient to justify regulation that may or may not prove effective. Indeed, if the concern is that firms use dark patterns to extract small additional revenue from a large number of consumers that may

[72] See discussion supra, at notes 16-17.

[73] *See, e.g.*, Michael S. Barr, Sendhill Mullainathan, Eldar Shafir, *Behaviorally Informed Home Mortgage Credit Regulation* (Joint Center for Housing Studies of Harv. U., Working Paper UCC08-12, 2008), *available* at https://papers.ssrn.com/sol3/papers.cfm?abstract_id=1121199.

be particularly at-risk of exploitation, caution may be particularly warranted: increasing regulatory compliance costs on these firms could result in them leaving markets entirely, leaving those consumers entirely unserved, rather than incurring compliance costs and facing potential enforcement actions if they do not comply correctly. We live in an imperfect world and need to be careful to judge proposed regulations by their likely real-world effects, not against a world of costless and perfectly effective regulation.[74]

It also unclear how much of this behavior is fraudulent or deceptive, and how much of it is simply advertising by another name. Calling a shopper's attention to a complementary product during a checkout flow *could* be called trickery, but it's not clear how it is materially different than showing the user an advertising they need to dismiss when they land on the site's home page. On the other hand, practices like cramming, slamming, and "sneak into cart" are much more likely to be harmful – the transaction costs of returning or cancelling unwanted items may exceed the value that the firm extracts from the consumer, leading the consumer to move on with her day and take the loss.

Research on the effects of dark patterns on consumers is still in its infancy. There probably is not enough today to justify any broad regulatory undertakings that would not incur substantial risk of unintended consequences. In all likelihood, the best regulatory approach – to the extent that one proves to be justified – will be one that is tailored to specific types of pattern. Such regulation could, for instance, make specific design practices (e.g., providing fraudulent information to consumers at or near the time of purchase) illegal, or could alternatively task or empower an agency such as the Federal Trade Commission to identify specific practices as violative of the FTC Act.

The Marketplace Is Working to Address These Problems

Even as some firms take advantage of dark patterns, other firms are voluntarily working to protect consumers from them. Google, to take one example, banned advertisers from its network that used pop-under ads, which it viewed as a poor design pattern providing a bad user experience.[75] Most major browsers now allow users to automatically block pop-up windows – another design practice designed to draw users attention similar to windows that

---

[74] Harold Demsetz, Information and Efficiency: Another Viewpoint, 12 *J. of L. & Econ.* 1, (1969) (elaborating the "Nirvana Fallacy," comparing the ideal scenario as more efficient than the real choices presented).

[75] Sarah Perez, *Google bans its ads on sites that use those annoying 'pop-unders'*, *Techcruch* (Jul. 11, 2017), https://techcrunch.com/2017/07/11/google-bans-its-ads-on-sites-that-use-those-annoying-pop-unders//.

cannot easily be closed. Malware and spyware frequently attempted to takeover a user's web browsing experience via browser hijacking – the installation of a software add-on that would permit third parties to interfere with and observe the web browsing of a user. As of Windows 10, Microsoft disabled the key behavior of web browsers that facilitated browser hi-jacking.

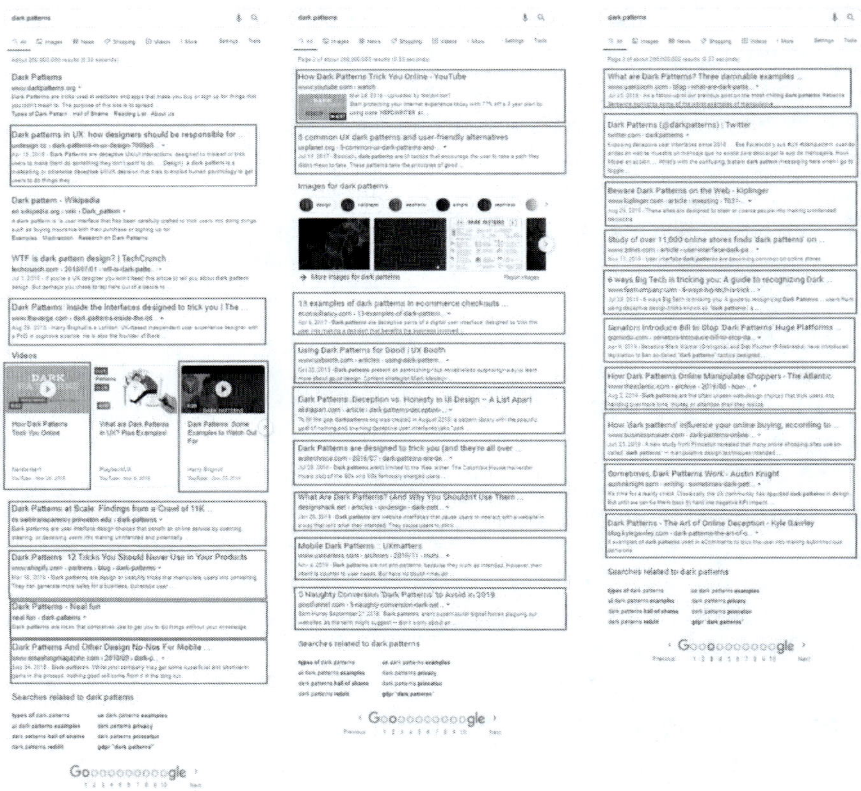

Those are all examples of platform-level efforts to combat these practices by disabling features needed to implement designs that are particularly likely to be harmful to users. There is also effort among industry professionals to combat the use by designers of dark pattern techniques. The figure below shows the first three pages of results for a Google search of the term "dark patterns." It shows that 27 of the top 30 results (marked in red boxes) for the search term "dark patterns" demonstrate a widespread understanding and condemnation of using dark patterns to trick users. These search results show that designers are warning peers not to use these and similar tactics and, where the practice may have value they offer alternative design tools. The remaining three search results link to more general discussions of dark patterns – these discussions all also describe use of them approach as problematic.

Given the complexity of design, there is reason to prefer to rely on the marketplace to address the concerns raised by dark patterns – particularly given that this market-based approach appears to be working. Some patterns that seem to be, or even in fact are being used in ways that are, problematic, may also have good uses. For instance, pop-up windows are generally problematic, but some websites make good use of them. Rather than prohibit them entirely, modern web browsers indicate to users when a website has tried to use a pop-up window and allow users to allow them on a case-by-case basis, for specific websites, or generally. This is a more nuanced approach than regulation is likely to implement. Moreover, this change was phased in over a period of time and across a range of browser platforms, allowing for industry to experiment and gather data on how best to implement this feature. And it is also notable that this feature was implemented at the browser (platform) level. Regulation of design features can be undertaken at any number of levels in the software stack – from the operating system to the protocols and programming languages use to send content to web browsers to the programmers who write the code that controls the design of the website to the browsers that render that code. To whom should regulation of design patterns apply? How does this choice affect the overall complexity of the design ecosystem?

Indeed, even aside from this problem, there is a great deal of value in maintaining stable interfaces, even where those interfaces may contain some poor design. Frequent design change is itself a dark pattern. Consumers are more likely to make mistakes – or to be tricked into doing things they would not otherwise do – if they are unfamiliar with a design or an interface.[76] Regulatory intervention into design could force widespread redesign of interfaces, especially if undertaken regularly or in a way that lacks the precision of changes that industry itself may be able to make. This, in turn, could have widespread adverse effects on consumers. Again, this is not to say that regulation is unwarranted or not possible – only that it must be undertaken with care and with due consideration to alternatives such as industry standardization (which would *increase* stability, both over time and across websites) and self-regulation.

---

[76] *See, e.g.*, Miranda, *supra* note 4.

The Sufficiency of Existing Law?

Existing law is sufficient to address many, possibly most, of the concerns raised by dark patterns. Most of the egregious dark patterns should fall within the ambit of the FTC's consumer protection authority. To the extent that they are harmful, most of these patterns involve making representations or engaging in practices that are designed to deceive consumers. Such conduct is covered by Section 5 of the FTC Act's prohibition against unfair and deceptive acts and practices.[77] In order to make out such a claim, the FTC Act, and the FTC's subsequently adopted Policy Statement on Deception,[78] the Commission must establish that the practice is likely to mislead the ordinary, reasonable, consumer in a way that is material to injury to that consumer.[79] The Commission may presume that express claims are material.[80] Thus, the Commission need only demonstrate injury – i.e., that some consumer did, in fact, make purchases that they otherwise would not have – to take action against firms employing design practices (dark patterns) such as falsely asserting that a certain number of people have recently purchased a product or that a specific limited number of unit remain available for sale. Other practices, such as obscuring how to close a window may require that a more substantial evidentiary burden by the Commission be met.

Should the FTC decide to take action against firms making use of dark patterns, there are several approaches that it could take. In general, like most regulatory agencies, the FTC has both adjudicative and rulemaking authorities – though its rulemaking authority is more involved than the traditional APA rulemaking procedures.[81] In general, the Commission may bring an administrative enforcement action to enjoin any conduct that the Commission determines (after an investigation and administrative hearing);[82] it may also seek damages for such action in federal court for conduct that "a reasonable man would have known under the circumstances was dishonest or fraudulent."[83] It may also issue rules that "define with specificity acts or

---

[77] 15 U.S.C. § 45(a).

[78] *Federal Trade Comm'n, Ftc Policy Statement on Deception (*1983), https://www.ftc.gov/system/files/documents/public_statements/410531/831014deceptionstmt.pdf.

[79] *Id.*

[80] *Id.* at note 48.

[81] *See* 15 U.S.C. § 57a. These procedures were amended in 1975 by the Magnuson-Moss Warranty—Federal Trade Commission Improvement Act of 1975, Pub. L. 93-637 to facilitate heightened Congressional oversight of FTC rules.

[82] 15 U.S.C. § 45(a)(2).

[83] 15 U.S.C. § 57b(a)(2).

practices which are unfair or deceptive."[84] Once enacted, it can enforce such rules through administrative action or directly in federal court (seeking both injunctive relief or damages).[85]

In recent decades, the FTC has been reluctant to engage in rulemaking proceedings, due largely to misunderstandings of both the FTC Act and general administrative law dating back to important judicial losses in the 1980s – but this does not mean that it lacks such authority.[86] Given the broad, and generally unexplored, depth of the FTC's authority directly relevant to the practice of dark patterns, it would be preferable for the FTC to take the lead in developing rules relating to dark patterns. It only makes sense for legislative approaches to be explored should the FTC's authority prove insufficient to the task.

It also bears note that, in addition to authority that the FTC has, it is established law that consent obtained through deception isn't valid.[87] Many dark patterns exploit the boundaries of consent. But this issue is broader than the issue of dark patterns, relating, for instance, to contracts of adhesion, the process of contract formation in the online setting, and the enforceability of contracts that are generally known to go unread. These are topics of significant and ongoing (arguably endless) discussion – to the extent that legislative attention should be given to this issue it should focus on the validity of consent, not on the sub-issue of dark patterns.

The Need for New Law or Regulation?

To the extent that existing legal rules are insufficient to address harms from dark patterns, it is likely either because the conduct is not clearly harmful or it may at times be beneficial. If such is the case, the conduct likely should not be prohibited. Nonetheless, this is a reasonable area of legislative concern where regulation, either today or in the future, may be warranted.

---

[84] 15 U.S.C. § 57a(a)(1)(B).

[85] 15 U.S.C. § 45(a)(2); 15 U.S.C. § 57b(a)(1).

[86] *See generally* Justin Hurwitz, *Chevron and the Limits of Administrative Antitrust*, 76 U. PITT. L. REV. 209 (2014). *See also* FTC Commissioner Rohit Chopra, Comment of Federal Trade Commissioner Rohit Chopra, Hearing #1 on Competition and Consumer Protection in the 21st Century (2018), *available* at https://www.ftc.gov/system/files/ documents/public_statements/1408196/chopra_-_comment_to_hearing_1_9-6-18.pdf.

[87] *See* RESTATEMENT (SECOND) OF TORTS § 892B.: CONSENT UNDER MISTAKE, MISREPRESENTATION OR DURESS (AM. LAW INST. 1979); RESTATEMENT (SECOND) OF CONTRACTS § 163.: WHEN A MISREPRESENTATION PREVENTS FORMATION OF A CONTRACT (AM. LAW. INST. 1981).

Should regulation be desired, a few ideas to keep in mind when approaching regulation in this area are discussed below.

This is an area well suited to industry self-regulation, where standardized industry practices are given some presumption of being inoffensive but entities deviating from those practices bear a burden of demonstrating that their design choices are in the interest of consumers. As discussed above, industry is, and has consistently been, working to improve the status quo and deter the use of pernicious dark patterns.[88] The most viable approach would likely be to allow firms to use contemporaneous documentation (that is, documentation supporting design decisions at the time those decisions were made) to demonstrate that design decisions were made with the interest of consumers and users in mind. Such a factor could be influential both for the development of standardized industry practices as well as for firms that deviate from those practices, by placing an expressly consumer-focused R&D element at the heart of the design practice. Such documentation would tend to suggest that pro-consumer justifications exist for design decisions. Moreover, to the extent that designers are not concerned with consumer experience today (such as if they are focused more narrowly on designs that are appealing on technological or aesthetic grounds but that may, in fact, be detrimental to the user experience of products), it would create an strong incentive for designers and industry groups to focus expressly on the effects of design decisions on consumers.

This may also be an area well-suited to the development of an expedited review and rulemaking process, such as that developed in the DMCA for the review of circumvention technologies.[89] For instance, the FTC could periodically report to Congress on practices that it is seeing that have the potential to harm consumers but fall outside of its existing statutory authority.

Ideas such as these would bolster the FTC's authority in this area without need for the enactment of a substantial new regulatory regime or enactment of ossifying laws. In general, the FTC should be encouraged to explore the limits of its authority to address these concerns, including through narrow legislative interventions such as discussed above or through FTC-generated reports on these issues, before implementing new, Congressionally-crafted, regulatory regimes. Importantly, administrative remedies should be limited to injunctions, with civil penalties only available through the federal courts. And, except in case of clearly intentional fraudulent behavior – such as would already be covered under existing Section 5 authority – the preferred initial

---

[88] See *supra* note 47 and nearby text.
[89] *See* 17 U.S.C. 1201(a)(1)(C).

remedy should be for firms to forego the problematic conduct, with the purpose of improving the overall standard of conduct of the industry in a non-adversarial manner.

To the extent the law proscribes certain designs, it must do so carefully, including thinking about what alternative designs may be adopted – both legitimate and illegitimate ones. As discussed above, design is hard[90] – these are complex systems – and any regulation puts regulators in the shoes of the designers. What's more, it ossifies design.

Finally, given that many dark patterns are used both online and offline – and more generally that the concerns created by dark patterns are not unique to the online setting, Congress should consider whether the scope of its interest in this area should be limited to the online setting. For instance, many firms engage in practices that make it difficult to cancel service or return products. To the extent that concern is justified about analogous online practices, it does not make sense to cabin that concern – or any exploration of it through reports or regulation – to the online setting. If new rules are adopted, regulators should consider whether any proscribed practices should be limited to online actors or whether they should be rules of more general applicability.

* * *

Ms. SCHAKOWSKY. So, Mr. Harris, you are recognized now for 5 minutes.

Statement of Tristan Harris, President and Cofounder, Center for Humane Technology

Mr. HARRIS. Thank you, Chairwoman Schakowsky and members. I really appreciate you inviting me here.

I am going to go off script. I come here because I am incredibly concerned. I actually have a lifelong experience with deception and how technology influences people's minds. I was a magician as a kid, so I have started off by seeing the world this way. And then I studied at a lab called the Stanford Persuasive Technology Lab, actually with the founders of Instagram. And so I know the culture of the people who build these products and the way that it is designed intentionally for mass deception.

---

[90] See *supra* notes 33-46.

I think there is—the thing I most want to respond to here is we often frame these issues as we have got a few bad apples. We have got these bad deepfakes, we have got to get them off the platform. We have got this bad content. We have got these bad bots. What I want to argue is this is actually—and we have got these dark patterns.

What I want to argue is we have dark infrastructure. This is now the infrastructure by which 2.7 billion people, bigger than the size of Christianity, make sense of the world. It is the information environment. And if someone went along, private companies, and built nuclear power plants all across the United States, and they started melting down and they said, "Well, it is your responsibility to have HazMat suits and, you know, have a radiation kit," that is essentially what we are experiencing now. The responsibility is being put on consumers when, in fact, if it is the infrastructure, it should be put on the people building that infrastructure.

There are specifically two areas of harm I want to focus on, even though when this becomes the infrastructure it controls all of our lives. So we wake up with these devices. We check our phones 150 times a day. It is the infrastructure for going to bed. Children spend as much time on these devices as they do at the hours at school. So no matter what you are putting in people's brains, kids' brains at school, you have got all the hours they spend, you know, on their phones.

And let's take the kids' issue. So as infrastructure, the business model of this infrastructure is not aligned with the fabric of society. How much have you paid for your Facebook account recently, or your YouTube account? Zero. How are they worth more than a trillion dollars in market value? They monetize our attention. The way they get that attention is by influencing you and using the dark patterns or tricks to do it.

So the way they do it with children is they say, "How many likes or followers do you have?" So they basically get children addicted to getting attention from other people. They use filters, likes, et cetera, beautification filters that enhance your self-image. And after two decades in decline, the mental health of teen girls, highdepressive symptoms—there is an image here that they will be able to show—went up 170 percent after the year 2010, with the rise of Instagram, et cetera. OK. These are your children. These are your constituents. This is a real issue. It is because we are hacking the self-image of children.

On the information ecology front, the business model, think of it like we are drinking from the Flint water supply of information. The business model is polarization, because the whole point is I have to figure out and calculate whatever keeps your attention, which means affirmation, not information, by default. It polarizes us by default.

There is a recent Upturn study that it actually costs more money to advertise across the aisle than it does to advertise to people with your own same beliefs. In other words, polarization has a home field advantage in terms of the business model. The natural function of these platforms is to reward conspiracy theories, outrage, what we call the race to the bottom of the brainstem. It is the reason why all of you at home have crazier and crazier constituents who believe crazier and crazier things, and you have to respond to them. I know you don't like that.

Russia is manipulating our veterans by—we have totally open borders. While we have been protecting our physical borders, we left the digital border wide open. Imagine a nuclear plant and you said we are not going to actually protect the nuclear plants from Russian cyber attacks. Well, this is sort of like Facebook building the information infrastructure and not protecting it from any bad actors until that pressure is there.

And this is leading to a kind of information trust meltdown, because no one even has to use deepfakes for essentially people to say, "Well, that must be a faked video, right?" So we are actually at the last turning point, kind of an event horizon, where we either protect the foundations of our information and trust environment or we let it go away.

And, you know, we say we care about kids' education, but we allow, you know, technology companies to basically tell them that the world revolves around likes, clicks, and shares. We say we want to, you know, come together, but we allow technology to profit by dividing us into echo chambers. We say America should lead on the global stage against China with its strong economy, but we allow technology companies to degrade our productivity and mental health, while jeopardizing the development of our future workforce, which is our children.

And so, while I am finishing up here, I just want to say that, instead of trying to design some new Federal agency, some master agency, when technology has basically taken all the laws of the physical world—taken all the infrastructure of the physical world and virtualized it into a virtual world with no laws—what happens when you have no laws for an entire virtualized infrastructure? You can't just bring some new agency around and regulate all of the virtual world.

Why don't we take the existing infrastructure, existing agencies who already have purview—Department of Education, Health and Human Services, Natural Institutes of Health—and have a digital update that expands their jurisdiction to just ask, well, how do we protect the tech platforms in the same areas of jurisdiction?

I know I am out of time, so thank you very much.

[The statement of Mr. Harris follows:]

Prepared Statement of Tristan Harris

Unregulated Tech Mediation → Inevitable Online Deception → Societal Harm

"Software is eating the world." (Marc Andreessen, founder of Netscape)

While we used to say that technology platforms have *eroded* the social fabric, it's more accurate to say that tech companies have *become* the social fabric. Tech has become the infrastructure that manage civilization's global "social organs" and our personal lives.

- *Broadcast:* YouTube's algorithms have effectively become the video broadcast infrastructure for the world, without any of the regulations that used to protect children or other ethical standards.
- *Social Relationships:* Facebook, Twitter, Instagram have become the *infrastructure for making sense of our social world* – shaping how we determine what the majority of people around us seem to believe or agree with, how popular or influential people are, how happy our ex-romantic partners seem to be, even how we track each other's psychological health.
- *Democracy:* Micro-targeting and lookalike models through Facebook and Google Ads have become the *infrastructure for competing in elections*, without any of the regulations ensuring equal-price slots for political candidates as regulated on TV.
- *Children:* While children may spend hours at school, they often spend *more hours* per day on their devices and platforms like YouTube, TikTok or Snapchat – often while at school – effectively becoming the *infrastructure for children's development and learning*.
- *Family and Relationships:* Look around you at dinner tables in homes or at restaurants, smartphones have *intermediated the private spaces*

that used to make up family time and meals, and set the background for our relationships.

- *News:* Facebook's algorithms have become the *news and social commentary infrastructure* for 2.7 billion people.
- *Communications:* WhatsApp, Instagram or FB Messenger have become the *primary communications infrastructure* for one-to-many broadcast communication.

Consider the scale. Facebook has more than 2.7 billion users, more than the number of followers of Christianity. YouTube has north of 2 billion users, more than the followers of Islam. Tech platforms arguably have more psychological influence over two billion people's daily thoughts and actions when considering that millions of people spend hours per day within the social world that tech has created, checking hundreds of times a day. In several developing countries like the Philippines, Facebook has 100% penetration. Philippines journalist Maria Ressa calls it the first "Facebook nation."

But what happens when infrastructure is left completely unprotected, and vast harms emerge as a product of tech companies' direct operation and profit?

Social Organs of Society, Left Open for Deception

These private companies have become the eyes, ears, and mouth by which we each navigate, communicate and make sense of the world. Technology companies manipulate our sense of identity, self-worth, relationships, beliefs, actions, attention, memory, physiology and even habit-formation processes, without proper responsibility. Technology has become the filter by which we are experiencing and making sense of the real world. In so doing, technology has directly led to the many failures and problems that we are all seeing: fake news, addiction, polarization, social isolation, declining teen mental health, conspiracy thinking, erosion of trust, breakdown of truth.

But while social media platforms have become our cultural and psychological infrastructure on which society works, commercial *technology companies have failed to mitigate deception on their own platforms from deception*. Imagine a nuclear power industry creating the energy grid infrastructure we all rely on, without taking responsibility for nuclear waste, grid failures, or making sufficient investments to protect it from cyber attacks. And then claiming that we are personally responsible for buying radiation kits to protect ourselves from possible nuclear meltdowns.

By taking over more and more of the "organs" needed for society to function, social media has become the de facto psychological infrastructure that has created conditions that incentivize mass deception at industrialized scales. There are three core aspects of the problem:

1. *For-profit companies operating for private interest have taken over critical, intimate functions in society that should – and used to – operate in the public interest.* Instead of operating for the public good they operate to their own benefit. Even though they have sensitive information about each of us, involuntarily given due to their infrastructure role, they are not required to treat that information with sensitivity – with regard to the wellbeing of the people or the cultures that they inherently affect.
2. *The infrastructure they built has both enabled and been left vulnerable to mass deception and manipulation by:*
    a) Directly taking advantage of our psychological vulnerabilities (self-image, addiction, infinite scrolling feeds) to capture attention necessary for their profits,
    b) Automating that attention with gameable algorithms and impersonated user identities, and
    c) Renting access to the manipulation and targeting of our deepest vulnerabilities with unprecedented precision for advertising purposes, unreviewable by any real regulatory process. The amount of deception that can be created far exceeds that of any realistic process of review.

    Technology companies have covertly "tilted" the playing field of our individual and collective attention, beliefs and behavior to their private commercial benefit. Naturally, these tools and capabilities tend to favor the sole pursuit of private profit far more easily and productively than any "dual purpose" benefits they may also have at one time – momentarily – and occasionally had for culture or society.
3. *Once becoming the obligate infrastructures that manage civilization's global "social organs" they have lead to myriad individual and collective harms (isolation, anxiety, depression, suicide, polarization, war).* Because this loss of unmediated interpersonal communication and relationship is beyond the means of the public to fight back or change, it is the equivalent of extortion. These platforms pollute the information environment and are

damaging to all forms of public deliberation and society, indirectly leading to many other collective problems (disease, pollution, collapse and other environmental damage).

Further critical and consequential outcomes occur *on top* of these lower level infrastructures managed by private companies, including the upbringing and education of the next generation, our national psychological health, and the information environment that determines the outcome of elections.

While tech has taken over each "organ" of the social fabric, they have failed to also take responsibility for managing that system in a healthy and integrated way. They are inherently acting in ways which are deeply harmful to the communities that they claimed they were in service to – "to connect all the people," so that they could "live more meaningful lives." While this is the dream, it is not the reality.

The private tech company takeover of social process poses enormous harms and risks to the people and to those societies that are using this tech, along with the greater civilization. Deep Fakes dismantle our shared capacity to make sense of the world, to determine what is true, what is real, and what we can or should trust. This leads to all sorts of consumer product advertising and marketing issues, hijacking of our election process, and creating a situation in which the most deceptive and least moral actors win, without accountability.

Truth Loses

Truth loses. In an *MIT Twitter study,*[91] fake news spread six times faster than true news. Someone limited to speaking only truths is *constrained*, it takes time and energy to investigate and carefully articulate accurately what is true. By contrast, those speaking falsehoods are unconstrained. You can say anything without exerting any energy to censor yourself. In a competition between the two, the least constrained (least ethical actor who's willing to say *whatever works)* wins. This incentivizes a "race to the bottom of the brain stem" to go lower and lower into unconstrained, fear, outrage, existential, trust-destroying conspiracy thinking to win. If you don't play the game, you lose.

Deception and distortion of our relationships, narrative, and social lives, of our sense of community meaning, takes advantage of our innate human vulnerabilities – the psychological bias that we all have built in. The

[91] https://news.mit.edu/2018/study-twitter-false-news-travels-faster-true-stories-0308.

development of tools for advertisers to leverage our natural social interests is at the root of what has gone wrong in our current use of technology. Both individually and collectively, the unrestrained use of content amplification and context manipulation capabilities are dismantling, directly disrupting, and disabling our democracy – our great nation is at risk of ruin.

They Have Become a "Digital Frankenstein" That Is Out of Control

The manipulation-for-profit (MFP) business model of large technology companies (Facebook, YouTube, Instagram or TikTok) are existential to the sustainability of the societies in which they operate, and cannot be allowed to continue with their current business model.

This manipulation occurs at multiple levels – manipulating our lizard brains to keep people hooked, and then using automated systems for routing content and ads that cannot distinguish between what is true or deceitful (fake accounts, fake users, deep fakes vs. regular content), because it is not profitable to pay actual human editors.

In each case, in support of paid marketing, technology enables the mass deception of consumers to think that things which are unhealthy are "good for them," that things which are false are "popular knowledge," and that things which are actually dangerous are "in the public good." Most of what is causing harm in technology can be broken down into exploitation of human weaknesses:

- Netflix exploits our *reliance on stopping cues* to keep kids and adults alike binge watching and losing sleep.
- "Likes" and "filters" *exploit teens' need for social validation and approval* from others.
- Notification sounds ("you have mail!") *exploits operant conditioning* and habit formation *to expect frequent rewards.*
- Infinite scrolling feeds, "pull to refresh" notifications are designed to operate like slot machines, offering "intermittent variable rewards" as you check for notifications, maximizing addiction.
- Moral outrage *exploits our vulnerability to anger*, fast agreement and desire for tribe membership.
- Fake news and conspiracy theories *exploit our need for significance and confirmation bias* – that what we feel is more important than what we think.

- Deepfakes (including bots, deeptext, etc) exploit the shortcuts our brains rely on to discern what's authentic or trustworthy, and have now become completely and fundamentally indistinguishable from the real thing. This is a trust-breaking deception. This is "checkmate."

A vehicle that results in people more likely getting hurt in car accidents is a product that could be purchased or not, or perhaps purchased from some other maker, because they had a better safety design and public reports. And there are regulations concerning what vehicles will be allowed on the road. Yet Metcalfe's law "winner take all" dynamics ensures that everyone is involved – willingly or not – in social media.

It is like the choice of a community to accept that some company wants to build a nuclear power plant. The people in the surrounding community will be affected, if something goes wrong, regardless. And in such an event, we do not expect that the general public to be responsible – to have their own radiation detectors, or hazmat suits, or to deal with radiation, fallout, etc. With infrastructure, the level of responsibility should be *higher* than it would for an automobile manufacturer. The Nuclear Regulatory Commission puts policies in place to protect the people, when it is clear that asking them to handle the hazards – to make them responsible for the errors of the company – is simply inappropriate. When radiation is everywhere, what does it mean to move away?

It is not a personal responsibility for people to protect themselves from grid attacks, from nuclear waste issues, from chemical spills, quack doctors, toxic food vendors, or anything else which is inherently a commons or utility. Asking "individuals" to be responsible for pollution effects of a business, or to assume that an industry can "regulate itself," is like asking a passenger to "be responsible" for flying the 737 Max plane, or to "take care of themselves" in a crash. Creating unsafe aircraft is not a pilot problem, nor is it a "personal problem." Dangerous and addictive drugs are FDA "controlled substances" for a reason. Gambling must be licensed and sanctioned by the state.

When you create infrastructure that millions or billions of people rely on for the daily function of their lives and their social contracts (information, news, etc.) you become responsible for the harms, direct or indirect, created by that infrastructure. This is the message of responsibility that we need to teach tech companies – like all other types of infrastructure businesses – to adhere to.

Unless the government acts, the competition between technology businesses' never-ending interest in capturing human attention, will irreversibly dismantle the information environment, accelerate polarization leading towards civil war, degrade the mental health of a generation of children and teenagers, and break down the basis for trust itself, leading to market collapse and near permanent civil disorder.

Currently, social tech companies are building infrastructure – but they are not acting responsibly – for the harms that that infrastructure is creating at both personal and societal levels. Therefore, the government must act, and not expect the industry regulate itself. It is not possible for an industry run on optimizing quarterly profits to think in the long term. Yet, it is inherent in the creation of public infrastructure to imply public responsibility and policy.

Therefore, as with all other forms of public works, infrastructure, and common utility, there is also with social tech, media, and communications companies, now a need for similarly clear, effective, and actionable government process, policy, and law, holding such commons infrastructure implementations to reasonable and responsible standards, designed to promote the public good. New law is needed to protect the health and welfare of the consumer, culture, and community, to restore and maintain the value of the commons, the practice of free and open commerce, and the vitality and utility of the digital environment as a whole.

Our current use and deployment of technology is not properly aligned with the limits and vulnerabilities of human nature. It is currently being implemented in a way to weaken us and to disadvantage nearly everyone, so as to favor only a few. Most of what is going wrong with technology today – harming and deceiving the consumer – is based on this misalignment.

Dismantled Shared Truth – The "Flint Water Supply" of Information

By creating 2.7 billion "Truman shows" (personalized channels of automated news feeds) keeping us engaged for hours by calculating what will most likely keep us glued to screens, social media has taken the shared narratives and facts that make society function and put it through an industrial-grade meat shredder.

Newspapers thought they were in the *truth* business but found out they were actually in the *attention* business. It costs money to pay journalists and editors that ultimately generate the attention sold to advertisers.

By allowing technology platforms to take the role of an information environment without journalistic standards, long-form investigation, fact-checking and some notion of care, we suffer the consequences. Exponential hearsay, gossip, "BREAKING" news, and cynical "hot take" commentary generated by the most outrageous voices have become the default information flows that make up how we see reality.

We are the free "gig workers" of the attention economy. Instead of investing in journalists and their protection, Facebook and YouTube turned each of us into unpaid "contractors" who create posts and share links to gain the attention of our friends to look at what we post, and doing it for free by manipulating to our honest desires for belonging and purpose. This has destroyed our way of making sense in the world.

This is not normal, and it is not sustainable. It is the "Flint water supply" of information run by privately-interested tech platforms.

Addiction & Public Health

What we call addiction is when technology manipulates and deceives our dopamine reward systems ("pull to refresh!" like a slot machine), our physiological workings of habit formation (link habit X with action Y), our reliance on stopping cues ("is there an end to scrolling this feed?"), and manipulation of vanity and desire for attention from others ("Look, I got more followers today than I did last week!"). Even Facebook's own founding president, Sean Parker, admitted that he, along with the founders of Instagram, Mark Zuckerberg, and others, knew they were designing their products to exploit vulnerabilities in human psychology and "we did it anyway."[92]

Most of all, this affects kids and teenagers. We are raising a generation of children who are more distracted, less creative, more narcissistic, and more vulnerable to bullying and teen suicides than in the last few decades. While we glorify U.S. tech companies as the crown jewels of our economy, we are profiting off of the harm to our own children, cannibalizing our national longevity and the well-being of our citizens.

Bragging about the U.S. economic growth from our most harmful tech companies, is like bragging about getting a plastic surgery while suffering from congestive heart failure. The organs that make up our society are failing.

Social Pressure & Deception of Self-Image

Social media is harming teenagers. After nearly two decades in decline, "high depressive" symptoms for 13-18 year old teen girls rose 170% between 2010 - 2017 which researchers such as NYU sociologist Jonathan Haidt link directly

---

92 https://www.theguardian.com/technology/2017/nov/09/facebook-sean-parker-vulnerability-brain-psychology.

to social media.[93] Tech products using beautification filters like Snapchat have led to "Body Dysmorphic Disorder" – where people's self-image is distorted by beautification filters, is harming mental health. In a survey of plastic surgeons, 55% said they'd seen patients whose primary motivation was to look better in selfies, up from 13% in 2016.[94] On YouTube, two years ago if a teen girl searched for "dieting" videos, the recommendation systems would recommend "anorexia" videos because they were better at keeping attention.[95]

Is it surprising that mental health problems surge when millions of kids negotiating their identity in public with immediate feedback are taught, "people like you... if only you looked different than you actually are."

An example of Snapchat Beautification filters.

Each time a child is admitted to a hospital, there is a real-life family dealing with a tragedy.

Moreover, parents are trapped in a "game" of social pressure controlled by companies that capture enough children in a community that essentially force all other children in that school or community to be on their service. Parents feel intense pressure to give in and let middle school kids have it only because everyone else has it.

[93] https://journals.sagepub.com/doi/full/10.1177/2167702617723376.
[94] https://www.aafprs.org/media/stats_polls/m_stats.html.
[95] https://www.wired.com/story/how-pro-eating-disorder-posts-evade-social-media-filters/.

A chart of high-depressive symptoms for teenage girls – whose sense of personal self-worth is much more likely to be defined in terms of the currency of the attention of their peers – rose 170% between 2010 and 2017.

Joe Camel ads from the tobacco industry also went directly after children to capture "early" market share.

Conspiracy Theories, Deepfakes and the Basis of Trust

70% of YouTube's traffic is driven by its recommendation engine. Multiplied by two billion people that use YouTube, this has vast consequences. Because the recommendation system is automated, it does not know what's valuable, ethical, or credible beyond what got the most clicks or watchtime.

Inadvertently, YouTube's algorithms have recommended countless conspiracy theories. Conspiracy theories like Flat Earth were recommended by YouTube hundreds of millions of times. Alex Jones InfoWars conspiracies were recommended 15 billion times before being removed.

While it might sound innocuous and funny, the Flat Earth conspiracy is particularly damaging because if taken seriously, it means that *all of science and the entirety of government has been lying to the public*. It means you can't trust *any of science*. That sentence is worth repeating.

Conspiracies are "trust bombs" because they eliminate all faith in science, reason and institutions. Using bot networks to amplify "the Election is rigged" becomes a common doubt – people are disenfranchised and no longer vote. Authoritarian regimes are recognizing their power to use these effects deliberately. In the Philippines, there is evidence of populist movements behind authoritarian president Roderigo Duterte promoting the Filipino Flat Earth conspiracies groups to sow distrust in the media and scientific establishment.[96]

Conspiracies can have lasting effects for decades. Famously, a Soviet disinformation campaign in 1983 seeded the idea that the HIV virus raging across the world was a bioweapon released by the United States, based on an *anonymous letter*[97] published in an Indian newspaper, and ended up becoming widely believed among those predisposed to distrust the Reagan administration. From Russian disinformation researcher Renée DiResta, "As late as 2005, *a study showed*[98] that 27 percent of African Americans still believed that HIV was created in a government lab."[99]

---

[96] https://blogs.lse.ac.uk/medialse/2019/08/28/beyond-conspiracy-the-ties-that-bind-filipino-flat-earthers-and-populist-supporters/.

[97] https://www.washingtonpost.com/news/made-by-history/wp/2018/03/12/the-russian-fake-news-campaign-that-damaged-the-united-states-in-the-1980s/.

[98] https://www.prb.org/conspiracybeliefsmaybehinderinghivpreventionamongafricanamericans/.

[99] https://www.washingtonpost.com/opinions/2019/11/15/heres-how-russia-will-attack-election-were-still-not-ready/.

Mass Deception – Trolling Elections, Civil Wars, and Geopolitics

Our minds operate on the principle of social proof: if others believe it and say it's true, we're more likely to believe that it's true. But with social media, it's never been easier to synthesize fake consensus, as detailed by this Russian troll:

> "We did it by dividing into teams of three," *he said.* "One of us would be the 'villain,' the person who disagrees with the forum and criticizes the authorities, in order to bring a feeling of authenticity to what we're doing. *The other two enter into a debate with him — 'No, you're not right; everything here is totally correct.' One of them should provide some kind of graphic or image that fits in the context, and the other has to post a link to some content that supports his argument. You see? Villain, picture, link."*[100]
> (Interview with Russian troll)

Foreign actors have also gone after U.S. veterans communities online to sow distrust of the military and government. In a report by social media research analytics firm Graphic telling the House Veterans Affairs Committee, Russia-linked ads from the 2016 election found *"at least 113 ads directed at veterans, or which used veterans as props in Russia's mission to divide Americans.* "Foreign actors have been targeting U.S. veterans across social media for at least eight years" Vlad Barash, says Graphicka's science director.

To this day, even after Twitter and other platforms have banned paid political ads, it's still incredibly cheap to buy influence as this is still the fundamental business model and it's impossible for them to fully distinguish paid political speech from any other speech. NATO recently discovered "At a cost of just 300 euros (about $333), NATO StratCom bought 3,530 comments, 25,750 likes, 20,000 views and 5,100 followers across the four platforms."[101]

Moreover, it's never been easier to impersonate being someone you're not. In one quarter alone, Facebook shut down 2.2 billion fake accounts. Tech platforms leave the doors open to anyone who would want to create a fake account to impersonate anyone else – so as to maintain plausible deniability. While we have been obsessed with closing down and protecting our physical borders, we've left the digital borders *wide open* for abuse by any actor.

Keeping in mind that Facebook and YouTube's commanding the daily attention of more than two billion users for hours a day, a psychological

---

[100] https://share.america.gov/trolls-everything-you-wanted-to-know/.

[101] https://www.buzzfeednews.com/article/albertonardelli/facebook-twitter-google-manipulation-nato-stratcom.

footprint greater than the followers of the Christian church, technology has become the *de facto information environment* by our civilization makes sense of the world: what is real, and what is true.

Platforms have disrupted the psychological logistics, by eliminating the capacity for people to have trust in what is true, our capacity to agree, or build consensus and take action instead of feeling hopeless. DARPA calls this "reality jamming" and the RAND Corporation calls this "truth decay."

The risks of disinformation continue to escalate into serious potential problems. The consequences can range from internal polarization, functionally biased elections, civil wars, escalation of international disputes to nuclear-armed conflict, as a civilization as a whole, all the way up to whether we can agree on whether we are actually facing existential threats at all. A report by the Toda Peace Institute's stated, "we have already seen six instances of social media playing a role in nuclear-prone conflicts occurring between August 2017 and January 2018" in the Asia-Pacific region.[102]

Will China Win? Or Will Democracy Survive?

Today's technology platforms have put our civilization into tremendous danger. If we continue to let the big tech company platforms continue to enable civilization's regression into a "Digital Dark Age," it will also be the case that the government will have failed its basic job to protect the land and the people.

> The real problem of humanity is that we have Paleolithic emotions, Medieval institutions, and God-like technology. (Dr. E.O. Wilson)

Our human physiology isn't changing any time soon – it evolves over many millennia. But our technology is growing exponentially more powerful, over a trillion times since the computer was invented in 1946.

Technology can either be used to create a kind of robustness that makes society and democracy work, or it can be used to disable that democracy completely. The culture, incentives, and protections must be shaped so technology's god-like power is always in service to human values – never the other way around. Any other arrangement is catastrophic to the human race, as god-like powers are expressed outside the control and wise guidance of humanity.

---

102 https://toda.org/assets/files/resources/policy-briefs/t-pb-66_peter-hayes_social-media-arrives-on-the-nuclear-stage.pdf.

We *can* live in a world of humane technology. One that is built on protecting the vulnerabilities and limits of human nature. It can align with the development of human sovereignty. To do that – to have any possibility of a bright future – we must give up the desire to allow it to continue to be used to exploit our natural human weaknesses.

Technology is not going away. We can't put the genie of these god-like powers back in the bottle. Technology can – and must – be implemented and used in a manner that is consistent with healthy society, communities, and the world.

Therefore, we must tame the tech, regulate its business model for the common good of the people, as the temptation to misuse it to take "advantage" of someone's short sighted personal ends, is too great for any one of us to manage by ourselves. We must reign-in such forces into an alignment with the well-being of our communities.

It is natural, therefore, to suggest that the government put regulations in place around any industry and its products, services and procedures, to prevent societal harms and/or to harness the technology in salutary ways – like any other fundamental infrastructure we live by, whether that's the auto industry, electric/power utilities, roads and transportation, or anything else.

Most people recognize the need and the benefits of government regulating various aspects of industries that operate common infrastructure. The Big Five – Facebook, Google, Amazon, Microsoft, Apple – is the new infrastructure of our social fabric. Representative democracies have the right to put the rules around companies that society has determined are necessary. Why should these Big Tech companies be any different?

Why should any private infrastructure company be allowed to collect, store or in any way use or manipulate our personal data? After all, the Post Office can't do it, FedEx and UPS can't do it. There are many businesses that are not allowed to use our data – whether personal data or location data – in these sorts of toxic ways. So why not just regulate the social tech infrastructure companies, and their services, the way these other businesses are regulated?

Federal criminal laws are designed to deter and punish trafficking in stalking and harassment by means of computer. If we define "stalking" as following the user everywhere, tracking and collecting photos and notes about everything that they are doing, as if every person in the world was a paparazzi target; then perhaps we should regard that each social infrastructure tech company is *stalking* each and every user on their platform, at industrial scales. If so, then there is a clear and present need for an anti-stalking law, to protect our children, ourselves, and our communities, from digital surveillance capitalism.

Some possible policy directions that can be explored:

1. *Mandate a "Digital Update"* to each of the regulatory bodies already charged with doing their job on these problems. Instead of creating a brand new Digital Federal agency to regulate all digital matters, we could extend all the existing agencies who already have jurisdiction over the areas with a "digital update" to deal with the public health, public education, election and broadcast issues, etc. The SEC could monitor fraud from tech platforms in the form of fake clicks, fake users and mandate regular reporting from tech companies. HHS and NIH could force quarterly reporting by technology companies on how many users are addicted, depressed, isolated etc for addressing the public health, addiction and teen suicide aspects, with quarter goals set with tech companies to issue product updates to address the problems. A "Digital Update" would also be popular with the American public who are increasingly alarmed about these issues and want to see government act to update our medieval institutions for the 21st century, let alone the 2020 decade.
2. *Apply the principles of broadcast law to technology platforms* that enable broadcasting of matching scale and reach, without any of the responsibility. There should be restrictions on developing and/or deploying tools for the creation of weaponized disinformation campaigns, or for the creation, dissemination, or distribution of ads targeting children, seniors, mentally disabled or developmentally disadvantaged, or other vulnerable populations. In the same way that you cannot simply just sell automatic weapons to anyone, that you cannot also grant unlimited broadcast license, beyond certain volumes, to just anyone who wants it.
3. *Require tech platforms that have asymmetrically powerful and sensitive information about what influences users' or communities' behavior and beliefs to have Fiduciary responsibilities to that membership.* We can't have private companies that privately profit for their own self-interest, while dumping harm and excess risk onto the balance sheets of society. Business interest cares about short-term self-interest, not long-term, societal-scale issues. We need government to represent the common long-term interest and well-being.

4. *Decouple profit from attention* and clean up the attention economy. Explore making attention, social, and voting manipulation markets should be illegal.
5. *Put sane limits* on the development and/or deploying of tools and technologies designed for the purpose of social capital value mining, extraction, and the aggressive re-purposing of cultural norms, sacred icons, religious morals, etc. This includes the use of deepfakes.
6. *Set up some forms of real and legal deterrence.* In China, the use of deep-fake technology without labeling it as such, for any reason, is simply illegal – treated as an information weapon and inherent moral hazard – and that people violating that law are put into prison. Our analog could be temporary platform bans. Citizens seeing actual enforcement of their own protection has the effect of supporting the building of reliable trust and identity infrastructures in community.

No regulation is perfect. Sometimes you kill some of the lesser notions of "good" while protecting against the more serious and significant harms. These harms accrue into a dystopia we cannot afford: a world without truth, mass social isolation, constant social pressure, and a whole generation of children and teenagers who never knew that life could be different.

Conclusion

I believe in a world where technology industry is remade in a manner that becomes a more empowering tool – something that serves humanity and life again. Where it is built around servicing our needs and strengthening the fabric of our society, not parasitically extracting value from the most vulnerable organs of society. Where technology strengths our capacity to see multiple perspectives, nuance and complexity – where there are no black and white answers.

We need technology to aid us in these endeavors for our civilization to survive.

While we all have base emotions, we also always have something unique to our species: a capacity for choice. The ability to do other than what would simply be predicted by past behavior, or whatever profit is dangled in front of our brains.

In a way this situation is a test: will we be the chimpanzees with predictable emotions drawn to economic growth, or will we recognize that no one else is going to put their hand on the steering wheel. You have to do it. You have to make a choice. That choice is now up to you.

* * *

Ms. SCHAKOWSKY. Thank you.

So now we have concluded our witnesses' opening statements. At this time, we will move to Member questions. Each Member will have 5 minutes to ask a question of our witnesses. I will begin by recognizing myself for 5 minutes.

So, as chair of the subcommittee, over and over again I am confronted with new evidence that Big Tech has failed in regulating itself. When we had Mark Zuckerberg here, I kind of did a review of all the apologies that we have had from him over the years, and I am concerned that Facebook's latest effort to address misinformation on the platforms leaves a lot out.

I want to begin with some questions of you, Ms. Bickert. So the deepfakes policy only covers video, as I understand it, that has been manipulated using artificial intelligence, or deep learning. Is that correct?

Ms. BICKERT. Thank you, Chairwoman Schakowsky. The policy that we announced yesterday is confined to the definition that we set forth about artificial intelligence being used in a video to make it appear that somebody is saying something——

Ms. SCHAKOWSKY. I only have 5 minutes. So the video, for example, of Speaker Pelosi was edited to make her look like she was drunk, wouldn't have been taken down under the new policy. Is that right, yes or no?

Ms. BICKERT. It would not fall under that policy, but it would still be subject to our other policies that address misinformation.

Ms. SCHAKOWSKY. And, as I read the deepfakes policy, it only covers video where a person is made to appear like they said words that they didn't actually say, but it doesn't cover videos where just the image is altered. Is that true?

Ms. BICKERT. Chairwoman Schakowsky, that is correct about that policy. We do have a broader approach to misinformation that would put a label—we would actually obscure the image and put a screen over it that says "false information," and directs people to information from fact checkers.

Ms. SCHAKOWSKY. So, Ms. Bickert, I really don't understand why Facebook should treat fake audio differently from fake images. Both can be highly misleading and result in significant harm to individuals and undermine democratic institutions.

Dr. Donovan, in your testimony, you noted that, quote, "cheapfakes," unquote, are more prevalent than deepfakes. Do you see any reason to treat deepfakes and cheapfakes differently?

Dr. DONOVAN. One of the things——

Ms. SCHAKOWSKY. Microphone.

Dr. DONOVAN. Of course, as if I am not loud enough.

One of the things that cheapfakes leverage is what is sort of great about social media, is that it makes things clippier, or smaller. And so I understand the need for separate policies, but also the cheapfakes issue has not been enforced. Speaking more broadly about social media platforms in general, there is completely uneven enforcement.

So you can still find that piece of misinformation within the wrong context in multiple places. And so the policy on deepfakes is both narrow—and I understand why—but also, one thing that we should understand is presently there is no consistent detection mechanism for even finding deepfakes at this point. And so I would be interested to know more about how they are going to seek out, either on upload, not just Facebook——

Ms. SCHAKOWSKY. I am going to have to cut you off at this point, because I do want to ask Mr. Harris.

Given the prevalence of deceptive content online, are platforms doing enough to stop the dissemination of misinformation, and what can government do to prevent such manipulation of consumers? Should government be seeking to clarify the principle that if it is illegal offline then it is illegal online?

Mr. HARRIS. Yes. A good example of that—so first is no, the platforms are not doing enough, and it is because their entire business model is misaligned with solving the problem. And I don't vilify the people because of that. It is just their business model is against the issue.

We used to have Saturday morning cartoons. We protected children from certain kinds of advertising, time/place/manner restrictions. When YouTube gobbles up that part of the attention economy, we lose all those protections. So why not bring back the protections of Saturday morning? We used to have fair-price/equal-price election ads on TV, the same price for each politician to reach someone. When Facebook gobbles up election advertising, we just removed all of those same protections.

So we are basically moving from a lawful society to an unlawful virtual internet society, and that is what we have to change.

Ms. SCHAKOWSKY. Thank you. I yield back.

And now the Chair recognizes Mrs. Rodgers, our subcommittee ranking member, for 5 minutes.

Mrs. RODGERS. Thank you, Madam Chair.

I referenced how misinformation is not a new problem, but certainly with the speed of information, how it can travel in the online world, its harm is increasing. That said, I have long believed that the way to address information is more transparency, more sources, more speech, not less. This is important, not just in an election cycle, but also in discussions around public health issues, natural disasters, or any number of significant events. I am worried about this renewed trend, where some want the government to set the parameters and potentially limit speech and expression. Ms. Bickert, how does free speech and expression factor into Facebook's content decisions, and can you please explain your use of third-party fact checkers?

Ms. BICKERT. Thank you. We are very much a platform for free expression. It is one of the reasons that we work with third-party fact-checking organizations, because what we do if they have ranked something false is, we share more information on the service. So we put a label over it, this is false information, but then we show people here is what fact checkers are saying about this story.

We work with more than 50 organizations worldwide, and those organizations are chosen after meeting high standards for fact checking.

Mrs. RODGERS. Thank you. As a followup, with the total volume of traffic you have, clearly human eyes alone can't keep up. So artificial intelligence and machine learning have a significant role to identify not only deepfakes but also other content that violates your terms of service. Would you just explain a little bit more to us how you use AI and the potential to use AI to fight fire with fire?

Ms. BICKERT. Absolutely. We do use a combination of technology, and people to identify potential information to send to fact checkers. We also use people and technology to try to assess whether or not something has been manipulated, media. That would be covered by the policy we released yesterday.

So, with the fact-checking program, we use technology to look for things like—let's say somebody has shared an image or a news story and people are—friends are commenting on that, saying, "Don't you know this is a hoax?" or "This isn't true." That is the sort of thing our technology can spot and send that content over to fact-checkers.

But it is not just technology. We also have ways for people to flag if they are seeing something that they believe to be false. That can send content over to fact checkers. And then the fact checkers can also proactively choose to rate something that they are seeing on Facebook.

Mrs. RODGERS. Thank you.

Professor Hurwitz, can you briefly describe how user interfaces can be designed to shape consumer choice and how such designs may benefit or harm consumers?

Mr. HURWITZ. They can be used—they can be modified, created, structured in any number of ways. We have heard examples: font size, text placement, the course of interaction with a website, or even just a phone menu system. These can be used to guide users into making uninformed decisions, or to highlight information that users should be paying attention to. This broadly falls into the category of nudges and behavioral psychology. That is an intensely researched area. It can be used in many ways.

Mrs. RODGERS. You highlighted some of that in your testimony. Would you explain how the FTC can use its existing Section 5 authority to address most of the concerns raised by dark pattern practices?

Mr. HURWITZ. Yes, very briefly. I could lecture for a semester on this, not to say that I have.

The FTC has a broad history, long history of regulating unfair and deceptive practices and advertising practices. Its deception authority—false statements, statements that are material to a consumer, making a decision that is harmful to the consumer. They can use adjudication. They can enact rules in order to take action against platforms or any entity, online or offline, that deceives consumers.

Mrs. RODGERS. Do you think that they are doing enough?

Mr. HURWITZ. I would love to see the FTC do more in this area, especially when it comes to rulemaking and in-court enforcement actions, because the boundaries of their authority are unknown, uncertain, untested. This is an area where bringing suits, bringing litigation, that tells us what the agency is capable of, which this body needs to know before it tries to craft more legislation or give more authority to an entity. If we already have an agency that has power, let's see what it is capable of.

Mrs. RODGERS. Right. OK. Thank you, everyone. I appreciate you all being here. Very important subject, and I appreciate the Chair for hosting, or having this hearing today.

Ms. SCHAKOWSKY. I thank the ranking member, who yields back. And now I recognize the chair of the full committee, Mr. Pallone, for 5 minutes.

Mr. PALLONE. Thank you, Madam Chair.

I have got a lot to ask here, so I am going to ask you for your responses to be brief, if possible. But, in your various testimonies, you all talked about a variety of technologies and techniques that are being used to deceive and manipulate consumers.

We have heard about user interfaces designed to persuade and sometimes trick people into making certain choices, deepfakes and cheapfakes, that show fictional scenarios that look real, and algorithms designed to keep people's eyes locked on their screens. And we know these things are happening. But what is less clear is how and the extent to which these techniques are being used commercially and on commercial platforms.

So first let me ask Dr. Donovan: As a researcher who focuses on the use of these techniques, do you have sufficient access to commercial platform data to have a comprehensive understanding of how disinformation and fraud is conducted and by whom?

Dr. DONOVAN. The brief answer is no, and that is because we don't have access to the data as it is. There are all these limits on the ways in which you can acquire data through the interface.

And then the other problem is that there was a very good-faith effort between Facebook and scholars to try to get a bunch of data related to the 2016 election. That fell apart, but a lot of people put an incredible amount of time, money, and energy into that effort, and it failed around the issues related to privacy and differential privacy.

What I would love to see also happen is, Twitter has started to give data related to deletions and account takedowns. We need a record of that so that, when we do audit these platforms for either financial or social harms, that the deletions are also included and marked. Because, even if you can act like a data scavenger and go back and get data, when things are deleted, sometimes they are just gone for good, and those pieces of information are often the most crucial.

Mr. PALLONE. Thank you.

Mr. Harris, should the government be collecting more information about such practices in order to determine how best to protect Americans?

Mr. HARRIS. Yes. Here is an example: So, unlike other addictive industries, for example—addiction is part of the deception that is going on here—the tobacco industry doesn't know which users are addicted to smoking, the alcohol industry doesn't know exactly who is addicted to alcohol. But, unlike that, each tech company does know exactly how many people are checking more than, you know, 100 times a day between certain ages. They know who is using it late at night.

And you can imagine using existing agencies—say, Department of Health and Human Services—to be able to audit Facebook on a quarterly basis and say, "Hey, tell us how many users are addicted between these ages, and then what are you doing next quarter to make adjustments to reduce that number?"

And every day they are the ones issuing the questions, and the responsibility and the resources have to be deployed by the actor that has the most of them, which in this case would be Facebook. And there is a quarterly loop between each agency asking questions like that, forcing accountability with the companies for the areas of their existing jurisdiction.

So I am just trying to figure out is that a way that we can scale this to meet the scope of the problem. You realize this is happening to 2.7 billion people.

Mr. PALLONE. Thank you. This week, Facebook released a new policy on how it will handle deepfakes. So, Ms. Bickert, under your policy deepfakes are—and I am paraphrasing—videos manipulated through artificial intelligence that are intended to mislead and are not parody or satire. Did I get that right?

Ms. BICKERT. Yes, that is right.

Mr. PALLONE. OK. Now, I understand that Twitter and YouTube either do not have or use the same definition for deepfakes, and that is indicative of a lack of consistent treatment of problematic content across the major platforms. Banned hate speech or abusive behavior on one site is permitted on another. There seems to be very little consistency across the marketplace, which leaves consumers at a loss.

So let me go to Dr. Donovan again. Is there a way to develop a common set of standards for these problematic practices so that consumers are not facing different policies on different websites?

Dr. DONOVAN. I think it is possible to create a set of policies, but you have to look at the features that are consistent across these platforms. If they do, for instance, use attention to a specific post in their algorithms to boost popularity, then we need a regulation around that, especially because bots or unmanned accounts, for lack of a better term, are often used to accelerate content and to move content across platforms.

These are things that are usually purchased off-platform, and they are considered a dark market product, but you can purchase attention to an issue. And so, as a result, there has to be something more broad that goes across platforms, but also looks at the features and then also tries to regulate some of these markets that are not built into the platform themselves.

Mr. PALLONE. All right. Thank you.

Thank you, Madam Chair.

Ms. SCHAKOWSKY. Thank you.

Mr. Bucshon, you are recognized for 5 minutes.

Mr. BUCSHON. Thank you, Madam Chairwoman. I am sorry, I have two of these hearings going on at the same time, so I am back and forth.

I appreciate the hearing and the opportunity to discuss the spread of misinformation on the internet, but I want to stress that I am concerned over the efforts to make tech companies the adjudicators of "truth," in quotation marks.

In a country founded on free speech, we should not be allowing private corporations, in my view, or, for that matter, the government to determine what qualifies as, again in quotation marks, the "truth," potentially censoring a voice because that voice disagrees with a mainstream opinion. That said, I totally understand the difficulty and the challenges that we all face together concerning this issue, and how we are, together, trying to work to address it.

Ms. Bickert, can you provide some more information on how Facebook might or will determine if a video misleads? What factors might you consider?

Ms. BICKERT. Thank you. Just to be clear, there are two ways that we might be looking at that issue. One is with regard to the deepfakes policy that we released yesterday. And we will be looking to see, specifically, were we seeing artificial intelligence and deep learning? Was that part of the technology that led to change or fabricate a video in a way that really wouldn't be evident to the average person? And that will be a fundamental part of determining whether there is misleading.

Separately——

Mr. BUCSHON. Can I ask a question? Who is the average—sorry, I will wait until you quit coughing so you can hear me.

Ms. BICKERT. I am sorry.

Mr. BUCSHON. The question then—I mean, I am playing devil's advocate here—who is the average person?

Ms. BICKERT. Congressman, these are exactly the questions that we have been discussing with more than 50 experts as we have tried to write this policy and get it in the right place.

Mr. BUCSHON. And I appreciate what you are doing. I am not trying to be difficult here.

Ms. BICKERT. No, these are real challenging issues. It is one of the reasons that we think, generally, the approach to misinformation of getting more information out there from accurate sources is effective.

Mr. BUCSHON. And you stated in your testimony that, once a fact checker rates a photo or video as false, or partly false, Facebook reduces the distribution. Is there a way for an individual who may have posted these things to protest the decision?

Ms. BICKERT. Yes, Congressman. They can go directly to the fact checker. We make sure there is a mechanism for that. And they can do that either if they dispute it or if they have amended whatever it was in their article that was the problem.

Mr. BUCSHON. Right. Because I would say—I mean, people with good lawyers can dispute a lot of things, but the average citizen in southwest Indiana who posts something online, there needs to be, in my view, a fairly straightforward process that the average person, whoever that might be, can understand to protest or dispute the fact that their distribution has been reduced. Thank you.

Mr. Hurwitz, you have discussed that the FTC has current authority to address dark pattern. However, I would be interested to know your thoughts on how consumers can protect themselves from these patterns and advertisements. Is the only solution through government action, or can consumer education help highlight these advertisement practices?

Mr. HURWITZ. The most important thing for any company, especially in the online context, is trust, the trust of the consumers. Consumer education, user education, is important, but I think that it is fair to say, with condolences perhaps to Ms. Bickert, Facebook has a trust problem. If consumers—if users stop trusting these platforms, if hearings such as this shine a light on bad practices, then they are going to have a hard time retaining users and consumers. That puts a great deal of pressure.

In addition, stability of practices. One dark pattern is to constantly change the user interface, so users don't know how it operates. If we have stability, if we have platforms that operate in consistent, predictable ways, that helps users become educated, helps users understand what the practices are, and learn how to operate in this new environment. Trust on the internet is different. We are still learning what it means.

Mr. BUCSHON. And I know you went over this, but can you talk again about how these dark pattern practices took place before the internet and are currently happening in brick-and-mortar stores and other areas, mail pieces that politicians send out.

I mean, I just want to reiterate again: This is a broader problem than just the internet, this is something that has been around for a while.

Mr. HURWITZ. Yes. Dark patterns, these practices, they go back to the beginning of time. Fundamentally, they are persuasion. If I want to convince you of my world view, if I want to convince you to be my customer, if I want to convince you to be my friend, I am going to do things that influence you. I am going to present myself to you in ways that are going to try and get you to like me or my product.

If you come into my store and ask for a recommendation—"What size tire do I need for my car?"—my sales representative is going to give you information. The store is going to be structured—these have been used consistently throughout——

Mr. BUCSHON. My time is expired. My point was is that, when we look at this problem, we need to, in my view, take a holistic approach about what has happened in the past and, with emerging technology, how we address that consistently and not just target specific industries.

Thank you. I yield back.

Ms. SCHAKOWSKY. The gentleman yields back.

I now recognize Congresswoman Castor for 5 minutes.

Ms. CASTOR. Well, thank you, Chairwoman Schakowsky, for calling this hearing.

You know, the internet and online platforms have developed over time without a lot of safeguards for the public. And government here, we exercise our responsibility to keep the public safe, whether it is the cars we drive, or the water we drink, airplanes, drugs that are for sale. And really, the same should apply to the internet and online platforms.

You know, there is a lot of illegal activity being promoted online, where the First Amendment just does not come into play. And I hope we don't go down that rabbit hole, because we are talking about human trafficking, terrorist plots, illicit sales of firearms, child exploitation.

And now, what we have swamping these online platforms that control the algorithms that manipulate the public are the deepfakes, these dark patterns, artificial intelligence, identity theft. But these online platforms, remember, they control these algorithms that steer children and adults, everyone in certain directions, and we have got to get a handle on that.

For example, Mr. Harris, one manipulative design technique is the autoplay feature. It is now ubiquitous across video streaming platforms, particularly billions of people that go onto YouTube or Facebook. This feature automatically begins playing a new video after the current video ends. The next video is determined using an algorithm. It is designed to keep the viewer's attention.

This platform-driven algorithm often drives the proliferation of illegal activities and dangerous ideologies and conspiracy theories. It makes it much more difficult for the average person to try to get truth-based content.

I am particularly concerned about the impact on kids, and you have raised that and I appreciate that. You discuss how the mental health of kids today really is at risk. Can you talk more about the context in which children may be particularly harmed by these addiction-maximizing algorithms and what parents can do to protect kids from becoming trapped in a YouTube vortex, and what you believe our responsibility is as policymakers?

Mr. HARRIS. Thank you so much for your question. Yes, this is very deeply concerning to me.

So laying it out, with more than 2 billion users, think of these on YouTube as 2 billion "Truman Shows." Each of you get a channel, and a super computer is just trying to calculate the perfect thing to confirm your view of reality. This, by definition, fractures reality into 2 billion different polarizing channels, each of which is tuned to bring you to a more extreme view.

The quick example is, imagine a spectrum of all the videos on YouTube laid out in one line, and on my left side over here, you have the calm Walter Cronkite, rational science side of YouTube, and the other side you have Crazy Town. You have UFOs, conspiracy theories, Alex Jones, crazy stuff.

No matter where you start on YouTube, you could start in the calm section or you could start in crazy. If I want you to watch more, am I going to steer you that way or that way? I am always going to steer you towards Crazy Town. So imagine taking the ant colony of 2.1 billion humans and then just tilting it like that.

Three examples of that per your kids example: 2 years ago on YouTube, if a teen girl watched a dieting video, it would autoplay anorexia videos, because those were more extreme. If you watched a 9/11 news video, it would recommend 9/11 conspiracy theories. If you watched videos about the moon landing, it would recommend flat Earth conspiracy theories.

Flat earth conspiracy theories were recommended hundreds of millions of times. This might sound just funny and, "Oh, look at those people," but actually this is very serious. I have a researcher friend who studied this. If the flat Earth theory is true, it means not just that all of government is lying to you, but all of science is lying to you. So think about that for a second. That is like a meltdown of all of our rational epistemic understanding of the world.

And, as you said, these things are autoplaying. So autoplay is just like [holds up cup]—it hacks your brain's stopping cue. So, as a magician, how do I know if I want you to stop? I put a stopping cue and your mind wakes up. It is like a right angle in a choice. If I stop drinking, if the water hits the bottom of the glass, I have to make a conscious choice, do I want more? But we can design it so the bowl never stops. We can just keep refilling the water, and you never stop. And that is how we basically have kept millions of kids addicted. In places like the Philippines, people watch YouTube for 10 hours a day. Ten hours a day.

Ms. CASTOR. This has significant cost to the public, and that is one of the points I hope people will understand. As Dr. Donovan says, there is economy of misinformation now. These online platforms now are passing along—they are monetizing, making billions of dollars. Meanwhile, public health costs, law enforcement costs are adding up to the public, and we have a real responsibility to tackle this and level the playing field.

Mr. HARRIS. And by not acting, we are subsidizing our societal self-destruction. I mean, we are subsidizing that right now. So yes, absolutely. Thank you so much.

Ms. SCHAKOWSKY. I recognize Representative Burgess for 5 minutes.

Mr. BURGESS. Thank you. Thanks for holding this hearing. I apologize. We have another Health hearing going on upstairs, so it is one of those days you got to toggle between important issues.

Mr. Hurwitz, let me start by asking you—and this is a little bit off topic, but it is important. In 2018, United States District Court for Western Pennsylvania indicted seven Russians for conducting a physical cyber hacking operation in 2016 against Western targets, including the United States Anti-Doping Agency, in response to the revelation of Russia's state-sponsored doping campaign. These hackers were representatives of the Russian military, the GRU. According to the indictment, the stolen information was publicized by the GRU as part of a related influence and disinformation campaign designed to undermine the legitimate interests of the victims. This information included personal medical information about United States athletes.

So these GRU hackers used fictitious identities and fake social media accounts to research and probe victims and their computer networks. While the methods we are talking about today are largely in the context of perhaps deceiving voters or consumers, the harmful potential effects is actually quite large.

So, in your testimony, you defined the dark pattern, the practice of using design to prompt desired, if not necessarily desirable, behavior. Can these dark patterns be used to surveil people and find ways to hack them in the service of broader state-sponsored operations?

Mr. HURWITZ. Yes, absolutely, they can. And this goes to the broader context in which this discussion is happening. We are not only talking about consumer protection, we are talking about a fundamental architecture. The nature, as I said before, of trust online is different. All of those cues that we rely on for you to know who I am when you see me sitting here. We have gone through some vetting process to be sitting here. We have identities. We have telltale cues that you can rely on to know who I am and who you are. Those are different online, and we need to think about trust online differently.

One example that I will highlight that goes to an industry-based solution and, more important, the nature of how we need to think about these things differently, in the context of targeted advertising and political advertising in particular, how do we deal with targeted misinformation for political ads?

Well, one approach which Facebook has been experimenting with is, instead of saying you can't speak, you can't advertise, if I target an ad at a group of speakers, Facebook will let someone else target an ad to that same group, or they have been experimenting with this.

It is a different way of thinking about how we deal with establishing trust or responding to untrustworthy information. We need more creative thinking. We need more research about how do we establish trust in the online environment.

Mr. BURGESS. Well, thank you, and thank you for those observations.

Ms. Bickert, if I ever doubted the power of Facebook, 3 years ago that doubt was completely eliminated. One of your representatives actually offered to do a Facebook event in the district that I represent in northern Texas. And it was not a political—it was a business-to-business. It is how to facilitate and run your small business more efficiently. And wanted to do a program, and we selected a Tuesday morning. And I asked how big a venue should we get, thinking maybe 20, 30. And I was told 2,000, expect 2,000 people to show up. I am like, "Two thousand people on a Tuesday morning for a business-to-business Facebook presentation? Are you nuts?"

The place was standing room only, and it was the power of Facebook getting the word out there that this is what we are doing. And it was one of the most well-attended events I have ever been to as an elected representative. So, if I had ever doubted the power of Facebook, it was certainly brought home to me just exactly the kind of equity that you are able to wield.

But recognizing that, do you have a sense of the type of information on your platforms that needs to be fact-checked, because you do have such an enormous amount of equity?

Ms. BICKERT. Yes, Congressman. And thank you for those words. We are concerned not just with misinformation—that is a concern, and that is why we developed the relationships we have now with more than 50 fact-checking organizations—but we are also concerned with abuse of any type. I am responsible for managing that, so whether it is terror propaganda, hate speech, threats of violence, child exploitation content, content that promotes eating disorders. Any of that violates our policies, and we go after it proactively to try to find it and remove it. That is what my team is.

Mr. BURGESS. Do you feel you have been successful?

Ms. BICKERT. I think we have had a lot of successes, and we are making huge strides. There is always more to do. We have begun publishing reports in the past year and a half or so, every 6 months, where we actually show across different abuse types how prevalent is this on Facebook from doing a sample, how much content did we find this quarter and remove, and how much did we find before anybody reported it to us?

The numbers are trending in a good direction, in terms of how effective our enforcement measures are, and we hope that will continue to improve.

Mr. BURGESS. As policymakers, can we access that fund of data to, say, for example, get the number of antivaccine issues that have been propagated on your platform?

Ms. BICKERT. Congressman, I can follow up with you on the reports we have and any other information.

Mr. BURGESS. Thank you. I will yield back.

Ms. SCHAKOWSKY. If I could just clarify that question. Is that information readily available to consumers, or no?

Ms. BICKERT. Chairwoman, the reports I just mentioned are publicly available, and we can follow up with any detailed requests as well.

Ms. SCHAKOWSKY. I recognize Mr. Veasey for 5 minutes for questioning.

Mr. VEASEY. Thank you, Madam Chair. Outside of self-reporting, what can be done to help educate communities that may be specifically targeted by, you know, all these different platforms?

I was wondering, Mr. Harris, if you could address that specifically, just because I think that a great deal of my constituency, and even on the Republican side, I think, a great deal of their constituencies, are probably being targeted, based on things like race and income, religion, and what have you.

And is there anything outside of self-reporting that can be done to just help educate people more?

Mr. HARRIS. Yes, there are so many things here. And, as you mentioned, in the 2016 election Russia targeted African-American populations. I think people don't realize—I think every time a campaign is discovered, how do we back-notify people, all of whom were affected, and say "You were the target of an influence operation"?

So right now, every single week, we hear reports of Saudi Arabia, Iran, Israel, China, Russia, all doing various different influence operations. Russia was recently going after U.S. veterans. Many veterans would probably say that is a conspiracy theory, right? But Facebook is the company that knows exactly who was affected, and they could actually back-notify every time there is an influence operation, letting those communities know that this is what happened, and that they were targeted.

We have to move from "This is a conspiracy theory" to "This is real." I have studied cult deprogramming for a while, and how do you wake people up from a cult when they don't know they are in? You have to show them essentially the techniques that were used on them to manipulate them. And every single time these operations happen, I think that has to be made visible to people.

And just like we said, you know, we have laws and protections. We have a Pentagon to protect our physical borders. We don't have a Pentagon to protect our digital borders, and so we depend on however many people Facebook chooses to hire for those teams. One example of this, by the way, is that the City of Los Angeles spends 25 percent of its budget on security. Facebook spends 6 percent of its budget on security, so it is underspending the City of L.A. by about 4 times.

So, you know, you can just make some benchmarks and say, "Are they solving the problem?" They have got 2.2 billion fake accounts, Facebook has, that they took down, fake accounts. So they have 2.7 billion real accounts, and then there were 2.2 billion fake accounts. And, you know, I am sure they got all of them I think would be the line to use here.

Mr. VEASEY. Ms. Bickert, you know, given the fact that it does seem like these foreign agents, these foreign actors, are targeting people specifically by their race, by their economics, by what region of the country that they live in, is Facebook doing anything to gather information or to look at how specific groups are being targeted?

If African Americans are being targeted for political misinformation, if whites that live in rural America, if they are being targeted for political misinformation, if people based on their likes—like, if you could gatherinformation, if these foreign actors could gather information based on people based on things that they like.

So let's say that you were white and you lived in rural America and you liked One America News and you like these other things and you may be more likely to believe in these sorts of conspiracy theories. Are you sure that some of the things that people are sharing on your platform, the likes and dislikes, aren't being used as part of that scheme as well?

Could you answer both of those?

Ms. BICKERT. Yes, Congressman. Thank you for the question. There are, broadly speaking, two things that we do. One is trainings and tools to help people—especially those who might be most at risk—recognize ways to keep themselves safe from everything from hacking to scams and other abuse.

Separately, whenever we remove influence operations under our, what we call this coordinated inauthentic behavior—we have removed more than 50 such networks in the past year—any time we do that, we are very public about it, because we want to expose exactly what we are seeing. And we will even include examples in our post saying, here is a network, it was in this country, it was targeting people in this other country, here are examples of the types of posts that they were putting in their pages. We think the more we can shine a light on this, the more we will be able to stop it.

Mr. VEASEY. Before my time expires, but if people are being scientifically—if their likes, and Dr. Burgess' district being specifically targeted because of certain television or news programming that they like, if they are African Americans that are being specifically targeted because Russian actors may think that they lean a certain way in politics, don't you think that information ought to be analyzed more closely instead of relying on—instead of just leaving it up to the user to be able to figure all of this out? Especially when people work odd hours and may only have time to digest what they immediately read, and they may not have an opportunity to go back and analyze something so deeply as far as what you are saying.

Ms. BICKERT. Congressman, I appreciate that. And I will say, attribution is complicated, and understanding the intent behind some of these operations is complicated. We think the best way to do that is to make them public.

And we don't just do this ourselves. We actually work hand-in-hand with academics and security firms who are studying these types of things, so that they can see. And sometimes we will say as we take down a network, "We have done this in collaboration or conversation with," and we will name the group.

So there are groups who can look at this and together hopefully shine light on who the actors are and why they are doing what they are doing.

Mr. VEASEY. Thank you. I yield back.

Ms. SCHAKOWSKY. I recognize Mr. Latta for 5 minutes.

Mr. LATTA. Well, thank you, Madam Chair, and thanks very much for holding this very important hearing today. And thank you to our witnesses for appearing before us. And it is really important for Americans to get this information.

In 2018, the experts out there estimated that criminals were successful in stealing over $37 billion from our older Americans through different scams through the internet, identity theft, friends, family abuse and impostor schemes. And last year in my district, I had the Federal Trade Commission and the IRS out for a senior event, so that the seniors could be educated on the threat of these scams and how to recognize, avoid, ward off, and how to recover from them.

Congress recognized that many of these scams were carried out through the use of manipulative and illegal robocalls. To combat these scams, I introduced the STOP Robocalls Act, which was recently signed into law as part of the tray stack, which I am very glad the President signed over the Christmas holiday.

While I am glad that we were able to get this done, I continue to be concerned with the ability of scammers to evolve and adapt to changes in the law by utilizing new technologies and techniques like deep- and cheapfakes.

And, Ms. Bickert, I don't want to pick on you, and I truly appreciate you being here today, especially since you are a little under the weather. And I also appreciated reading your testimony last night. I found it very interesting and enlightening.

I have several questions. As more and more seniors are going online and joining Facebook to keep in contact with their family, friends, and neighbors, in your testimony, you walk us through Facebook's efforts to recognize misinformation and what the company is doing to combat malicious actors using manipulated media. Is Facebook doing anything specifically to help protect seniors from being targeted on the platform, or educating them on how to recognize fake accounts or scams?

Ms. BICKERT. Thank you for the question. We are, indeed. And that includes both in-person trainings for seniors, which we have done and will continue to do. We also have a guide that can be more broadly distributed that is publicly available that is a guide for seniors on the best ways to keep themselves safe.

But I want to say more broadly, and as somebody who was a Federal criminal prosecutor for 11 years, looking at that sort of behavior, this is something we take seriously across the board. We don't want anybody to be using Facebook to scam somebody else, and we look proactively for that sort of behavior and remove it.

Mr. LATTA. Just a quick followup. I think it is really important because, you know, from what we have learned in a lot of times is that seniors don't want to report things, because they are afraid that, boy, you know, "I have been taken. I don't want to tell my relatives, I don't want to tell my friends," because they are afraid of losing some of what they might have, and not just on the money side, but how they can get out there.

And so, I think it is really important that we always think about our seniors, and just to follow up, because at the workshop that we had in the District last year, the FTC stated that one of the best ways to combat scams is to educate the individuals on how to recognize the illegal behavior so they can turn that into educating their friends and neighbors.

In addition to your private-sector partnerships, would Facebook be willing to partner with agencies like the FTC to make sure the public is informed about scammers operating on their platform?

Ms. BICKERT. Congressman, I am very happy to follow up on that. We think it is important for people to understand the tools that are available to keep themselves safe online.

Mr. LATTA. Ms. Donovan.

Dr. DONOVAN. Yes, one of the things that we should also consider is the way in which people are targeted by age for—I have looked at reverse mortgage scams, retirement funding scams, fake healthcare supplements. You know, when you do retire, it becomes very confusing. You are looking for information. And if you are looking primarily on Facebook and then posting about it, you might be retargeted by the advertising system itself.

And so, even when you are not information-seeking, Facebook's algorithms and advertising are giving other third parties information, and then serving advertising to seniors. And so it is a persistent problem.

Mr. LATTA. Thank you. Again, Ms. Bickert, if I can just follow up quickly with my remaining 30 seconds. Many of the scammers look for ways to get around Facebook's policies, including through the development and refinement of new technologies and techniques.

Is Facebook dedicating the resources and exploring ways to proactively combat scams instead of reacting after the fact?

Ms. BICKERT. Yes, Congressman, we are. I have been overseeing content policies at Facebook for about 7 years now, and in that time I would say that we have gone from being primarily reactive in the way that we enforce our policies to now primarily proactive. We are really going after abusive content and trying to find it. We grade ourselves based on how much we are finding before people report it to us, and we are now publishing reports to that effect.

Mr. LATTA. Thank you very much.

Madam Chair, my time is expired, and I yield back.

Ms. SCHAKOWSKY. The gentleman yields back.

And I now recognize Mr. O'Halleran for 5 minutes.

Mr. O'HALLERAN. I want to thank the chairwoman for holding this important and timely meeting here today—hearing. I echo the concerns of my colleagues. The types of deceptive online practices that have been discussed today are deeply troubling. I have continually stressed that a top priority for Congress should be securing our U.S. elections.

We could see dangerous consequences if the right tools are not in place to prevent the spread of misinformation online. This is a national security concern. As a former law enforcement officer, I understand that laws can be meaningless if they are not enforced. I look forward to hearing more from our witnesses about the FTC's capabilities and resources to combat these deceptive online practices.

Dr. Donovan, in your testimony you say that regulatory guardrails are needed to protect users from being misled online. I share your concerns about deception and manipulation online, including the rise in use of the dark patterns, deepfakes and other kinds of bad practices that can harm consumers.

Can you explain in more detail what sort of regulatory guardrails are necessary to prevent these instances?

Dr. DONOVAN. I will go into one very briefly. One of the big questions is, if I post something online that is not an advertisement, you know, I am just trying to inform my known networks. The problem isn't necessarily always that there is a piece of fake content out there. The real problem is the scale, being able to reach millions.

In 2010, 2011, we lauded that as a virtue of platforms. It really emboldened many of our important social movements and raised some incredibly important issues. But that wasn't false information. It wasn't meant to deceive people. It wasn't meant to siphon money out of other groups. At that time too, you weren't really able to scale donations. It was much harder to create networks of fake accounts and pretend to be an entire constituency.

And so, when I talk about regulatory guardrails, we have to think about distribution differently than we think about the content. And then we can also assuage some of the fears that we have about freedom of expression by looking at what are the mechanisms by which people can break out of their known networks? Is it advertising? Is it the use of fake accounts? How are people going viral? How are posts going viral, information going viral?

The other thing I would like to know from the government perspective is, does the FTC have enough insight into platforms to monitor that, to understand that? And if they don't, if they don't know why and how tens of millions of dollars are being siphoned out of Trump's campaign, then that is also another problem, and we have to think about what does transparency, what does auditing look like in a very meaningful way.

Mr. O'HALLERAN. Doctor, do you believe, then, that the FTC has the adequate authority under Section 5 of the FTC Act to take action against individuals and companies engaged in deceptive behavior practices online? And I do want to point out a Wall Street Journal report that said of the millions of dollars—200-and-some million dollars—of fines, that they have only collected about $7,000 since 2015.

Dr. DONOVAN. Wow. I think that you do have to look a lot closer at what the FTC has access to and how they can make that information actionable. For example, proving that there is substantial injury, if only one group has access to the known cost or knows the enormity of a scam, then we have to be able to expedite the transfer of data and the investigation in such a way that we are not relying on journalists or researchers or civil society organizations to investigate. I think that the investigatory powers of the FTC have to also include assessing substantial injuries.

Mr. O'HALLERAN. Thank you, Doctor.

Mr. Harris, do you believe the agency has enough resources to responsibly, swiftly, and appropriately address the issues? And I just want to point out that we flat-line them all the time. And on the other side, industry continues to expand at exponential rates.

Mr. HARRIS. That is the issue that you are pointing to, is that the problem-creating aspects of the technology industry, because they operate at exponential scales, create exponential issues, harms, problems, scams, et cetera. And so how do you, you know, have a small body reach such large capacities? This is why I am thinking about how can we have a digital update for each of our different agencies who already have jurisdiction over, whether it is public health or children or scams or deception, and just have them ask the questions that then are forced upon the technology companies to use their resources to calculate, report back, set the goals for what they are going to do in the next quarter.

Mr. O'HALLERAN. Thank you, Mr. Harris.

And I yield.

Ms. SCHAKOWSKY. The Chair now recognizes Mr. Carter for 5 minutes.

Mr. CARTER. Thank you, Madam Chair.

And thank all of you for being here. This is extremely important, and extremely important to all of our citizens.

I want to start by saying that, you know, when we talk about deepfake and cheapfake, to me, that is somewhat black and white. I can understand it. But, Mr. Hurwitz, when we talk about dark patterns, I think that is more gray in my mind. And I will just give you an example.

I was a retailer for many years. And I grew up in the South, OK? We had a grocery store chain, some of you may be familiar with it: Piggly Wiggly. Now, I always heard that the way they got their name—and I tried to fact-check it, but I couldn't find it, but anyway—I always heard the way they got their name is they arranged their stores to when you went in you had to kind of wiggle all the way around before you could get back out so that you would buy more things. It was like a pig wiggling through the farmyard or something. And they came up with Piggly Wiggly. Well, that is marketing.

And, you know, another example is all of us go to the grocery store. When we are at the grocery store and you are in the checkout line, you got all these things up there that they are trying to get you to buy. They are not necessarily—you could argue that they are impulse items. But then again, you could also make the argument that when you get home you say, "Geez, I wish I had gotten that at the grocery store. I wish I would have gotten these batteries or Band-Aids" or whatever.

How do you differentiate between what is harmful and what is beneficial?

Mr. HURWITZ. A great question, because it is gray. And, as I said previously, dark patterns, the term itself is a dark pattern intended to make us think about this as dark. There are some clear categories, clear lies, clear false statements, where we are talking about classic deception. That is pretty straightforward.

But when we are talking about more behavioral nudges, it becomes much more difficult. Academics have studied nudges for decades at this point, and it is hard to predict when they are going to be effective, when they are not going to be.

In the FTC context, the deception standard has a materiality requirement. So there needs to be some demonstration that a practice is material to the consumer harm, and that is a good sort of framework. If we don't have some sort of demonstrable harm requirement and causal connection there—I am a law professor, causation is a basic element of any legal claim. If you don't have some ability to tie the act to the harm, you are in dark waters for due process.

Mr. CARTER. So do you think we should be instructing the FTC to conduct research on this as to what is going on here?

Mr. HURWITZ. I think more information is good information. The FTC is conducting some hearings already. I think greater investigation is very powerful, both so that the FTC understands what they should be doing so they can use this information to establish rules. Where materiality is difficult to establish, the FTC can issue a rule, go through a rulemaking process which makes it easier to substantiate an enforcement action subsequently.

And even to respond, in part, to a previous question, to the extent that one of the FTC's core powers, even if it doesn't lack this as an enforcement authority, is to report to this body and say, "Look, we are seeing this practice. It is problematic. We don't have the authority. Can you do something about it?" And perhaps this body will act and give it power, perhaps this body will take direct action, or perhaps the platforms and other entities will say, "Oh, wow, the jig's up, we should change our practices before Congress does something that could be even more detrimental to us."

Mr. CARTER. Right. Mr. Harris, did you have something?

Mr. HARRIS. Yes. I have studied this topic for also about a decade. So you asked what is different about this. You have got the pig going through the thing. You have got the supermarket aisle. You have got the last-minute of, sort of last-minute-purchase items. There are two distinct things that are different.

The first is that this is infrastructure we live by. When you talk about children waking up in the morning and you have autoplay, that is not like the supermarket where I occasionally go there and I just made some purchases and I am at the very end of it, and that is the one moment, the one little microsituation of deception or marketing, which is OK.

In this case, we have children who are, like, spending 10 hours a day. So imagine a supermarket, you are spending 10 hours a day, and you wake up in that supermarket. And so that is the degree of intimacy and sort of scope in our lives. That is the first thing.

The second thing is the degree of asymmetry between the persuader and the persuadee. So, in this case, you have got someone who knows a little bit more about marketing who is arranging the shelf space so that the things in the top are at eye level versus at bottom level. That is one very small amount of asymmetry.

But in the case of technology, we have a supercomputer pointed at your brain, meaning like the Facebook news feed sitting there, and using the vast resources of 2.7 billion people's behavior to calculate the perfect thing to show you next and to not be discriminant about whether it is good for you, whether it is true, whether it is trustworthy, whether it is credible. And so, it knows more about your weaknesses than you know about yourself, and the degree of asymmetry is far beyond anything we have experienced.

Mr. CARTER. And you want the Federal Government to control that?

Mr. HARRIS. I think we have to ask questions about—when there is that degree of asymmetry, about intimate aspects of your weaknesses, and its business model is to exploit that asymmetry. It is as if a psychotherapist who knows everything about your weaknesses uses it with a for-profit advertising business model.

Mr. HURWITZ. The challenge is that can also go the other way. It can used to strengthen.

Mr. CARTER. Yes, yes.

Mr. HURWITZ. Mr. Harris used the example earlier of what if autoplay is shifting us towards conspiracy theories. OK, that is a dark pattern, that is bad. What if, instead, it was using us to shift us the other way, to the light, to greater education. If we say autoplay is bad, then we are taking both of those options off the table.

This can be used for good, and the question that you asked about how do we differentiate between good uses and bad, that is the question.

Mr. CARTER. Thank you, Madam Chair. I yield back.

Ms. SCHAKOWSKY. Mr. Ca´rdenas is recognized for 5 minutes.

Mr. CÁRDENAS. Thank you, Madam Chair, and thank you so much for holding this very important hearing that, unfortunately, I think most Americans don't understand how important this is to every single one of us, especially to our children and future generations.

There is an app, TikTok, question mark. Is it a deepfake maker? Five days ago, TechCrunch reported that ByteDance, the parent company of the popular video-sharing app TikTok, may have secretly built a deepfake maker. Although there is no indication that TikTok intends to actually introduce this feature, the prospect of deepfake technology being made available on such a massive scale and on a platform that is so popular with kids raises a number of troubling questions.

So my question to you, Mr. Harris, is in your testimony you discuss at length the multitude of ways that children are harmed by new technology. Can you talk about why this news may be concerning?

Mr. HARRIS. Yes. Thank you for the question.

So deepfakes is a really complex issue. I think if you look at how other governments are responding to this—I don't mean to look at China for legal guidance, but they see this as so threatening to their society, the fabric of truth and trust in their society, that if you post a deepfake without labeling it clearly as a deepfake, you can actually go to jail.

So they are not saying if you post a deepfake you go to jail. They are saying if you post it without labeling it, you go to jail. You can imagine a world where Facebook says, "If you post a deepfake without labeling it, we actually maybe suspend your account for 24 hours, so that you sort of feel—and we label your account to other people who see your account——"

Mr. CÁRDENAS. Hold on a second. My colleague on the other side of the aisle just warned, quote, "And you want to have the government control this?" You just gave an example of where private industry could, in fact, create deterrents——

Mr. HARRIS. That is right.

Mr. CA´RDENAS [continuing]. To bad behavior, not the government, but actual industry. OK, go ahead.

Mr. HARRIS. So that is right. And so they can create—and that is the point, is instead of using these AI Whac-a-Mole approaches where the engineers at Facebook—how many engineers at Facebook speak the 22 languages of India where there was an election last year? They are controlling the information infrastructure not just for this country, but for every country, and they don't speak the languages of the countries that they operate in, and they are automating that.

And, instead of trying to use AI where they are just missing everything going by—yes, they have made many investments, we should celebrate that, there are people working very hard, it is much better than it was before—but they have created a digital Frankenstein where there is far more content, advertising, variations of texts, lies, et cetera, than they have the capacity to deal with.

And so you can't create problems way beyond the scope of your ability to address them. It would be like creating nuclear power plants everywhere with the risk of meltdown, without actually having a plan for security.

Mr. CÁRDENAS. Now, getting back to your example where industry could, in fact, for example, Facebook could say "We are going to suspend your account for 24 hours" or something like that, with all due respect, in that example, Facebook might lose a little bit of revenue, as well as the person that they are trying to deter from bad action is likely going to lose revenue as well, correct?

Mr. HARRIS. That is correct. But maybe that is an acceptable cost, given we are talking about the total meltdown of trust.

Mr. CÁRDENAS. Yes, but maybe it is acceptable when you look at it intellectually and honestly, but when you look at it from whether or not private industry is going to take it upon themselves to actually impact their shareholders' revenue, that is where government has a place and space to get involved and say, proper actions and reactions need to be put in place so that people can understand that you can't and you shouldn't just look at this from a profit center motive.

Mr. HARRIS. That is right.

Mr. CÁRDENAS. Because in this world sometimes the negative actions are more profitable for somebody out there than positive, good actions. And that is one of the things that is unfortunate.

And you talk about languages around the world, but the number one target, in my opinion, for these bad actions for both financial gain and also the tearing down of the fabric of the democracy of the greatest nation on the planet, the United States, is the United States, we are the biggest target for various reasons.

Two main reasons are because we are supposed to be the shining light on the hill for the rest of the world for what a good democracy should be like. And secondly, we are by far and away the largest economy, the biggest consumer group of folks on the planet.

So, therefore, there is a motive for people to focus on profit and focus on their negative, bad intentions against our interests, the interests of the American people. Is that accurate?

Mr. HARRIS. That is exactly right. And this is a national security—I see this as a long-term—I mean, the polarization dynamics are accelerating towards civil war-level things, hashtag civilwariscoming.

Our colleague Renée DiResta says, "If you can make it trend, you can make it true." When you are planting these suggestions and getting people to even think those thoughts because you can manipulate the architecture, we are profiting, as I said, we are subsidizing our own self-destruction if the government doesn't say that these things can't just be profitable.

Mr. CÁRDENAS. Thank you to the witnesses. And thank you, Mr. Harris. I have run out of time. I wish I had more time. Thank you.

Ms. SCHAKOWSKY. The gentleman yields back.

And now I recognize Mr. Soto for 5 minutes.

Mr. SOTO. Thank you, Madam Chair.

It has been my experience that a lie seems to be able to travel faster on the internet than the speed of light, while the truth always goes at such a snail's pace. I suppose that is because of the algorithms we see.

I want to start with deepfakes and cheap fakes. We know through *New York Times* v. *Sullivan* that defamation of public figures requires actual malice. And some of these just appear to be malicious on their face.

I appreciate the labeling, Ms. Bickert, that Facebook is doing now. That is something that we actually were pondering in our office as well. But why wouldn't Facebook simply just take down the fake Pelosi video?

Ms. BICKERT. Thank you for the question.

Our approach is to give people more information so that, if something is going to be in the public discourse, they will know how to assess it, how to contextualize it. That is why we work with the fact checkers.

I will say that in the past 6 months it is feedback from academics and civil society groups that has led us to come up with stronger warning screens.

Mr. SOTO. Would that be labeled under your current policy now as false, that video?

Ms. BICKERT. I am sorry, which video?

Mr. SOTO. Would the fake Pelosi video be labeled as false under your new policy?

Ms. BICKERT. Yes. And it was labeled false. At the time we did— we think we could have gotten that to fact checkers faster, and we think the label that we put on it could have been more clear. We now have the label for something that has been rated false. You have to click through it so it actually obscures the image. And it says "false information." And it says "This has been rated false by fact checkers." You have to click through it, and you see information from the fact-checking source.

Mr. SOTO. Thanks.

In 2016 there was a fake Trump rally put together by Russians in Florida, complete with a Hillary Clinton in a prison and a fake Bill Clinton.

Could a fake rally be created today through Facebook in the United States by the Russians under existing technology?

Ms. BICKERT. The network that created that was fake and inauthentic, and we removed it. We were slow to find it.

I think our enforcement has gotten a lot better. And, as a data point for that, in 2016 we removed one such network. This past year, we removed more than 50 networks. Now, that is a global number all over the world. But these are organizations that are using networks of accounts—some fake, some real—in an attempt to obscure who they are or to push false information.

Mr. SOTO. So could it happen again right now?

Ms. BICKERT. Our enforcement is not perfect. However, we have made huge strides, and that is shown by the dramatic increase in the number of networks that we have removed.

And I will say that we do it not just by ourselves, but we work with security firms and academics who are studying this to make sure we are staying on top of it.

Mr. SOTO. What do you think Facebook's duty is, as well as other social media platforms, to prevent the spread of lies across the internet?

Ms. BICKERT. I am sorry. Could you repeat that?

Mr. SOTO. What you do think Facebook and other social platforms' duty is to prevent the spread of lies across the internet?

Ms. BICKERT. I can speak for Facebook. We think it is important for people to be able to connect safely and with authentic information. And my team is responsible for both.

So there is our approach to misinformation where we try to get people—label contented as false and get them accurate information. And then there is everything we also do to remove abusive content that violates our standards.

Mr. SOTO. Thank you, Ms. Bickert.

Dr. Donovan, I saw you reacting to the fake Trump rally aspect. Could that still happen now under existing safeguards in social media?

Dr. DONOVAN. Yes. And the reason why it can still happen is because the platform's openness is now turning into a bit of a vulnerability for the rest of society.

So what is dangerous about events like that is the kind of research we do, we are often trying to understand, well, what is happening online? And what happens when the wires—the interaction between the wires and the weed? Like when people start to be mobilized, start to show up places, that to us is one order of magnitude much more dangerous.

Mr. SOTO. What do you think we should be doing as government to help prevent something like that?

Dr. DONOVAN. There are ways in which I think, when people are using particularly events features, group features, there has to be added transparency about who, what, when, where those events are being organized by.

And there have been instances in Facebook very recently where they have added transparency pages, but it is not always clear to the user who is behind what page and for what reason they are launching a protest.

What is dangerous, though, is that actual constituents show up, real people show up as fodder for this. And so we have to be really careful that they don't stage different parties like they did in Texas across the street from one another at the same time. And so we don't want to have manipulation that creates this serious problem for law enforcement, as well as others in the area.

Mr. SOTO. Thanks. My time has expired.

Ms. SCHAKOWSKY. I now recognize Congresswoman Matsui for 5 minutes.

Ms. MATSUI. Thank you very much, Madam Chair. And I really appreciate the witnesses here today, especially on this really important issue.

I introduced the Blockchain Promotion Act with Congressman Guthrie to direct the Department of Commerce to convene a working group of stakeholders to develop a consensus-based definition of blockchain. Currently there is no common definition, which has hindered its deployment.

Blockchain technology could have interesting applications in the communication space, including new ways of identity verification. This technology is unique in that it can help distinguish between credible and noncredible news sources in a decentralized fashion, rather than relying on one company or organization to serve as a sole gatekeeper.

I have a lot of questions. I would like succinct answers to this. Ms. Donovan, do you see value in promoting impartial, decentralized methods of identity verification as a tool to combat the spread of misinformation?

Dr. DONOVAN. I think in limited cases, yes, especially around purchasing of advertising, which is allowing you to break out of your known networks and to reach other people, especially if those advertising features do allow you to target very specific groups.

I am interested in learning more about this consensus on definition, because I also think it might help us understand what is a social media company, what are their—how do we define their broadcast mechanisms, how do we define them related to the media, media company, as well as the other kinds of products that they build. And I think it would also get us a lot further in understanding what it is we say when we say deepfakes or even AI.

Ms. MATSUI. OK. The European Commission has recently announced that it will be supporting research to advance blockchain technology to support a more accurate online news environment.

The entire panel, just a yes or no is sufficient.

Do you believe the U.S. should be keeping pace with Europe in this space? Yes or no?

As far as blockchain, do you think that the European Commission is supporting research to advance blockchain technology to support a more accurate online news development? Do you believe that the U.S. should be keeping pace with Europe regarding this?

Ms. BICKERT. This is not my area.

Ms. MATSUI. OK. Dr. Donovan, I probably would say——

Dr. DONOVAN. Yes, more research could help us understand this better.

Ms. MATSUI. Mr. Hurwitz, yes or no?

Mr. HURWITZ. Around the world, many are outpacing us in blockchain.

Ms. MATSUI. OK.

Mr. Harris?

Mr. HARRIS. It is not my area, but I know that China is working on a decentralized currency and could basically get all of the countries in which it is indebting them to their infrastructure with these huge Belt and Road plans. If they switch the global currency to their decentralized currency, that is a major national security threat and would change the entire world order. I think much more work has to be done in the U.S. to protect against China gaining currency advantage and changing the world of reserve currency.

Ms. MATSUI. Thank you.

It is an undisputed fact, reaffirmed by America's intelligence agencies, that Russia interfered in our 2016 and 2018 elections through targeted and prolonged online campaigns. We know that Russia is ramping up for 2020, and the American voters will once again be exposed to new lies, falsehoods, and misinformation designed to sow division in our democratic process.

While I was glad to see the recent funding bill included $425 million in election security grants, this is only part of a much larger solution. To protect the most fundamental function of our democracy, social media companies need to take clear, forceful action against foreign attempts to interfere with our elections.

Mr. Harris, how have the various election interference strategies evolved from the 2016 and 2018 election cycles?

Mr. HARRIS. You know, I am actually not an expert on exactly what Russia is doing now. What I will say is I think that we need a mass public awareness campaign to inoculate the public. Think of it as like a cultural vaccine.

And there is actually precedent in the United States for this. So, back in the 1940s, we had the Committee for National Morale and the Institute for Propaganda Analysis that actually did a domestic awareness campaign about the threat of fascist propaganda.

You have probably seen the videos from—they are black and white—from 1947. It was called "Don't Be a Sucker." And they had us looking at a guy spouting fascist propaganda, someone starting to nod, and then the guy taps him on the shoulder and says, "Now, son, that is fascist propaganda, and here is how to spot it."

We actually saw this as a deep threat, a national security threat to our country. We could have another mass public awareness campaign now, and we could have the help of the technology companies to collectively use their distribution to distribute that inoculation campaign so everybody actually knew the threat of the problem.

Ms. MATSUI. Does the rest of the panel agree with Mr. Harris on this, to have this public awareness campaign?

Mr. HURWITZ. Probably. I will just note that it runs the risk of being called a dark pattern if the platforms are starting to label certain content in certain ways. So there is a crosscurrent for our discussion to note there.

Ms. MATSUI. OK. Well, we don't come to any solutions now, but I appreciate it. And I have run out of time. Thank you very much.

Ms. BICKERT. Congresswoman, I would just point to the ads library that we have put in place over the past few years, which has really brought an unprecedented level of openness to political advertising. So people can now see who is behind an ad, who paid for it, and we verify the identity of those advertisers.

Ms. MATSUI. I think it is difficult for most people out there to really do that, unless it is right in front of them. But I am glad that that is happening. But I think we should have much more exposure about this.

Thank you.

Ms. SCHAKOWSKY. I now recognize Mr. McNerney for 5 minutes.

Mr. MCNERNEY. I thank the chair.

And I thank the witnesses. Your testimony has been helpful, and I appreciate it. But I have to say, with big power comes big responsibility, and I am disappointed, in my opinion, that Facebook hasn't really stepped up to that responsibility.

Back in June, I sent a letter to Mr. Zuckerberg, and I was joined by nearly all the Democrats on the committee. In this letter we noted that we are concerned about the potential conflict of interest between Facebook's bottom line and addressing misinformation on its platform. Six months later, I remain very concerned that Facebook is putting its bottom line ahead of addressing misinformation.

Ms. Bickert, Facebook's content monetization policy states that content that depicts or discusses subjects in the following categories may face reduced or restricted monetization, and misinformation is included on the list. It is troubling that your policy doesn't simply ban misinformation.

Do you think there are cases where misinformation can and should be monetized? Please answer yes or no.

Ms. BICKERT. Congressman, no. If we see somebody that is intentionally sharing misinformation, and we make this clear in our policies, they will lose the ability to monetize.

Mr. MCNERNEY. OK. Well, that sounds different than what is in your company's stated policy.

But the response I received from Facebook to my letter failed to answer many of my questions. For example, I asked the following question that was left unanswered, and I would like to give you a chance to answer it today. How many project managers does Facebook employ whose full-time job it is to address misinformation?

Ms. BICKERT. Congressman, I don't have a number of PMs. I can tell you that across my team, our engineering teams, and our content review teams, this is something that is a priority. Building that network of the relationships with more than 50 fact-checking organizations is something that has taken the efforts of a number of teams across the company.

Mr. MCNERNEY. Does that include software engineers?

Ms. BICKERT. It does, because there for any of these programs you need to have an infrastructure that can help recognize when something might be misinformation, allow people to report when something might be misinformation, get things over to the fact-checking organization.

Mr. MCNERNEY. OK. So I am going to ask you to provide that information, how many full-time employees, including software engineers who were employed in that, to identify misinformation.

Ms. BICKERT. We are happy to try to follow up and answer.

Mr. MCNERNEY. Another question that was left unanswered is, on average, from the time a content is posted on Facebook's platform, how long does it take for Facebook to flag suspicious content to third-party fact checkers, third-party fact checkers to review the content, and Facebook to take remedial action once the content— once the review is completed?

Ms. BICKERT. Congressman, the answer depends. This could happen very quickly. We actually allow fact-checking organizations to proactively rate content they see on Facebook. So they——

Mr. MCNERNEY. You think that would be fast enough to keep deepfakes from going viral or other misinformation from going viral?

Ms. BICKERT. If they rate something proactively then it happens instantly. And we also use technology and use the reporting to flag content to them, and we often see that they will rate it very quickly.

Mr. MCNERNEY. Well, moving on, I am very concerned that Facebook is not prepared to address misinformation on its platform in advance of this year's election. Will you commit to having a third-party audit conducted by June 1 of Facebook's practices for combating the spread of disinformation on its platform and for the results of this audit to be made available to the public?

Ms. BICKERT. Congressman, we are very happy to answer any questions about how we do what we do. We think transparency is important. And we are happy to follow up with any suggestions that you have.

Mr. MCNERNEY. I would request a third-party audit—I am not talking about the civil rights audit—an independent third-party audit be conducted at Facebook by June 1.

Ms. BICKERT. Congressman, again, we are very transparent about what our policies and practices are, and we are happy to follow up with any specific suggestions.

Mr. MCNERNEY. Mr. Harris.

Mr. HARRIS. I was going to say, their third-party fact-checking services are massively understaffed, underfunded, and a lot of the people are dropping out of the program. And the amount of information flowing through that channel is far beyond their capacity to respond.

More or less, fact checking isn't even really the relevant issue. I think if you look at the clearest evidence of this, is Facebook's own employees wrote a letter to Mark Zuckerberg saying, "You are undermining our election integrity efforts with your current political ads policy."

That says it all to me. That letter was leaked to The New York Times about a month ago, I think that those people, because they are closest to the problem, they do the research queries, they understand how bad the issue is.

We are on the outside. We don't actually know. It is almost like they are Exxon, but they also own the satellites that would show us how much pollution there is. So we don't actually know on the outside. So all we can do is trust people like that on the inside that are saying this is far less than what we would like to do. And they still have not updated their policy.

Mr. MCNERNEY. Thank you. I yield back.

Ms. SCHAKOWSKY. I recognize Congresswoman Dingell for 5 minutes for questions.

Mrs. DINGELL. Thank you, Madam Chair.

And thank you all of you for being here today. This is a subject that really matters to me, like it does to all of us. But in the past we have treated what little protections people have online as something that is separate from those we have in our day-to-day lives offline. But the line between what happens online and offline is virtually nonexistent. Gone are the days when we can separate one from the other.

Millions of Americans have been affected by data breaches and privacy abuses. The numbers are so large that you can't even wrap your head around them. I mean, I have talked to Members here and they don't even at times understand what has happened or how people have collected data about us.

The resources to help folks protect themselves after the fact are desperately needed. But what is really happening is that the cost of failure to protect sensitive information is being pushed on millions of people who are being breached and not trying to do anything. It is a market externality.

And that is where the government, I believe, must step in. You go to the pharmacy to fill a prescription, you assume that the medicine you are going to get is going to be safe, it is not going to kill you. If you go outside, you assume that the air you breathe—you assume—is going to be safe, or we are trying to make it that way.

And that is because we have laws that protect people from have a long list of known market externalities and the burden isn't placed on their ability to find out is the medicine you are taking OK, safe, and is the air you are breathing clean. We are still working on that, but it is one we have identified. It shouldn't be any different for market externalities that are digital.

Ms. Bickert, I will admit I have sent a letter to Facebook today which has a lot of questions that didn't lend themselves to answer here, so I hope that they will be answered.

But I would like to get yes-or-no answers from the panel on the following questions. And I am going start this way, with Mr. Harris, because we always start with you, Ms. Bickert, and we will give you a little—and thank you for being here even though you are sick.

Do you believe that the selling of real-time cell phone location without users' consent constitutes a market externality?

Mr. Harris?

Mr. HARRIS. I don't know with that specific one, but the entire surveillance capitalism system produces vast harms that are all on the balance sheets of societies, whether that is the mental health of children, the manipulation of elections, the breakdown of polarization.

Mrs. DINGELL. But it is a market externality.

Mr. HARRIS. Absolutely, all market externality.

Mrs. DINGELL. OK, let's go down.

Mr. Hurwitz?

Mr. HURWITZ. Based on the economic definition of an externality, no, it is not. However, it can be problematic.

Mrs. DINGELL. Dr. Donovan?

Dr. DONOVAN. I am in line with Gus.

Mrs. DINGELL. Ms. Bickert?

Ms. BICKERT. I am not an economist, but we do think user consent is very important.

Mrs. DINGELL. Second question: Yes or no, do you believe that having 400 million pieces of personally identifiable information made public, including passport numbers, names, addresses, and payment information, is a market externality?

Mr. Harris?

Mr. HARRIS. Similarly, on sort of classic economic definition, I don't know if that would specifically qualify, but it is deeply alarming.

Mr. HURWITZ. Same answer.

Dr. DONOVAN. Agreed.

Ms. BICKERT. Same answer.

Mrs. DINGELL. So are you all agreeing with Mr. Harris?

Mr. HURWITZ. Same answer as I gave previously. It is not the technical economic definition.

Mrs. DINGELL. I just wanted to see if we had gotten you to understand what a bother it is.

Three, do you believe that having 148 million individuals' personally identifiable information, including credit card numbers, driver's license, and Social Security numbers, made public is a market externality?

Mr. Harris?

Mr. HARRIS. I can see it is sort of like an oil spill externality.

Mrs. DINGELL. Mr. Hurwitz?

Mr. HURWITZ. The same answer.

Mrs. DINGELL. So you don't think it is a problem.

Mr. HURWITZ. I don't—I don't not think it is a problem. I wouldn't characterize it as an externality and use it as a——

Mrs. DINGELL. Do you not think we have got to protect people from that?

Mr. HURWITZ. No, that is not what I am saying. I have an economics background. I rely on a more technical definition of an externality.

Mrs. DINGELL. Dr. Donovan?

Dr. DONOVAN. It is an incredibly important problem.

Mrs. DINGELL. Ms. Bickert?

Ms. BICKERT. Yes, I would echo Dr. Donovan.

Mrs. DINGELL. Do you believe that having the data of 87 million users taken and used for nefarious and political purposes is a market externality?

Mr. Harris?

Mr. HARRIS. I think it is the same answer as before.

Mr. HURWITZ. If I break into your house and steal your stuff and sell it on the black market, that is not an externality. However, it is a problem.

Mrs. DINGELL. Dr. Donovan?

Dr. DONOVAN. Well, I wouldn't characterize it as a break-in. It was facilitated by the features built into the platform, and it is a huge problem.

Mrs. DINGELL. Thank you. Ms. Bickert?

Ms. BICKERT. Again, we think that user control and consent is very important.

Mrs. DINGELL. Last question. I am out of time, so you are going to have to be fast.

And finally, do you believe that simply asking whoever took it to please delete it is an appropriate response?

Mr. Harris?

Mr. HARRIS. It is very hard to enforce that. And once the data is out there, it is distributed everywhere. So we have to live in a world where now we assume that this is just out there.

Mr. HURWITZ. You need to solve the problem on the front end.

Mrs. DINGELL. Dr. Donovan?

Dr. DONOVAN. That never should have been allowed in the first place.

Mrs. DINGELL. Ms. Bickert?

Ms. BICKERT. Again, we think that it is very important to give people control over their data, and we are doing our best to make sure that we are doing that.

Mrs. DINGELL. So I am out of time. Thank you, Madam Chair.

Ms. BLUNT ROCHESTER [presiding]. Thank you. The gentlewoman yields. And I recognize myself for 5 minutes.

Thank you to the chairwoman in her absence, and thank you to the panelists.

This is a vitally important conversation that we are having. What I have noticed is that technology is outpacing policy and the people. And so we are feeling the impacts in our mental health, we are feeling it in our economy, we are feeling it in our form of government. And so this is a very important conversation.

And I would like to start with a few questions that are kind of off of the dark patterns and those issues but really do deal with the idea of deceptive and manipulative practice. And it is just a basic question, so yes or no, and it is really surrounding the platforms that we have and the ability for people with disabilities to use them.

Are each of you, or any of you, familiar with the term universal design? And I will just ask Mr. Harris.

Mr. HARRIS. Vaguely, yes.

Ms. BLUNT ROCHESTER. Mr. Hurwitz?

Mr. HURWITZ. Vaguely, yes.

Dr. DONOVAN. Yes.

Ms. BLUNT ROCHESTER. Yes.

Ms. BICKERT. Vaguely, yes.

Ms. BLUNT ROCHESTER. Vaguely. OK. So there are a lot of vaguelies, and I don't have time to really talk about what universal design is. But I think, as we look at how people are treated in our society, universal design and looking at people with disabilities is one of the areas that I would like to follow up with each of you on.

I would now like to turn my time to a discussion about dark patterns. And every single Member of Congress and every one of our constituents, virtually everyone, has been affected by this in some respect. Every day, whether it is giving up our location data, or manipulated into purchasing products that they don't need, or providing sensitive information that enables scams, many of us are targeted.

And, while the failure to address dark patterns harms individuals, one of the areas that is of deeper concern to me is the challenge for us as a society as a whole. Cambridge Analytica, that scandal in and of itself was a great example for all of us of it wasn't just an individual that was harmed, it was our society, and we see some of the remnants of it to this day.

And so I heard someone say to me yesterday that they hoped that this hearing was not just a hearing, but a real wakeup call, a wakeup call to our country. And so my first question is to Mr. Harris.

Do you believe that oversight of dark patterns and the other deceptive and manipulative practices discussed here are well suited for industry self-regulation?

Mr. HARRIS. No, absolutely not.

Ms. BLUNT ROCHESTER. And I would like to follow up with Ms. Bickert.

Does Facebook have a responsibility to develop user interfaces that are transparent and fair to its users?

Ms. BICKERT. We definitely want that. And, yes, I think we are working on new ways to be transparent all the time.

Ms. BLUNT ROCHESTER. Does Section 230 of the Communications Decency Act provide immunities to Facebook over these issues?

Ms. BICKERT. Section 230 is an important part of my team being able to do what we do. So, yes, it gives us the ability to proactively look for abuse and remove it.

Ms. BLUNT ROCHESTER. But does it provide immunities? You would say yes?

Ms. BICKERT. I am sorry, what is the specific—Section 230 does provide us certain protections. The most important from my standpoint is the ability for us to go after abuse on our platform. But separately it is also an important mechanism for people who use the internet to be able to post to platforms like Facebook.

Ms. BLUNT ROCHESTER. I guess one of my concerns here for asking that question is we are having a big conversation about the balance of freedom of speech, in addition to the ability for people to yell fire in a crowded place. And so I am going to turn back to Mr. Harris.

How do you think that we in Congress can develop a more agile and responsive response to the concerning trends on the internet? You mentioned a digital update of Federal agencies. Can you talk a little bit about that as well?

Mr. HARRIS. Just as you said, that the problem here is we have— this is E.O. Wilson—the problem of humanity is we have paleolithic emotions, medieval institutions, and accelerating. Godlike technology. When your steering wheel goes about a light year behind your accelerating, godlike technology, the system crashes.

So the whole point is, we have to give a digital update to some of the existing institutions—Health and Human Services, FCC, FTC, you can imagine every category of society—and saying where do we already have jurisdiction about each of these areas, and ask them to come up with a plan for what their digital update is going to be and put the tech companies in a direct relationship where every quarter there is an audit and there is a set of actions that are going to be taken to ameliorate these harms.

That is the only way I can see scaling this, absent creating a whole new digital Federal agency, which will be way too late for these issues.

Ms. BLUNT ROCHESTER. I know I am running out of time, but my other question really was going to be to Ms. Bickert on the role that you see of government. I think we are having a lot of conversations here about freedom of speech and also the role of government.

And so as a followup, I would like to have a conversation with you about what you see as that role of government versus self-regulation and how we can make something happen here. The bigger concern is for us to make sure that we are looking at this both as an individual level, but also as a society.

And I yield my time and recognize the gentlewoman from New York, Ms. Clarke.

Ms. CLARKE. Thank you very much, Madam Chair.

And I thank our ranking member, I thank our panelists for their expert witness here today.

Deepfakes currently pose a significant and an unprecedented threat. Now more than ever, we need to prepare for the possibility that foreign adversaries will use deepfakes to spread disinformation and interfere in our election, which is why I have successfully secured language in the NDAA requiring notification be given to Congress if Russia or China seek to do exactly this.

But deepfakes have been and will be used to harm individual Americans. We have already seen instances of women's images being superimposed on fake pornographic videos. As these tools become more affordable and accessible, we can expect deepfakes to be used to influence financial markets, discredit dissidents, and even incite violence.

That is why I have introduced the first House bill to address this threat, the DEEPFAKES Accountability Act, which requires creators to label deepfakes as altered content, updates our identity theft statutes for digital impersonation, and requires cooperation between the government and private sector to develop detection technologies. I am now working on a second bill specifically to address how online platforms deal with deepfake content.

So, Dr. Donovan, cheap fakes. We have often talked about deepfakes, where the technology footprint of the content has changed. But can you talk a bit more about the national security implications of cheap fakes, such as the Pelosi video, where footage is simply altered instead of entirely fabricated?

Dr. DONOVAN. One of the most effective political uses of a cheap fake is to draw attention and shift the entire media narrative towards a false claim. And so particularly what we saw last week with the Biden video was concerning because you have hundreds of newsrooms kick into gear to dispute something, a video, and platforms have allowed it to scale to a level where the public is curious and are looking for that content, and then are also coming into contact with other nefarious actors and networks.

Ms. CLARKE. What would you say can be done by government to counteract the threat?

Dr. DONOVAN. There has to be—I think you are moving very much in the direction I would go to, where we need to have some labels, we need to understand the identity threat that it poses, and that there needs to be broader cooperation between governments.

As well I think that the cost to journalism is very high, because all of the energy and resources that go into tracking, mapping, and getting public information out there, I think the platform companies can do a much better job of preventing that harm up front by looking at content when it does seem to go wildly out of scale with the usual activity of an account and to proactively look at things where, if you do see an uptick of 500,000 views on something, maybe there needs to be proactive content moderation.

Ms. CLARKE. Very well.

Ms. Bickert, Facebook is a founding member of the Deepfake Technology Challenge, but detection is only partially a technology issue. We also need to have a definition of what fake is and a policy for which kind of fake videos are actually acceptable.

Last summer you informed Congress that Facebook is working on a precise definition for what constitutes a deepfake. Can you update us on those efforts, especially in light of your announcement yesterday? And specifically how do you intend to differentiate between legitimate deepfakes, such as those created by Hollywood for entertainment, and malicious ones?

Ms. BICKERT. Thank you for the question.

The policy that we put out yesterday is designed to address the most sophisticated types of manipulated media, and this fits within the definition of what many academics would call deepfakes, so that we can remove it.

Now, beyond that, we do think it is useful to work with others in industry and civil society and academia to actually have common definitions so we are all talking about the same thing. And those are conversations that we have been a part of in the past 6 months. We will continue to be a part of those. And we are hoping that, working together with industry and other stakeholders, we will be able to come up with comprehensive definitions.

Ms. CLARKE. Should the intent of the deepfake or rather its subject matter be the focus?

Ms. BICKERT. I am sorry. Could you repeat that?

Ms. CLARKE. Should the intent of the deepfake or the subject matter be the focus?

Ms. BICKERT. From our standpoint, it is often difficult to tell intent when we are talking about many different types of abuse, but also specifically with deepfakes for misinformation, and that is why if you look at our policy definition it doesn't focus on intent so much as what the effects would be on the viewer.

Ms. CLARKE. Thank you very much. I yield back.

I thank you, Madam Chair, for allowing my participation today.

Ms. SCHAKOWSKY [presiding]. That concludes the questioning.

I have things I want to put into the record, and maybe the ranking member does as well. But I did want to make an ending comment, and I would welcome her to do the same if she wishes.

So we had a discussion that took us to the grocery store, but we are now in a new world that we are discussing that is hugely bigger when we talk about Facebook. And as you say in your testimony, Facebook is a community of more than 2 billion people spanning countries, cultures, and languages across the globe.

But I think that there is now such an incredible and justified distrust of how we are being protected. We know in the physical world we do have laws that apply and that expectations of consumers are that those will be somehow there to protect us. But in fact they aren't.

We live, then, in the virtual world and the digital world in a place of self-regulation. And it seems to me that that has not satisfied expectations of consumers correctly. And we don't have institutions right now, even when they have the authorities, have the funding, have the expertise—I am thinking of the Federal Trade Commission, just as an example—to do what it needs to do.

But we don't have a regulatory framework at all that I think, hopefully in a bipartisan way, we can think about. And it may include things like just the kinds of audits that you were talking about, Mr. Harris, which would not necessarily create new regulatory laws, but we may need to.

And to me, that is the big takeaway today. When you have communities that are bigger than any country in the entire world that are essentially making decisions for all of the rest of us, and we know that we have been victimized, that the Government of the United States of America does need to respond. That is my takeaway from this hearing.

And I would appreciate hearing from the ranking member.

Mrs. RODGERS. I thank the chair, and I thank everyone for being here. I think it is important that we all become more educated.

I wanted to bring to everyone's attention that the FTC is holding a hearing on January 28 regarding voice cloning. I think that it is important that all of us are participating, becoming better educated, and helping make sure we are taking steps as we move forward.

Clearly, this is a new era, and on one hand we can celebrate that America has led the world in innovation and technology and improving our lives in many ways. There is also this other side that we need to be looking at and making sure that we are taking the appropriate steps to keep people safe and secure.

So we will continue this important discussion and continue to become better educated. Today's hearing was a great part of that. Thank you, Chair.

Ms. SCHAKOWSKY. Thank you very much.

I would like to insert into the record the—I seek unanimous consent to enter the following documents into the record: a letter from the SAG–AFTRA, a letter from R Street, a paper written by Jeffrey Westling of the R Street Institute, a report from the ATHAR Project on Facebook. And so I seek unanimous consent.

Without objection, so ordered.

[The information appears at the conclusion of the hearing.[103]]

Ms. SCHAKOWSKY. So let me thank all of our witnesses today. We had good participation from Members despite the fact that there were other hearings going on.

I remind Members that, pursuant to committee rules, they have 10 business days to submit additional questions for the record to be answered by the witnesses, and hopefully in a reasonably short time. We hope that there will be prompt answers.

And at this time, the subcommittee is adjourned. [Whereupon, at 1:00 p.m., the subcommittee was adjourned.] [Material submitted for inclusion in the record follows:]

---

[103] The Westling paper and the ATHAR report have been retained in committee files and also are available at https://docs.house.gov/Committee/Calendar/ByEvent.aspx?EventID=110351.

Submitted Material for the Record

SAG·AFTRA.

The Honorable Janice D. Schakowsky, Chair
Subcommittee on Consumer Protection & Commerce
House Committee on Energy & Commerce
2125 Rayburn House Office Building
Washington, DC 20515

The Honorable Cathy McMorris Rodgers, Ranking Member
Subcommittee on Consumer Protection & Commerce
House Committee on Energy & Commerce
2322 Rayburn House Office Building
Washington, DC 20515

January 8, 2020

Chair Schakowsky & Ranking Member McMorris Rodgers:

The Screen Actors Guild-American Federation of Television and Radio Artists (SAG-AFTRA) is greatly appreciative of the United States House Committee on Energy and Commerce Subcommittee on Consumer Protection and Commerce for holding the hearing on "Americans at Risk: Manipulation and Deception in the Digital Age." This is an issue of great importance to us, as SAG-AFTRA represents 160,000 actors, singers, dancers, broadcasters, and recording artists who are uniquely misappropriated by bad actors in the marketplace to defraud consumers into purchasing products and services.

As technological innovation continues, the danger of digital manipulation of our members whether to sell a product they have not endorsed, appear in a fake newscast to endorse a product, or feature their likeness in pornography increases exponentially. This is a grave concern to our members as it is threatening their greatest and most personal commodity, their image. The internet has made enforcement of these rights near impossible. Even if a victim can successfully take down a fake site or advertisement, another quickly repopulates. Technology allows these bad actors to hide behind almost untraceable, anonymous accounts.

Recently, two of our members, Ellen DeGeneres and Sandra Bullock, filed a lawsuit under state right of publicity law and federal false endorsement law for the unauthorized use of their likenesses to sell products on the internet. What makes this lawsuit novel is it targets affiliate marketing and pop-up advertisements. Consumers are tricked to enter e-commerce sites by clicking on an advertisement for products claimed to be endorsed by a celebrity. For example, one ad may depict Sandra Bullock to sell an anti-aging cream. This is a serious consumer protection issue as it may deceive consumers into purchasing products that may be ineffective or even dangerous or it may lock them into ongoing payment contracts they cannot easily escape.

SAG-AFTRA is grateful to the Committee for tackling these issues and we look forward to working with Members to address productive solutions.

Sincerely,

Kerri Wood Einertson

Kerri Wood Einertson
SAG-AFTRA
National Director, Government Affairs & Public Policy

* * *

January 8, 2020

Hon. Janice Schakowsky, Chairwoman
Subcommittee on Consumer Protection and Commerce
House Energy & Commerce Committee
U.S. House of Representatives
2125 Rayburn House Office Building
Washington, D.C. 20515

Hon. Cathy McMorris Rodgers, Ranking Member
Subcommittee on Consumer Protection and Commerce
House Energy & Commerce Committee
U.S. House of Representatives
2322 Rayburn House Office Building
Washington, D.C. 20515

RE: Hearing on "Americans at Risk: Manipulation and Deception in the Digital Age"

Dear Chairwoman Schakowsky and Ranking Member McMorris Rodgers,

My name is Jeffrey Westling and I am a Technology & Innovation Policy Fellow at the R Street Institute (R Street). I would like to commend you and the Subcommittee for holding this hearing on "Americans at Risk:

Manipulation and Deception in the Digital Age."[104] Understanding how and why disinformation spreads online remains a key challenge for researchers. As we better understand what drives trust and sharing of disinformation online, we can better alleviate the harms associated with them.

At the same time, the Subcommittee should be mindful of the actual harms associated with new technologies as it begins to consider any legislative response. As the technologies used to create disinformation advance, it can seem like new technologies create unprecedented problems that require unprecedented solutions. But this is not necessarily the case.

Realistic AI-generated audio and video forgeries, known as "deep fakes," are the latest development in a long line of tools and techniques used for deception.[105] It's important to note that overreactions to this new technology can have serious unintended consequences and limit the numerous beneficial uses the technology can provide. What's more, increased focus on new technologies can shift attention away from more rudimentary forms of disinformation that better exploit the psychological factors driving trust and sharing online.[106]

I write this letter to provide a paper for the Subcommittee's consideration as it explores the impacts of deep-fake media.[107] The paper puts deep fakes in historical context and examines the likely societal response to the new technology. I argue that society will adapt independently to the introduction of deep-fake media, and over time the harms associated with the new technology will diminish. This is not to say that harms will not occur, and Congress may indeed have a role to play in limiting their impact. However, any response to the advent of deep fakes must address the actual harms associated with their use and not impose overbearing regulations on the market.

I applaud the Subcommittee for holding this hearing and exploring this issue in depth. I look forward to working with you and the Subcommittee as you consider potential legislation in this area.

---

[104] House Energy & Commerce Committee, "Americans at Risk: Manipulation and Deception in the Digital Age," (Jan. 8, 2020), https://bit.ly/2ZSv61a.

[105] Jeffrey Westling, "Deep Fakes: Let's Not Go Off the Deep End," *Techdirt* (Jan. 30, 2019), https://bit.ly/39KzlAv.

[106] Jeffrey Westling, "Deception & Trust: A Deep Look at Deep Fakes," *Techdirt* (Feb. 28, 2019), https://bit.ly/2QWHE3E; Jeffrey Westling, "Fool Me...You Can't Get Fooled Again," *Morning Consult* (June 3, 2019), https://bit.ly/2ZWlhiT.

[107] Jeffrey Westling, "Are Deep Fakes a Shallow Concern? A Critical Analysis of the Likely Societal Response to Deep Fakes," *TPRC 19* (last revised Oct. 11, 2019), https://bit.ly/39MFH23.

Sincerely,
Jeff Westling, Technology & Innovation Policy Fellow
R Street Institute

CC:
Hon. Frank Pallone, Chairman
House Energy & Commerce Committee
U.S. House of Representatives
2125 Rayburn House Office Building
Washington, D.C. 20515

Hon. Greg Walden,
Ranking Member
House Energy & Commerce Committee
U.S. House of Representatives
2322 Rayburn House Office Building
Washington, D.C. 20515

* * *

February 21, 2020

Chairman Frank Pallone, Jr.
Ranking Member Greg Walden
U.S. House Committee on Energy and Commerce
Subcommittee on Consumer Protection and Commerce
Attn: Chloe Rodriguez
2125 Rayburn House Office Building
Washington, D.C. 20515

Dear·Chairman Pallone, Ranking Member Walden, Subcommittee Chairwoman Schakowsky, Subcommittee Ranking Member McMon is Rodgers, and Members of the Subcommittee:

Thank you for your questions for the record from the Janua1y 8, 2020 hearing entitled Americans at Risk: Manipulation and Deception in the Digital Age. Per your request, attached are the answers for the record to your questions.

Sincerely,
Facebook, Inc.

Questions from Chairwoman Schakowsky

1. *According to The Antiquities Trafficking and Heritage Anthropology Research (ATHAR) Project, there are at least three different extremist groups recorded in a new report that details traffickers and terrorists selling illicit antiquities on Facebook – the terrorist activity was recorded as occurring primarily over the past three years, a time period when Facebook was allegedly increasing their counter terrorism enforcement.*
   Isn't it true that Facebook's features (Groups, Pages, marketplace, "buy and sell," etc.) allow for and make it easier for terrorist groups to sell material on Facebook to finance their terror activities?

Organizations or individuals that proclaim a violent mission or are engaged in violence, including organizations or individuals involved in terrorist activity, are not allowed on Facebook. This policy is based on the actor, which means that we don't allow terrorist organizations or terrorists to have a presence on our platform for any purpose—including by having an account, Page, Group, etc. We also have a policy prohibiting people from facilitating, organizing, promoting, or admitting to certain criminal or harmful activities targeted at people, businesses, or property.

If we find content that praises or supports terrorists or terrorist organizations, we remove it. Indeed, we remove the vast majority of such content before anyone reports it. In the second and third quarters of 2019, we removed over 98% of such content before users reported it. And in the first three quarters of 2019, we took action on over 12 million pieces of such content.

Products sold on Facebook must comply with our Community Standards and Commerce Policies. As mentioned previously, our Community Standards prohibit terrorists or terrorist organizations from using Facebook, including Marketplace. When someone creates a listing on Marketplace, before it goes live, it is reviewed against our Commerce Policies using automated tools. Based on that review, the listing may be approved, rejected, or, in some cases, sent for further manual review. When we detect that a listing violates our policies, we reject it.

2. *Does Facebook archive terrorism data or posts related to sale of illicit goods and share the information with relevant authorities? Are there instances when Facebook has deleted the data without archiving it thus making it unavailable for law enforcement investigations?*

We will take steps to preserve account records in connection with official criminal investigations for 90 days pending our receipt of formal legal process. Law enforcement may submit formal preservation requests through Facebook's Law Enforcement Online Request System or by mail.

3. *Why are Al Qaeda and ISIS the only two terrorist organizations addressed in Facebook's counterterrorism policies?*

Facebook's Dangerous Organizations and Individuals policy applies to organizations outside of Al Qaeda and ISIS, and always has. We do not allow organizations or individuals that proclaim a violent mission or are engaged in violence from having a presence on Facebook. Our definition of terrorism is behavioral; terrorist organizations and terrorists include any non-state actor that:

- Engages in, advocates, or lends substantial support to purposive and planned acts of violence,
- Which causes or attempts to cause death, injury, or serious harm to civilians, or any other person not taking direct part in the hostilities in a situation of armed conflict, and/or significant damage to property linked to death, serious injury, or serious harm to civilians
- With the intent to coerce, intimidate and/or influence a civilian population, government, or international organization
- In order to achieve a political, religious, or ideological aim.

We also remove content that expresses support or praise for groups, leaders, or individuals involved in these activities. Additionally, we have a robust program to abide by legal restrictions, including those related to US-designated Foreign Terrorist Organizations ("FTO") and entities sanctioned by the US Treasury Department.

4. *Does Facebook track other terrorist groups? If yes, which ones?*

As discussed in the responses to your previous questions, we remove terrorists, terrorist organizations, and posts that support terrorism whenever we become aware of them. When we receive reports of accounts or posts that may support terrorism, we review them urgently and carefully. We use a range of tools to combat such content, including artificial intelligence, content matching, specialized human review, industry cooperation, and counterspeech training.

Because we proactively screen for terrorist content, we remove much of it before it is reported. In the third quarter of 2019, we removed 5.2 million pieces of content for violating our rules on terrorist material, 98.5% of which we identified proactively before it was reported by users. While it is difficult to accurately measure the content posted on behalf of terrorist organizations because the total is so small, our estimates indicate that, during that time period, fewer than 0.04% of views on Facebook were of content that violated our standards for terrorist propaganda. In other words, fewer than 4 of every 10,000 views on Facebook contained violating terrorist content.

Questions from Representative Blunt Rochester

1. *At the January 8, 2020 hearing, you indicated that you were familiar with the concept of universal design. Do you think online service providers, like Facebook, should follow universal design concepts as a best practice on all of their platforms?*

Facebook's mission is to bring the world closer together—and that means everyone. Our goal is to make it possible for anyone, regardless of ability, to access the information and connections that happen on Facebook. Access is opportunity, and when everyone is connected, we all benefit. That's why we're investing in accessibility, sharing our work publicly so others can learn from it, advancing accessibility training in higher education, and contributing to web standards that help make the internet accessible.

We have made significant investments in AI and video captioning. Our automatic photo captioning tool describes objects in photos to people with vision loss. New facial recognition features help people with vision loss to know more about who is in their photos. We also have several closed captioning features to help people who are hearing impaired: closed captions for videos on Facebook via text file upload, automatic video captioning for ads and Pages in the US, and real-time captioning in Facebook Live broadcasts.

We want to drive innovation in accessibility that extends beyond Facebook, which is why we're proud to support the Teach Access initiative. Announced on the 25th anniversary of the Americans with Disabilities Act in July 2015, Teach Access brings industry, academia, and advocacy together to create models for teaching and training students about technology to create accessible experiences. Teach Access has launched an online tutorial covering best practices for accessible software design in order to advance accessibility training in higher education.

For more information on the features and technologies that help people with disabilities, such as vision loss and deafness, get the most out of Facebook, please visit our accessibility Facebook Page at https://www.facebook.com/accessibility and our Help Page at https://www.facebook.com/help/accessibility.

2. *What is Facebook's strategy for screening ads that subtly exclude protected classes by focusing on certain geographies or language? And who, if anyone, does Facebook notify when it discovers such activity?*

Facebook prohibits advertisers from discriminating against people based on personal attributes such as race, ethnicity, color, national origin, religion, age, sex, sexual orientation, gender identity, family status, disability, and medical or genetic conditions. Our Advertising Policies prohibit advertisers from using targeting options to discriminate against, harass, provoke, or disparage users or to engage in predatory advertising practices. Discrimination and discriminatory advertising have no place on Facebook's platform, and we remove such content as soon as we become aware of it.

Our policies have long prohibited discrimination, and we have made significant changes to prevent advertisers from misusing our tools to discriminate in their ad targeting. As part of settlement agreements with civil rights organizations like National Fair Housing Alliance, and based on ongoing input from civil rights experts, we have taken the industry lead by changing the way advertisers may select the audience for housing, employment, and credit ("HEC") ads. Specifically, we have eliminated the ability to target HEC ads based on age, gender, or zip code, and we have severely restricted the number of interest category targeting options available.

These restrictions apply across all the tools businesses use to buy ads. Even before we made these changes last year, advertisers were prohibited from using any multicultural affinity interest segments, either for inclusion or exclusion, when running HEC ads. We've also added a housing ad section in the Ad Library, so it will be easy to search for and view US ads about housing opportunities. People can search for and view all active housing opportunity ads targeted at the US that started running—or were edited—on or after December 4, 2019, regardless of the advertiser's intended audience. People will be able to search the housing ad section by the name of the Page running an ad or the city or state to which the ad is targeted. This year, we'll also include ads that offer employment or credit opportunities in the Ad Library. We're actively working with civil rights groups to inform our approach as we prepare to roll this out. We've also committed to studying the potential for algorithmic bias, including in our ad algorithms, with input from the civil rights community, industry experts, and academics.

3. *Does Facebook acknowledge a responsibility for the ads they host and, potentially, the connection to disreputable third-party websites that may lead to even more egregious privacy violations?*

All ads must comply with our Community Standards and our Advertising Policies. Ads must not contain spyware, malware, or any software that results in an unexpected or deceptive experience. This includes links to sites containing these products. Similarly, ads must not direct people to non-functional landing pages, including landing pages that automatically download files to a person's computer.

Ads are subject to Facebook's ad review system, which relies primarily on automated tools to check ads against these policies. We use human reviewers to improve and train our automated systems and, in some cases, to review specific ads. This review happens before ads begin delivering, but may also happen after, if people hide, block, or provide negative feedback about an ad. When we detect an ad that violates our Advertising Policies, we disapprove it.

Facebook has also been certified by the Trustworthy Accountability Group's ("TAG") "Certified Against Fraud" program for Direct and Intermediary ad sales: https://www.tagtoday.net/certified-against-fraud-programcompliantcompanies/. TAG is an industry organization focused on eliminating fraudulent digital advertising traffic, combating malware, fighting ad-supported internet piracy to promote brand integrity, and promoting brand safety through greater transparency. Our certification has been determined by independent validation, not just self-attestation (like most companies that are TAG-certified).

We will continue our work to detect malicious behavior directed towards our platform and to enforce against violations of our Terms and Advertising Policies. As part of our ongoing efforts to keep people safe and combat abuse of our ad platform, Facebook recently filed suit in California against one entity and two individuals for violating our Terms and Advertising Policies. Creating real-world consequences for those who deceive users and engage in malicious practices is important for maintaining the integrity of our platform.

4. *I acknowledge that Facebook prohibits ads for guns and drugs. Does Facebook screen for manipulative ads, like those that portray false testimonials or false claims to the limited availability of products?*

All ads must comply with our Community Standards and our Advertising Policies, which prohibit ads promoting products or services using misleading or deceptive claims. We also prohibit ads promoting products, services, or schemes using deceptive or misleading practices, including those meant to scam people out of money or personal information.

As discussed in the response to your previous question, ads are subject to Facebook's ad review system, which relies primarily on automated tools to check ads against these policies. We use human reviewers to improve and train our automated systems and, in some cases, to review specific ads. This review happens before ads begin delivering, but may also happen after, if people hide, block, or provide negative feedback about an ad. When we detect an ad that violates our Advertising Policies, we disapprove it.

If we're made aware of an advertiser in violation of a specific law or regulation by an authorized government entity, we will investigate and take appropriate enforcement action.

Questions from Representative Castor

1. *What techniques do internet platforms employ to keep their users engaged? What types of techniques are harmful? What types of techniques are harmless? Are there industry standards? If so, what are they? If not, what should they be?*

Facebook was built to bring people closer together and build relationships. What we've found is that what's more important than *whether* people are engaged is *how* people interact online—that is, ensuring that people are able to have quality interactions with people and organizations they care about. For example, we've heard that people value active engagement with others (sending messages, posting, commenting, reminiscing about past interactions) over passive consumption like scrolling or clicking links, so we've worked to build experiences that enable that type of active interaction.

We have made many changes to facilitate people using Facebook in ways that support the goal of enabling healthy interactions. For example, we've made significant changes to News Feed to prioritize meaningful interactions, and we've redesigned our comments feature to encourage more discussion and better conversations. People can also "snooze" or mute content from a person, Page, or Group for 30 days if they need a break from certain content. And we've added "time spent" tools that help people manage their experience on Facebook and Instagram.

We are devoting substantial resources to understanding more about well-being online and we welcome the opportunity to work together with Congress and others in the industry to develop industry-wide standards.

Facebook is a supporter of the bipartisan, bicameral Children and Media Research Advancement ("CAMRA") Act, which would provide funding for the National Institutes of Health to study the impact of technology and media on the cognitive, physical, and socio-emotional development of children and adolescents. We also participated in the bipartisan roundtable hosted by Senators Markey and Blunt on this topic in February 2019.

2. *What techniques do internet platforms employ to manipulate their users? What types of techniques are harmful? What types of techniques are harmless? Are there industry standards? If so, what are they? If not, what should they be?*

Please see the response to your previous question. To be clear, we have no intention of manipulating our users.

A user's News Feed is informed by the user's own Facebook activity, such as their likes, comments, and other content. We work to offer a variety of tools to help people understand what they're seeing on Facebook and why, like the "Why Am I Seeing This?" feature, which gives users information about why they're seeing a post or ad. We also have built new and improved tools to help people access information associated with their Facebook account and to provide transparency and control around how we use data. For example, the Access Your Information and Download Your Information tools are available to Facebook users in their account settings. And we have been rolling out new ways to allow users to view and control data we receive when they use apps and websites off Facebook via our new Off-Facebook Activity tool, which allows users to see which apps and websites send us information about users' activity and allows users to disconnect this information from their accounts. We also have detailed notifications settings that allow people to customize their experiences on Facebook.

As discussed above, Facebook is a supporter of the bipartisan, bicameral Children and Media Research Advancement ("CAMRA") Act, and we welcome the opportunity to work together with Congress and others in the industry to develop industry-wide standards.

3. *The word algorithm is used frequently in discussions over internet engagement. What is an algorithm? Who designs the algorithms? What are the benefits/harms to internet platforms using algorithms? How do algorithms use artificial intelligence? Can internet platforms fully explain why an algorithm produces certain results? Do internet platforms have knowledge of all the information fed into the algorithms they use?*

An algorithm is a formula or set of steps for solving a particular problem. At Facebook, we use algorithms to offer customized user experiences and to help us achieve our mission of building a global and informed community. For example, we use algorithms to help generate and display search results (see https://about.fb.com/news/2018/11/inside-feed-how-search-works/), to prioritize the content people follow with their personalized News Feed (see https://about.fb.com/news/2018/05/inside-feed-news-feed-ranking/), and to serve ads that may be relevant to them.

As a company, we are committed to helping our users understand how we use algorithms. We publish a series of blog posts called News Feed FYI (see https://about.fb.com/news/category/news-feed-fyi/) that highlight major updates to News Feed and explains the thinking behind them. We also recently launched a new feature called "Why am I seeing this post?" (see https://about.fb.com/news/2019/03/why-am-i-seeing-this/) to help people on Facebook better understand and more easily control what they see from friends, Pages, and Groups in News Feed. This feature (which is similar to another tool we recently improved called "Why am I seeing this ad?") is based on user feedback asking for more transparency around what appears in News Feed and easier access to News Feed controls.

We are also working with external stakeholders on ethics and artificial intelligence ("AI"). We are part of various multi-stakeholder consortia working on issues of algorithmic fairness, transparency, and accountability. For example, we co-founded the Partnership on AI, a collaborative and multi-stakeholder organization that was established to study and formulate best practices on AI technologies, to advance the public's understanding of AI, and to serve as an open platform for discussion and engagement about AI and its influence on people and society. We are constantly seeking ways to collaborate with external stakeholders on these issues. For example, we partnered with the Technical University of Munich ("TUM") to support the creation of an independent Institute for Ethics in Artificial Intelligence. We have also collaborated with the Digital Ethics Lab of the University of Oxford to assess, map, and explore how AI can help meet the United Nations Sustainable Development Goals. We seek to harness the power of AI to promote human understanding and well-being and work to ensure AI is developed and used in a responsible and ethical manner.

4. *What should be considered healthy engagement with an internet platform? Is healthy engagement defined differently for children? If so, what should be considered healthy engagement with an internet platform for children?*

Regarding healthy engagement, please see the response to your Question 1.

Regarding engagement by children, Facebook requires everyone to be at least 13 years old before they can create an account. The safety and well-being of 13- to 17-year-olds on our platform is very important to us. That is why teams from across the company, including our Policy, Product, and Legal teams, work to ensure we have the right precautions and procedures in place. We work with parents and families; experts in child development, online safety, and children's health and media; and lawmakers to ensure that we are building better products for families. The safeguards we put in place include everything from extra in-app education regarding friending and posting publicly to age-gating and warnings to prevent exposure to certain content.

For example, the team that works on the development of our product policies consults with experts to ensure that our policies properly account for the presence of 13- to 17-year-olds on our platform and this work has resulted in the age-gating of certain content. Our team that works on privacy policies, in consultation with experts, has helped develop unique education moments regarding friending and posting publicly for our 13- to 17-year-old users. They also have worked with our product teams to ensure we remove certain information, like a user's school, from search for minors. Our safety policy team works across all internal teams at Facebook to ensure we are taking a 360-degree approach to minors' safety and building the best policies, tools, programs, and resources to ensure the safety of minors on our platform.

Our efforts also include giving parents the information, resources, and tools they need to set parameters for their children's use of online technologies and to help them develop healthy and safe online habits. For example, as part of our Safety Center, we have a Parent Portal (https://www.facebook.com/safety/parents) and a Youth Portal (https://www.facebook.com/safety/youth), which are both focused on fostering conversations around online safety, security, and well-being. Those portals give parents and young people access to the information and resources they need to make informed decisions about their use of online technologies. We remain dedicated to examining our own practices and the resources we make available for the safety and security of people who use our services.

In 2018, Facebook announced a partnership with the National Parent Teacher Association ("National PTA") to launch Digital Families Community events across the country. In 2019, 200 community safety events took place in all 50 states to help families address tech-related challenges, from online safety and bullying prevention to digital and news literacy. The toolkits for these events were developed with experts including the Youth and Media Team at the Berkman Klein Center for Internet and Society at Harvard. The events included interactive workshops for families on healthy online habits and a family tech talk around family social media values and social media and phone "off times."

Facebook also has a product for children called Messenger Kids. Messenger Kids is a messaging and video chat app that is designed for children under 13 to connect with friends and family. We designed Messenger Kids with the guidance and input of thousands of parents and experts, and with the Children's Online Privacy Protection Act ("COPPA") in mind. Parental controls are core to the Messenger Kids experience. For example, parents or guardians have control over who can communicate with their child through Messenger Kids. And we've recently launched additional tools and features for parents or guardians to manage their child's experience in Messenger Kids.

Parents or guardians can also set predetermined "off times" for the app on a child's device.

We are committed to continuing our work to foster safe, kind, and supportive communities for everyone.

5. *When does engagement with an internet platform turn into addiction? How are classic signs of addiction measured in the digital context? Is the addiction connected to internet platforms similar to manifestations of addiction in other situations? How is it similar? How is it different?*

Facebook is designed to bring people together. We want Facebook to be a place for meaningful interactions with your friends and family—enhancing your relationships offline, not detracting from them. After all, that's what Facebook has always been about.

To better understand this issue, we employ social psychologists, social scientists, and sociologists, and we collaborate with top scholars to better understand well-being. And because this isn't just a Facebook issue, but an internet issue, we collaborate with leading experts and publish in the top peer-reviewed journals. We work with leading academics at Carnegie Mellon, UC Riverside, and the Greater Good Science Center at UC Berkeley, and we have partnered closely with mental health clinicians and organizations like Save.org and the National Suicide Prevention Lifeline.

Facebook is a supporter of the bipartisan, bicameral Children and Media Research Advancement ("CAMRA") Act, which would provide funding for the National Institutes of Health to study the impact of technology and media on the cognitive, physical, and socio-emotional development of children and adolescents. We also participated in the bipartisan roundtable hosted by Senators Markey and Blunt on this topic in February 2019.

We have also pledged $1 million towards research to better understand the relationship between media technologies, youth development, and well-being. Facebook is teaming up with experts in the field to look at the impact of mobile technology and social media on children and teens, as well as how to better support them as they transition through different stages of life. Facebook is committed to bringing people together and supporting well-being through meaningful interactions on Facebook.

We've also developed and implemented tools to help people manage their time on Facebook and Instagram: an activity dashboard, a daily reminder, and ways to limit notifications. We developed these tools based on collaboration and inspiration from leading mental health experts and organizations, academics, our own extensive research, and feedback from our community. We want the time people spend on Facebook and Instagram to be intentional, positive, and inspiring. Our hope is that these tools give people more control over the time they spend on our platforms.

6. *Why are repeat engagement with or addiction to an internet platform harmful to the individual or society as a whole? What are the costs? For example, what are the economic costs?*

Facebook was built to bring people closer together and build relationships. What we've found with well-being is that it's not about time spent, but about how people interact online.

In general, when people spend a lot of time passively consuming information—reading but not interacting with people—they report feeling worse afterward. Though the causes aren't clear, researchers hypothesize that reading about others online might lead to negative social comparison—perhaps even more so than offline, since people's online posts are often more curated and flattering. Another theory is that the internet takes people away from social engagement in person.

On the other hand, actively interacting with people—especially sharing messages, posts, and comments with close friends and reminiscing about past interactions—is linked to improvements in well-being. This ability to connect with relatives, classmates, and colleagues is what drew many of us to Facebook in the first place, and it's no surprise that staying in touch with these friends and loved ones brings us joy and strengthens our sense of community.

As discussed in the responses to your previous questions, we have made many changes to facilitate people using Facebook in ways that are healthy. And we are partnering with leading experts and dedicating significant resources to better understand these challenging issues. At the end of the day, we're committed to bringing people together and supporting well-being through meaningful interactions on Facebook.

7. *Why are manipulative techniques employed by internet platforms harmful to the individual or society as a whole? What are the costs? For example, what are the economic costs?*

Please see the responses to your previous questions.

8. *How do internet platforms monetize repeat engagement or addiction? Why does this model benefit internet platforms? What are the benefits?*

Facebook's mission is to give people the power to build community and bring the world closer together. Facebook is not designed to be addictive. We want Facebook to be a place for meaningful interactions with your friends and family—enhancing your offline relationships, not detracting from them.

Like many other free online services, we sell advertising space to third parties. Doing so enables us to offer our services to consumers for free. This in turn allows us to fulfill one of our principles, which is to serve everyone—because everyone deserves access to these tools.

At the same time, we want ads to be as relevant and useful to our users as the other posts they see. This is important for businesses too, because users are less likely to respond to ads that are irrelevant or annoying. If we do this effectively, people will see ads about products and services they care about, and advertising on Facebook can help businesses large and small increase their sales and hire more people.

9. *How do internet platforms monetize manipulation? Why does this model benefit internet platforms? What are the benefits?*

Please see the response to your previous question.

10. *What tools are at internet platform users' disposal to stop repeat engagement or addiction? Should companies provide or fund those tools?*

We've developed and implemented tools to help people manage their time on Facebook and Instagram: an activity dashboard, a daily reminder, and a way to limit notifications. We developed these tools based on collaboration with and inspiration from leading mental health experts and organizations, academics, our own extensive research, and feedback from our community. We want the time people spend on Facebook and Instagram to be intentional, positive, and inspiring. Our hope is that these tools give people more control over the time they spend on our platforms.

Over the past few years, we've also introduced a number of tools to help people better control their experience on Facebook and Instagram. On Facebook, we improved News Feed quality to show people the most relevant posts with features like See First, Hide, and Unfollow. On Instagram, we launched powerful tools to proactively care for the community—like the "You're All Caught Up" message in Feed, keyword filtering, sensitivity screens, and offensive comment and bullying filters.

We want to help people understand how much time they spend on our platforms so they can better manage their experience. At the end of the day, we're committed to bringing people together and supporting well-being through meaningful interactions on our platforms.

Facebook's 2019 Global Safety and Well-Being Summit focused on some of the tools Facebook provides to help people better control their experience, as well as the perspectives of outside experts on other tools and resources to help us innovate responsibly and intentionally. For more information, please visit https://about.fb.com/news/2019/05/2019-global-safety-well-being-summit.

11. *What tools are at internet platform users' disposal to stop manipulation? Should companies provide or fund those tools?*

Please see the response to your previous question.

12. *What role should Congress play in combating repeat engagement with or addiction to internet platforms?*

We are committed to working with all stakeholders to ensure that we're bringing people together and supporting well-being through meaningful interactions on Facebook. We've dedicated significant resources to studying these issues, and we've had many conversations with academics, experts, and industry leaders to make sure that we are hearing from a broad range of perspectives. Of course, this isn't just a Facebook issue; it's an internet issue, and we would welcome Congress's involvement in facilitating research that can benefit users across internet platforms.

As discussed in the responses to your previous questions, Facebook is a supporter of the bipartisan, bicameral Children and Media Research Advancement ("CAMRA") Act, which would provide funding for the National Institutes of Health to study the impact of technology and media on the cognitive, physical, and socio-emotional development of children and adolescents. We also participated in the bipartisan roundtable hosted by Senators Markey and Blunt on this topic in February 2019.

13. Should Congress fund more research studying the techniques utilized by internet platforms to increase engagement and manipulate users and their effects? Should some of that research focus on the effect techniques utilized by internet platforms to increase engagement and manipulate users have on children?

Please see the response to your previous question.

14. Section 5 of the FTC Act prohibits "unfair or deceptive acts or practices in or affecting commerce." What types of manipulation should be considered unfair or deceptive? What types should not be considered unfair or deceptive? Should a different standard be developed for manipulative techniques used by internet platforms? If so, what should that standard be? What manipulative techniques should be allowed for adults but not for children?

The Federal Trade Commission ("FTC") has guidance interpreting its authority under Section 5 of the FTC Act, as well as longstanding policies and principles for what it considers to be an unfair or deceptive practice. Facebook is regulated under the FTC Act and therefore follows the FTC's guidance.

We would welcome the opportunity to work together with regulators, Congress, and others in the industry to develop industry-wide standards.

15. Does the application of section 230 of the Communications Decency Act (section 230) enable increased manipulation and repeat engagement/addiction? If so, how does section 230 enable increased manipulation and repeat engagement/addiction and what are the potential fixes?

Section 230 of the Communications Decency Act has been essential to protecting free expression and innovation on the internet, and we believe its provisions are consistent with operating safe products that give consumers choice. In fact, it is the legal protections afforded by Section 230 that allow us to proactively restrict certain types of harmful content on our platforms, regardless of whether that content is otherwise protected.

Questions from Representative Guthrie

1. *Ms. Bickert, can you explain how the Global Internet Forum to Counter Terrorism works, and how you and other companies are working together to remove terrorist content and disrupt violent extremists' ability to promote themselves and their propaganda online?*

In the summer of 2017, Facebook, YouTube, Microsoft, and Twitter came together to form the Global Internet Forum to Counter Terrorism ("GIFCT"). The objective of the GIFCT has always been to substantially disrupt terrorists' ability to promote terrorism, disseminate violent extremist propaganda, and exploit or glorify real-world acts of violence on our services. We do this by joining forces with counterterrorism experts in government, civil society, and the wider industry around the world. Our work has been centered around three interrelated strategies:

- Joint Tech Innovation;
- Knowledge Sharing; and
- Conducting and Funding Research.

For example, through the GIFCT, we have expanded a database in which thirteen companies share "hashes," or digital fingerprints, to better enable companies to identify terrorist content. The database now contains hashes for more than 200,000 visually distinct images, and more than 10,000 visually distinct videos. Facebook was the 2019 chair for the GIFCT, and we worked to expand its capabilities, including increased sharing of hashes and hashing technology.

In the summer of 2019 and building on the commitments we made as part of the Christchurch Call to Action, we added a fourth pillar to our work that focuses on crisis response. Specifically, we developed a joint content incident protocol for responding to emerging or active events like the horrific terrorist attack in Christchurch, so that relevant information can be quickly and efficiently shared, processed, and acted upon by all member companies. GIFCT member companies have developed, refined, and tested the protocol through workshops with Europol and the New Zealand Government. Our teams are in regular contact to share information about violent events.

Conducting and funding research to study counterterrorism and terrorism is another critical part of our work and was a key focus last year. In 2019, we supported the first phase of the GIFCT Academic Research Network, the Global Research Network on Terrorism and Technology. This phase was led by the Royal United Services Institute and produced thirteen original independent research papers looking at different aspects of terrorism. Phase 2 of the GIFCT Academic Research Network, the Global Network on Extremism and Technology, began recently and is being led by the International Centre for the Study of Radicalisation.

The GIFCT also announced last year that it will become an independent organization led by an Executive Director and supported by dedicated technology, counterterrorism, and operations teams. Evolving and institutionalizing the GIFCT's structure from a consortium of member companies will build on our early achievements and deepen industry collaboration with experts, partners, and government stakeholders—all in an effort to thwart increasingly sophisticated efforts by terrorists and violent extremists to abuse digital platforms.

FRANK PALLONE, JR., NEW JERSEY
CHAIRMAN

GREG WALDEN, OREGON
RANKING MEMBER

ONE HUNDRED SIXTEENTH CONGRESS

Congress of the United States

House of Representatives

COMMITTEE ON ENERGY AND COMMERCE
2125 Rayburn House Office Building
Washington, DC 20515–6115
Majority (202) 225–2927
Minority (202) 225–3641

January 30, 2020

Joan Donovan, Ph.D.
Research Director of the Technology and Social Change Project
Shorenstein Center on Media, Politics, and Public Policy
Harvard Kennedy School
79 John F. Kennedy St.
Cambridge, MA 02138

Dear Dr. Donovan:

Thank you for appearing before the Subcommittee on Consumer Protection and Commerce of the Committee on Energy and Commerce on Wednesday, January 8, 2020, to testify at the hearing is entitled, "Americans at Risk: Manipulation and Deception in the Digital Age." We appreciate the time and effort you gave as a witness before the Committee on Energy and Commerce.

Pursuant to Rule 3 of the Committee on Energy and Commerce, members are permitted to submit additional questions to the witnesses for their responses, which will be included in the hearing record. Attached are questions directed to you from members of the Committee. In preparing your answers to these questions, please address your responses to the member who has submitted the questions using the Word document provided with this letter.

To facilitate the publication of the hearing record, please submit your responses to these questions by no later than the close of business on Thursday, February 13, 2020. As previously noted, your responses to the questions in this letter, as well as the responses from the other witnesses appearing at the hearing, will all be included in the hearing record. Your written responses should be transmitted by email in the Word document provided to Chloe Rodriguez, Policy Analyst with the Committee, at Chloe.Rodriguez@mail.house.gov. You do not need to send a paper copy of your responses to the Committee. Using the Word document provided for submitting your responses will also help maintain the proper format for incorporating your answers into the hearing record.

Thank you for your prompt attention to this request. If you need additional information or have other questions, please contact Ms. Rodriguez at (202) 225-2927.

Sincerely,

Frank Pallone, Jr.
Chairman

Attachments

cc: The Honorable Greg Walden
Ranking Member
Committee on Energy and Commerce

The Honorable Jan Schakowsky
Chairwoman
Subcommittee on Consumer Protection and Commerce

The Honorable Cathy McMorris Rodgers
Ranking Member
Subcommittee on Consumer Protection and Commerce

[Dr. Donovan did not answer submitted questions for the record by the time of publication.]

Additional Questions for the Record

Subcommittee on Consumer Protection and Commerce
Hearing on
"Americans at Risk: Manipulation and Deception in the Digital Age"
January 8, 2020

Joan Donovan, Ph.D., Research Director of the Technology and Social Change Project
Shorenstein Center on Media, Politics, and Public Policy
Harvard Kennedy School

The Honorable Kathy Castor (D-FL)

1. What techniques do internet platforms employ to keep their users engaged? What types of techniques are harmful? What types of techniques are harmless? Are there industry standards? If so, what are they? If not, what should they be?
2. What techniques do internet platforms employ to manipulate their users? What types of techniques are harmful? What types of techniques are harmless? Are there industry standards? If so, what are they? If not, what should they be?
3. The word algorithm is used frequently in discussions over internet engagement. What is an algorithm? Who designs the algorithms? What are the benefits/harms to internet platforms using algorithms? How do algorithms use artificial intelligence? Can internet platforms fully explain why an algorithm produces certain results? Do internet platforms have knowledge of all the information fed into the algorithms they use?
4. What should be considered healthy engagement with an internet platform? Is healthy engagement defined differently for children? If so, what should be considered healthy engagement with an internet platform for children?
5. When does engagement with an internet platform turn into addiction? How are classic signs of addiction measured in the digital context? Is the addiction connected to internet platforms similar to manifestations of addiction in other situations? How is it similar? How is it different?
6. Why are repeat engagement with or addiction to an internet platform harmful to the individual or society as a whole? What are the costs? For example, what are the economic costs?

7. Why are manipulative techniques employed by internet platforms harmful to the individual or society as a whole? What are the costs? For example, what are the economic costs?

8. How do internet platforms monetize repeat engagement or addiction? Why does this model benefit internet platforms? What are the benefits?

9. How do internet platforms monetize manipulation? Why does this model benefit internet platforms? What are the benefits?

10. What tools are at internet platform users' disposal to stop repeat engagement or addiction? Should companies provide or fund those tools?

11. What tools are at internet platform users' disposal to stop manipulation? Should companies provide or fund those tools?

12. What role should Congress play in combating repeat engagement with or addiction to internet platforms?

13. Should Congress fund more research studying the techniques utilized by internet platforms to increase engagement and manipulate users and their effects? Should some of that research focus on the effect techniques utilized by internet platforms to increase engagement and manipulate users have on children?

14. Section 5 of the FTC Act prohibits "unfair or deceptive acts or practices in or affecting commerce." What types of manipulation should be considered unfair or deceptive? What types should not be considered unfair or deceptive? Should a different standard be developed for manipulative techniques used by internet platforms? If so, what should that standard be? What manipulative techniques should be allowed for adults but not for children?

15. Does the application of section 230 of the Communications Decency Act (section 230) enable increased manipulation and repeat engagement/addiction? If so, how does section 230 enable increased manipulation and repeat engagement/addiction and what are the potential fixes?

The Honorable Lisa Blunt Rochester (D-DE)

1. At the January 8, 2020 hearing, you indicated that you were familiar with the concept of universal design. Do you think online service providers, like Facebook, should follow universal design concepts as a best practice on all of their platforms?

2. I am concerned that sometimes our laws and regulations are too reactive and do not anticipate future developments in technology and their societal impacts. Frankly, it often seems that technology has outpaced people and policy. We need to be more proactive.

How do you think we in Congress can develop a more agile and effective response to these concerning trends on the internet?

<u>**The Honorable Robin L. Kelly (D-IL)**</u>

1. Dr. Donovan, in your opening statement you mention that "platforms must address the power of amplification." Do you believe that companies have a responsibility for when content goes viral on their platforms? How do you propose companies monitor content when it looks like it's going viral and may be deceptive or manipulative?

2. When discussing deception online, one thing in particular that concerns me is phishing schemes used to obtain individuals' personally identifiable information, such as credit cards and health data. This is of particular concern for vulnerable populations such as those for whom English is a second language, as well as seniors or other populations with lower tech literacy rates. What opportunities exist to provide consumers with the confidence that the website requesting their information is legitimate? Twitter has the blue check mark. Is there a way to provide an equally easy and identifiable verification of websites requesting PII?

Additional Questions for the Record, Submitted by Mr. Justin (Gus) Hurwitz, Director of Law and Economics Programs, International Center for Law and Economics

The Honorable Kathy Castor (D-FL)

1. *What techniques do internet platforms employ to keep their users engaged? What types of techniques are harmful? What types of techniques are harmless? Are there industry standards? If so, what are they? If not, what should they be?*

This is an exceptionally broad question to which there are no simple answers. Internet platforms, as a category, are as varied as any market or market actors. In general, Internet platforms keep their users engaged by providing those users with content, goods, services, or other things that their users find value in consuming.

2. *What techniques do internet platforms employ to manipulate their users? What types of techniques are harmful? What types of*

techniques are harmless? Are there industry standards? If so, what are they? If not, what should they be?

This, too, is an exceptionally broad question to which there are no simple answers. Indeed, what "manipulates" one user may help another. Short of cases of abject fraud, it is difficult to call any given conduct manipulative. Indeed, even the effects of certain fraud may be relative, and beneficial to some individuals or in some contexts. It is well within the range of common human experience that lies, in certain cases, can be useful or appreciated. This same observation is true even for attempted manipulations that fall short of fraud. Consider the framing of this question, the phrasing of which presupposes the deliberate use of manipulation by Internet platforms and is designed to elicit responses that support that presupposition. Such manipulations are commonplace and largely accepted in civil society – both because their effects are generally innocuous and because it is exceptionally difficult (arguably impossible) to ask a question (or design an interface) that is not based on some assumptions and therefore will not "manipulate" some individuals.

Looking to existing legal standards, tools such as the FTC's authority to proscribe deceptive conduct are illustrative of tools for identifying harmful conduct that we may think of as manipulative. The key element in a deception inquiry is whether the conduct *materially* contributed to the harm.

3. *The word algorithm is used frequently in discussions over internet engagement. What is an algorithm? Who designs the algorithms? What are the benefits/harms to internet platforms using algorithms? How do algorithms use artificial intelligence? Can internet platforms fully explain why an algorithm produces certain results? Do internet platforms have knowledge of all the information fed into the algorithms they use?*

There is no accepted formal definition of algorithm. The meaning of the term is the subject of vigorous academic research and debate. At a general level, the term roughly means nothing more than a structured process of doing something. The "algorithm" to start many cars is "insert the key into the ignition; press the brake pedal and hold it in the pressed position; turn the key to the start position and hold it there until the engine has started; turn the key to the run position." Elementary school students learn "algorithms" for long division or calculating square roots. Computers use algorithms to convert a sound wave into an audio file, or to display an image file onto a screen.

Given what an algorithm is, asking "what are the benefits/harms to internet platforms using algorithms" is synonymous with "what are the benefits/harms to internet platforms existing." Algorithms are merely the instructions that tell the computers on which the platforms operate how to carry any – or, literally every – thing that they do.

Algorithms do not use artificial intelligence. Artificial intelligence uses algorithms to identify patterns or correlations in data and, in turn uses those patterns or correlations as an input into algorithms.

It is often the case that computer engineers cannot explain, or cannot easily, explain, the behavior of algorithms. This is the case both with many complex algorithms designed entirely by computer engineers or by algorithms that rely on machine leaning ("artificial intelligence") as an input into the operation of algorithms.

If it were easy to fully understand how an algorithm works, computer software would not have bugs. As anyone who has ever used a computer knows, all software has bugs. This is not because computer engineers are lazy or incompetent. It's because designing and implementing algorithms is exceptionally, incomparably, incomprehensibly, difficult to do. One of the first concepts that any computer scientists learns is the Halting Problem, which, in essence, states that it is possible to prove that *any* algorithm beyond a trivial level of complexity *can not* be fully understood without devoting an impossibly large amount of resources to it. Fully characterizing the algorithmic behavior of even the simplest of modern computer programs would take modern supercomputers a period of time longer than the Universe has existed.

The use of modern computers and algorithms is, in a sense, always a calculated risk – albeit one where the benefits generally outweigh the risks by thousands of orders magnitude. Any efforts to regulate based upon "algortihms" will be as effective as simplifying math by legislatively defining π to equal 3. Rather, regulation should focus on the effects of algorithms, not their design or inputs.

4. *What should be considered healthy engagement with an internet platform? Is healthy engagement defined differently for children? If so, what should be considered healthy engagement with an internet platform for children?*

5. *When does engagement with an internet platform turn into addiction? How are classic signs of addiction measured in the digital context? Is the addiction connected to internet platforms similar to manifestations of addiction in other situations? How is it similar? How is it different?*

Comprehensive answers to questions 4 and 5 are outside of my areas of expertise, beyond general familiarity of the work of various individual researchers who do work in these areas. It is my general understanding that these are contentious issues subject to vigorous debate among experts in the field.

6. *Why are repeat engagement with or addiction to an internet platform harmful to the individual or society as a whole? What are the costs? For example, what are the economic costs?*
7. *Why are manipulative techniques employed by internet platforms harmful to the individual or society as a whole? What are the costs? For example, what are the economic costs?*

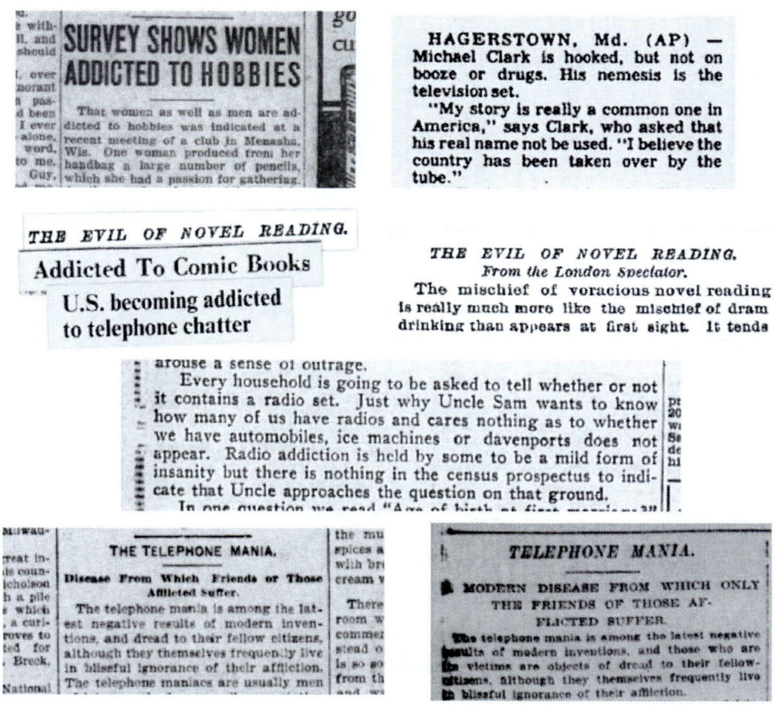

SURVEY SHOWS WOMEN ADDICTED TO HOBBIES

That women as well as men are addicted to hobbies was indicated at a recent meeting of a club in Menasha, Wis. One woman produced from her handbag a large number of pencils, which she had a passion for gathering.

HAGERSTOWN, Md. (AP) — Michael Clark is hooked, but not on booze or drugs. His nemesis is the television set.

"My story is really a common one in America," says Clark, who asked that his real name not be used. "I believe the country has been taken over by the tube."

THE EVIL OF NOVEL READING.

Addicted To Comic Books

U.S. becoming addicted to telephone chatter

THE EVIL OF NOVEL READING.
From the London Spectator.
The mischief of voracious novel reading is really much more like the mischief of dram drinking than appears at first sight. It tends

arouse a sense of outrage.
Every household is going to be asked to tell whether or not it contains a radio set. Just why Uncle Sam wants to know how many of us have radios and cares nothing as to whether we have automobiles, ice machines or davenports does not appear. Radio addiction is held by some to be a mild form of insanity but there is nothing in the census prospectus to indicate that Uncle approaches the question on that ground.

THE TELEPHONE MANIA.
Disease From Which Friends or Those Afflicted Suffer.
The telephone mania is among the latest negative results of modern inventions, and dread to their fellow citizens, although they themselves frequently live in blissful ignorance of their affliction. The telephone maniacs are usually men

TELEPHONE MANIA.
A MODERN DISEASE FROM WHICH ONLY THE FRIENDS OF THOSE AFFLICTED SUFFER.
The telephone mania is among the latest negative results of modern inventions, and those who are its victims are objects of dread to their fellow-citizens, although they themselves frequently live in blissful ignorance of their affliction.

8. *How do internet platforms monetize repeat engagement or addiction? Why does this model benefit internet platforms? What are the benefits?*
9. *How do internet platforms monetize manipulation? Why does this model benefit internet platforms? What are the benefits?*
10. *What tools are at internet platform users' disposal to stop repeat engagement or addiction? Should companies provide or fund those tools?*
11. *What tools are at internet platform users' disposal to stop manipulation? Should companies provide or fund those tools?*

In general, the response to questions 6 through 11 is that overwhelmingly Internet platforms approach all of these issues largely in the same way as other businesses, technologies, and platforms have approached them in the past. There are technological and economic differences between all of these platforms – to the extent that there are meaningful differences between Internet platforms and past businesses, technologies, and platforms, it is unclear whether these effects ultimately militate for or against the need for regulatory intervention. Just as platforms may have some greater ability to act in ways that are ultimately harmful (or beneficial) to consumers, consumers or competitors may similarly have greater ability in the modern technological era to protect themselves from or take action against such potentially harmful conduct.

12. *What role should Congress play in combating repeat engagement with or addiction to internet platforms?*
13. *Should Congress fund more research studying the techniques utilized by internet platforms to increase engagement and manipulate users and their effects? Should some of that research focus on the effect techniques utilized by internet platforms to increase engagement and manipulate users have on children?*

In response to questions 12 and 13, any Congressional response to the concerns evinced above should be based in empirical assessment of effects on consumers that compare the relative costs and benefits to consumers to plausible counterfactual worlds. Congress should absolutely fund, or encourage funding of, significant research into these areas. Importantly, the framing of that research is important – lest Congress itself be engaged in the practice of dark patterns. For instance, soliciting research "to study techniques used by Internet platforms to manipulate their users and the effects of these manipulations" *will* produce results that find that platforms do manipulate their users and that effects of these manipulations are adverse to users' interests. Such a study – and the funding behind it – would be political legerdemain (or, since relatively transparent politicking, merely manipulation)

14. *Section 5 of the FTC Act prohibits "unfair or deceptive acts or practices in or affecting commerce." What types of manipulation should be considered unfair or deceptive? What types should not be considered unfair or deceptive? Should a different standard be developed for manipulative techniques used by internet platforms? If so, what should that standard be? What manipulative techniques should be allowed for adults but not for children?*

The FTC's Section 5 authority is an exceptional model for how to approach these issues. Critical to its deception authority, in particular, is the requirement that for any conduct to be deceptive it have a material adverse effect on consumers.

Questions about differential regulation of platforms for adults and children is an exceptionally difficult subject. As the Supreme Court unanimous said in *Reno v. ACLU*, "the Government may not reduce the adult population to only what is fit for children." In general, the First Amendment requires that we not limit a forum intended broadly for use by adults to content and form suitable for children.

15. *Does the application of section 230 of the Communications Decency Act (section 230) enable increased manipulation and repeat engagement/addiction? If so, how does section 230 enable increased manipulation and repeat engagement/addiction and what are the potential fixes?*

Section 230 has only the barest and most attenuated of relevance to these issues. Section 230 has two functions: it immunizes platforms from liability for content created by its users, and it allows platforms to moderate that content, if they so elect, without assuming liability for content created by its users. To the extent that Congress is concerned about the conduct of Internet platforms, the first provision is wholly irrelevant. To the extent that Congress is concerned about users of platforms engaging in problematic conduct, the second provision facilitates action by platforms to curtail that problematic conduct. Both of these provisions are fundamentally sympathetic to any concern Congress may have, and supportive of Congressional efforts to curtail problematic conduct.

This is not to say that Section 230 is perfect. I have proposed narrow revisions to the statute that would bring it more into line with todays technological realities by enabling individuals engaging in harmful conduct to be identified, and subject to legal process, by parties harmed by their conduct. But proposals such as this are narrow and designed not to disrupt the fundamental operation of an exceptionally important law that has been overwhelmingly beneficial to American consumers and industry alike.

The Honorable Lisa Blunt Rochester (D-DE)

1. *At the January 8, 2020 hearing, you indicated that you were familiar with the concept of universal design. Do you think online service providers, like Facebook, should follow universal design concepts as a best practice on all of their platforms?*

Universal design is a laudable design goal and valuable is a principle that should be incorporated into design practices. However, it cannot be – as a technical matter – be reduced to or implemented as a design requirement. Requiring any firm to abide by the principles of universal design under penalty of law is tantamount to requiring that firm to successfully balance – in effect solve – all of society's competing tradeoffs and to face legal sanction for failure to do so. Researchers have studies questions related to these issues for hundreds of years and widely understand that there is no single, stable, equilibrium that maximizes the myriad competing values required by the principles of universal design.

This is not to say that universal design is not a good idea. Rather, it is necessarily aspirational. Firms that abide by it should be lauded and rewarded in the marketplace. Congress may choose to require firms to follow specific aspects of universal design, or, more likely, to meet narrow prescriptive goals required by those aspects under certain conditions. But the idea of requiring a firm to follow universal design concepts cannot be reduced to enforceable law – and any effort to do so would be a textbook example of a law that was unconstitutionally void.

2. *I am concerned that sometimes our laws and regulations are too reactive and do not anticipate future developments in technology and their societal impacts. Frankly, it often seems that technology has outpaced people and policy. We need to be more proactive. How do you think we in Congress can develop a more agile and effective response to these concerning trends on the internet?*

This is a generational effort – and not one that Congress can address on its own. There is no simple answer to this question. My recommendation is to create (that is, fund) more opportunities for interdisciplinary engagement between the fields of law, business, and engineering. To whit, I am currently in the process of establishing a new center at the University of Nebraska, the Nebraska Governance and Technology Center, that does precisely this.

In general, Congress always has been and always will be reactive to technological change. That is the nature of technology. The solution is not figure out how to bring greater technological knowledge into Congress. By the time problems created by any new technology reach the level of Congressional attention it will be too late for Congress to be anything but reactive – the horse will have already left the barn. Rather than bring greater understanding of technology into the legislative and policy process, we need to bring greater understanding of the legislative and policy process into the engineering and business sides of technology development.

The Honorable Brett Guthrie (R-KY)

1. *There is clearly a spectrum of business practices as it pertains to influencing consumer choices. On one end, these practices are legitimate and on the other, such practices have the potential to harm consumers. Professor Hurwitz, how do we draw the line between legitimate business behavior designed to influence users and exploitative "dark pattern" interfaces that may harm consumers?*

The best approach is to focus on the effects of these practices on consumers, not on the practices themselves. This approach has long been central to the Federal Trade Commission's authority to proscribe "deceptive" acts or practices. In order to be deceptive, an act or practice needs to have a *material* effect on consumers. In other words, and without getting into the details of FTC regulations, consumers need to be harmed because of the act or practice. It is not enough that an act or practice *could* conceivable cause harm – there needs to be some causal relationship between the conduct and actual harm. This requirement, of course, is not unique to consumer protection law – causation is a basic element of most areas of law.

It is often the case that design practices that appear likely to harm consumers have little, or even beneficial effects – and, conversely, that design practices that appear likely to benefit consumers may actually harm them. For instance, it is widely believed that supermarkets stock their checkout lines with "impulse" purchases that consumers are unlikely to buy unless "tricked" into buying them. While there is likely some truth to this, supermarket layout is intensively studied. Supermarkets often stock their checkout lanes either with products that consumers are likely to have forget to put in their carts (a benefit to consumers) or with curiosities that consumers are likely to engage with but not buy (e.g., tabloid magazines), which improves the customer experience. Or consider "ban-the-box" legislation, intended to give individuals with criminal records a better chance at getting jobs by preventing employers from asking them to indicate (check "the box") whether they have a criminal record on job applications. While a laudable goal, the result of these efforts has often been to reduce the likelihood that African American men get jobs at all – unable to ask about criminal history on applications directly, employers instead assume that men with names that "sound" African American are more likely to have criminal records and simply don't interview any such individuals. This is an example of a simple design intervention (ban the box) with a laudable goal (give more people opportunities to get jobs) that in many cases has had the opposite effect (even African Americans without criminal records now have a harder time of getting a job).

The only way to understand whether a design practice is beneficial or harmful is to focus on the actual effects of that practice.

2. *Professor Hurwitz, how is product design used to attract consumers? If the federal government were to regulate how companies may or may not design their products, what effect do you expect that to have on the free market and competition?*

Product design is used to attract consumers in myriad ways – most often by demonstrating of highlighting the value of products to consumers. Sometimes this value is superficial (consider a flashy but low-performance sports car), but sometimes even these superfices are valuable to consumers (consider the driver who enjoys having world think he owns a fancy sports car).

Importantly, product design is often used precisely to *attract* consumers – to get them in the door, not to close the sale. Most products in the economy are not commodities, where every firm sells identical products. Rather, they are differentiated products, where different firms sell products that are similar but not identical. Consider cars: Honda, Ford, Toyota, BMW, and many other companies sell sedans – but no to companies sell identical sedans. Companies will highlight aspects of their products, sometimes trivial or irrelevant ones, in order to get the attention of consumers. Importantly, this practice generally makes it more likely that consumers will compare more products from differentiated firms, which increases competition between those firms and decreases prices paid by consumers. That is, a cute advertisement of a dog driving car actually lowers the price that consumers pay for all cars, even though the advertisement communicates nothing of substance about the actual product.

In general, the best response to concerns about design is to rely on competition to address them. Poor design decisions create opportunities for competitors to enter the market with better products.

Regulating product design runs two parallel risks. Fist, as discussed in my response to the previous question, it is very likely that the government regulation will get things wrong and will make consumers worse off. Such regulations may proscribe designs that are counterintuitively beneficial to consumers or may mandate designs that are actually harmful to them. And, second, by specifying practices that firms must or cannot use, it reduces opportunities for innovation, experimentation, and competition. This is likely both to harm consumers today as well as to deprive future generations of beneficial technologies.

This is not to say that Congress and regulators should not be concerned about potentially problematic design practices. But any decision to regulate should be narrowly tailored to address design practices that can be demonstrated to have material harmful effects on consumers.

Additional Questions for the Record, Submitted by Mr. Tristan Harris, Executive Director, Center for Humane Technology

The Honorable Kathy Castor (D-FL)

1. *What techniques do internet platforms employ to keep their users engaged? What types of techniques are harmful? What types of techniques are harmless? Are there industry standards? If so, what are they? If not, what should they be?*

Techniques:

- Slot machine rewards ("pull to refresh")
- Loot boxes in games
- Removal of stopping cues (Infinite auto-backfilling news feeds, auto play on countdown)
- Designing to maximize tightly interconnected "infinite worlds" (never-ending, tightly interlinked worlds of content, like on Twitter, where links to more and more content never end)
- Personalized recommendation systems and algorithms that know us better than we know ourselves (e.g., YouTube "Up Next" recommendations, Instagram or TikTok News Feeds). They are supercomputers pointed at our brains making increasingly accurate predictions about which posts or videos will keep each brain most engaged.
- Social tagging and puppeteering ("You've been tagged in a photo," "X endorsed you, endorse them back?," "Say hi with a wave!," "Suggested users to follow")
- Attention-seeking hacking (# of followers, # of likes, # subscribers, etc.)
- "Come back" emails to "resurrect" idle or dormant users (tech as "digital drug lords")
- Beautification Filters that affect teenager's self-worth and identity through positive social feedback limited to unrealistic standards of beauty. ("people like you, if only you look different than you actually do")

There are no industry standards on what practices are allowed or not. The "race to the bottom of the brain stem" to strip mine human attention knows no boundaries, except when there's rare surges of public pressure that occasionally have them limit certain features – such as Instagram testing the removal of "Likes" in certain markets.

What should those standards be?

- No auto playing videos in feeds
- No automated countdowns for the next video, by default
- No bottomless, infinite scrolling feeds without pauses, "speed bumps" or self-imposed random friction and slowdowns – either in the form of a "Load more" button or a breathing gap
- Consider limiting people under the age of 18 to 90 minutes of playing time on weekdays and three hours on weekends and holidays – as they do in China.
- No loot boxes. This mirrors policies already passed in Japan.
- Ban time-spent and engagement-maximizing business models and algorithms

2. *What techniques do internet platforms employ to manipulate their users? What types of techniques are harmful? What types of techniques are harmless? Are there industry standards? If so, what are they? If not, what should they be?*

- Micro-targeting unchecked, unregulated computationally generated messages and images of vitriolic content with no accountability

All of the above techniques can be used in ways that lead to harms – addiction, polarization (over personalization), distraction, depression and suicide, bullying, vanity culture, loneliness, micro-targeted disinformation, seeding conspiracies and extremism.

There are no common industry standards or practices to protect against these harms. The industry should be held accountable to a new body, a Attention Economy Agency whose job is to monitor for the standardized set of harms that must be reduced or eliminated from technology, create public pressure, and set quarterly targets for harm-reduction across these areas from participating tech companies.

New standards:

- Ban micro-targeting
- Ban recommendation systems, which must be oriented around positive values, not engagement
- Ban time-spent and engagement-maximizing business models and algorithms

3. *The word algorithm is used frequently in discussions over internet engagement. What is an algorithm? Who designs the algorithms? What are the benefits/harms to internet platforms using algorithms? How do algorithms use artificial intelligence? Can internet platforms fully explain why an algorithm produces certain results? Do internet platforms have knowledge of all the information fed into the algorithms they Use?*

An algorithm is, "a process or set of rules to be followed in calculations or other problem-solving operations" according to Oxford Internet Dictionary. Algorithms produce automated decisions – and power everything from what content you see in news feeds, what order it appears in, which ads you see, when notifications on your phone get delivered, to which Uber car gets notified when you hit "Request Ride." Some algorithms are backed by artificial intelligence, which are more advanced algorithms where the machine "learns" its own strategies and rules to most efficiently reach specified goals or outcomes.

It is impossible for internet platforms to fully explain why an algorithm produces certain results. Recommendation and news feed algorithms powering services like Facebook or YouTube often use millions of variables to determine what we see – let alone the fact that there are trillions of possible combinations or orderings of content they could show.

There is also a direct tradeoff between what's called "algorithmic explainability" – the degree to which an algorithm can be explained, and how accurate it is at producing outcomes or predictions. An algorithm that uses a trillion invisible parameters is harder to explain, but more accurate at producing the intended goals, than an algorithm with 10 parameters that is easier to explain, but less accurate at producing the intended goals.

4. *What should be considered healthy engagement with an internet platform? Is healthy engagement defined differently for children? If so, what should be considered healthy engagement with an internet platform for children?*

It's tempting to define healthy use as simply spending less time on today's existing internet platforms like YouTube, Facebook, etc. However, that is deeply insufficient. That would be like a government advocating that every citizen have a "healthy daily habit" of cigarettes and limit it to three per day. We can't recommend "healthy use" of cigarettes when they are designed to be addictive, just like we cannot recommend "Healthy engagement" when commercial interests from asymmetrically powerful systems know how to manipulate each user and externalize cultural harms that affect everyone. So long as platforms' business models are based on extracting and mining attention at all costs, and billion-dollar profits depend on it, their design decisions won't have the best interests of society, or stakeholders in our society, in mind.

We shouldn't be aiming for "healthy engagement" as much as we should aim for the notion of "humane technology" that does not asymmetrically override and manipulate users for the best interests of business. Humane technology does not prey on human vulnerabilities for commercial interest.

A phone app that lets children make audio and FaceTime calls to each other, for example, is not manipulating children with news feeds, beautification filters, social feedback and ratings (e.g., Likes and Followers). A plain telephone is like a tool, like a hammer, waiting patiently to be used. Tools or hammers aren't harmful. Engagement-maximizing services, driven by the corrosive, unbounded business model of advertising that seeks to consume and extract human attention, is what is existentially harmful. Given their business model, a human being is simply worth more if they are addicted, isolated, outraged, narcissistic, voyeuristic, polarized and disinformed (because of ads), than if they are a sovereign human being.

5. *When does engagement with an internet platform turn into addiction? How are classic signs of addiction measured in the digital context? Is the addiction connected to internet platforms similar to manifestations of addiction in other situations? How is it similar? How is it different?*

Defining a clinical threshold for addiction is a distraction from the existential issues at stake. Tech companies will happily stall that debate for decades as governments enter never-ending debates about clinical thresholds and measurements everyone can agree on. What matters is that business models of asymmetrically powerful, and ever-growingly more powerful tech companies, who know more about each user than they know about themselves, have a runaway unbounded incentive to exploit that asymmetric understanding of your vulnerabilities.

Imagine a patient sitting unconscious in the operating room of a doctor. The patient's life is in their hands. They are vulnerable to whatever the doctor chooses to do. The patient also trusts the doctor who knows more about medicine and their personal information and differential vulnerabilities than they know about themselves, not to exploit their vulnerability as they lie on the operating table, unconscious. We have to redefine the asymmetric relationship between users and tech companies into a "fiduciary" relationship. That means technology platforms cannot be allowed to operate with business models based on exploiting their users and the societies in which they operate.

6. *Why are repeat engagement with or addiction to an internet platform harmful to the individual or society as a whole? What are the costs? For example, what are the economic costs?*

Addiction is the least of the harms. Platforms that create individualized, addiction-maximizing "Truman shows" with never-ending AFFIRMATION instead of INFORMATION, due to the business model that reinforces what keeps each of us clicking, destroys shared truth and facts, drives polarization, and is existential to the function of democracy and policy-making.

If no one agrees on what any given policy is, or what it will do, then no consensus can exist. For existential issues like climate change that can *only* be addressed by passing policies that bind market forces to reduce and reverse emissions, that's game over for all of humanity.

7. *Why are manipulative techniques employed by internet platforms harmful to the individual or society as a whole? What are the costs? For example, what are the economic costs?*

The complete breakdown of democracies all around the world. The inability of humanity to address climate change, immigration, democracy deficit, fake news and many other important issues.

8. *How do internet platforms monetize repeat engagement or addiction? Why does this model benefit internet platforms? What are the benefits?*

Because their business model is based on showing as many ads as possible to users, they make money the more time they can manipulate users into coming back and spending ever more time on their platform to see more ads, which allows the platforms to make even better predictions with their virtual models of each user. This business model has made these advertising-based technology platforms the most profitable corporations in history.

9. *How do internet platforms monetize manipulation? Why does this model benefit internet platforms? What are the benefits?*

Manipulation is the very basis of each design decision of advertising-backed platforms – not because of the *advertisement* as manipulation, but because each design decision surrounding the delivery of the ads is based on manipulating the user and strip-mining their attention in order to serve the user up to advertisers. Follow the money, and you will understand how and why they manipulate users.

10. *What tools are at internet platform users' disposal to stop repeat engagement or addiction? Should companies provide or fund those tools?*

They lack sufficient tools. "Screen Time" features like on iPhone only allow you a theoretical limit. Research suggests this hardly works, and very few people opt into these tools. It is equivalent to telling someone who is a smoker, "well you shouldn't keep smoking, just limit yourself to two cigarettes a day." A product designed with scientifically precise addictive capacity cannot be dealt with through serving size limits. The better solution is to re-align the business model and incentives of technology to align with the interests of users and society. In other words, acting like "attention utilities" who, like any public utility, must be regulated to operate for the public interest and come with certain safety standards.

11. *What tools are at internet platform users' disposal to stop manipulation? Should companies provide or fund those tools?*

They do not have access to tools to stop manipulation. They cannot opt out of micro-targeting or advertising or the ways that the news feed content, groups, events, etc., themselves can be manipulated by nefarious actors. If they did that, it would kill the goose that lays the golden eggs, from the company point of view. Manipulation is core to these platforms' money-making machines; it is core to their business model. Regulation and rules from the government are badly needed, because these companies cannot and will not regulate themselves.

12. *What role should Congress play in combating repeat engagement with or addiction to internet platforms?*

Congress is way behind the need to put rules and regulations around the business models of these companies. These companies have been able to establish their own rules for many years now, and as a result have created a business model that is destructive to children, families and society at large. I can't emphasize this enough – it is the BUSINESS MODEL of these companies that is the problem, not the technologies themselves. These companies use engagement and manipulation tricks because they are trying to keep us glued to their websites, because the longer we are glued, the more ads we see and the more money they make. So, you have to fundamentally break the connection between the money-making machine and the engagement.

There are several ways to do that. You could limit or even forbid advertising on these platforms. Just as the Highway Beautification Act of 1965 forbids the construction or showing of billboards on almost every piece of private property in the US, digital platform companies would not construct or show any advertisements on a user's web page on that platform. The digital platform may, however, provide a link to an advertising page that any viewer may visit if she/he wishes.

Alternatively, Congress could use legislative encouragement to push these platforms towards a subscription model. We should closely examine whether a business model based on free services in exchange for our personal data, which then is harvested for advertising, persuasion and the spread of disinformation, is the appropriate one for these platforms which have essentially created the "new digital infrastructure" for the 21st century. A subscription model, like the one used for cable TV in which companies charge a monthly fee and must adhere to a digital license of conditions, would be a better match for this crucial infrastructure sector. European Commission Vice President Margrethe Vestager, who is also the Commissioner on Competition for the EU, has called for a Facebook based on a subscription with "no tracking and advertising and *the full benefits of privacy.*" Keep in mind a paid, subscription version of Facebook wouldn't just be the same service we get today – without the ads. It would be an entirely different kind of service built around helping us get the most out of our lives with friends, like Mark Zuckerberg's original 2005 description of Facebook as a "social utility" to help us connect with our friends.

13. *Should Congress fund more research studying the techniques utilized by internet platforms to increase engagement and manipulate users and their effects? Should some of that research focus on the effect techniques utilized by internet platforms to increase engagement and manipulate users have on children?*

Yes, Congress should fund more research, not only concerning children but also the impact of these techniques on polarization, fake news, democratic discourse, elections and more. Internet platforms represent an existential threat to our democracy. But the need for ongoing research should not be an excuse for inaction. And research aiming to study the existing harms would simply take too long to make the necessary changes. Research would provide us with a more accurate record of how the social fabric, truth and mental health melted in front of our eyes, instead of funding research immediately into new platforms that would reverse and prevent this process. There already have been a number of studies done about the techniques utilized by Internet platforms, at this point the effects are well-known among researchers. See the book Surveillance Capitalism, which references a number of studies on the impacts of these Internet platforms and their toxic methods.

In fact, these platforms and their techniques should be subject to ongoing "Attention Impact Analyses" (AIA). – akin to an environmental impact analysis – which assess potential impacts on fake news and info-sharing, democracy, social polarization and mental health before deployment of new techniques. An AIA should apply a "precautionary principle" – a kind of Hippocratic oath of "first, do no harm" – to their business model. This would put society on a healthier footing for the safe use and enjoyment of these technologies.

In that light, the US badly needs to create a watchdog Attention Economy Agency (AEA). Like the Environmental Protection Agency was created in 1970 to oversee and consolidate the watchdog function of protecting the environment, the Attention Economy Agency would play a regulatory and watchdog role for this sector that is increasingly becoming central to every aspect of our economy, culture and society. This AEA also would facilitate other federal agencies engaging in a "digital update" and "harms audit" of how the new attention economy is impacting the legal and regulatory frameworks under its purview.

For example, there are restrictions on violence and advertising for Saturday morning cartoons and other programming for children, resulting from laws like the Children's Television Act passed in 1990. Yet Google's YouTube/YouTubeKids violates these regulations and norms of decency on a regular basis. The Federal Communications Commission should examine how to apply existing law to the online digital platforms. Other federal agencies, as well as state governments, should do the same. The AEA would help facilitate this kind of re-examination and update.

> 14. *Section 5 of the FTC Act prohibits "unfair or deceptive acts or practices in or affecting commerce." What types of manipulation should be considered unfair or deceptive? What types should not be considered unfair or deceptive? Should a different standard be developed for manipulative techniques used by internet platforms? If so, what should that standard be? What manipulative techniques should be allowed for adults but not for children?*

Their entire business model is "unfair and deceptive." How many people realize that every app on their cell phone, every platform company they interact with, is tracking them, grabbing their data, monitoring their email, and generally using powerful methods of surveillance and manipulation of their every next move that would have made the Nazis or the Stasi envious? And then they use that information to build psychographic profiles on each and every one of us, and then advertisers pay for access to those profiles. These platforms are pointing powerful supercomputers at our brains in order to more perfectly predict, more and more successfully, how to get us to think, feel and do things – click on the link, agree with a personalized micro-targeted message, read a popular but fake or extreme news article (because the algorithms cannot distinguish between "popular" and true). On and on and on. This entire practice is "unfair and deceptive."

Sure, we could break it down more minutely, look at which forms of engagement, recommendations, micro-targeting, auto feed, social tagging and more are the most destructive. But by singling out any one or two or three of these techniques, we missed the 800-pound gorilla in the room – the entire business model is unfair and deceptive.

15. *Does the application of section 230 of the Communications Decency Act (section 230) enable increased manipulation and repeat engagement/addiction? If so, how does section 230 enable increased manipulation and repeat engagement/addiction and what are the potential fixes?*

Yes, undoubtedly. Section 230 has made it so that these platforms are not legally or financially responsible for any of the content that their billions of users are spreading with the assistance of these platforms' global reach. Because they are not legally or financially responsible, they make very few efforts to stop bad actors. Look at Facebook, which has violated multiple consent decrees agreed to with the FTC and the Department of Justice, showing that even when it agreed to certain rules, it broke them because they were not afraid of strong enforcement. The New York Times ran a series about how live streams on Facebook, as well as on other platforms like Zoom, are being used by bad actors to live stream outrageous activities such as the Christchurch killer who live streamed his mass murder of Muslims in New Zealand; or Zoom and Google, being used to live stream sexual child abuse in real time, with participants observing and shouting encouragement to the abusers; or Buddhist extremists in Myanmar who used Facebook to whip up anti-Muslim hysteria against the Rohingya minority. This is horrific and when confronted about it most often the platform companies try to evade both action as well as responsibility. They get away with this because of section 230.

The harsh reality that everyone needs to come to grips with is that the same technology that is used for posting our children or puppy photos, or finding an old college roommate, or for live streaming important meetings, is also being used to do terrible things. Are we supposed to simply throw up our hands and say, "Oh well, that's the price for being able to post cute puppy photos?" Or can we find a way to regulate these extremely powerful technologies?

Section 230 became law in the mid-1990s, when all of these platforms were still rather small. It seemed like a good idea at the time to encourage the growth of the Internet. Now, we see That section 230 is part of an "Attention economy" ecosystem that is harming individuals, families, communities (Like the Rohingya in Myanmar), societies in general, our democracies. Section 230 needs to be modified in such a way as to rein in the harms and retain the good.

This can be done, following some of the proposals we have recommended above.

The Honorable Lisa Blunt Rochester (D-DE)

1. *At the January 8, 2020 hearing, you indicated that you were familiar with the concept of universal design. Do you think online service providers, like Facebook, should follow universal design concepts as a best practice on all of their platforms?*
2. *I am concerned that sometimes our laws and regulations are too reactive and do not anticipate future developments in technology and their societal impacts. Frankly, it often seems that technology has outpaced people and policy. We need to be more proactive. How do you think we in Congress can develop a more agile and effective response to these concerning trends on the internet?*

New technology frequently drives change that exceeds that capacity of government to respond. The nature of this evolutionary process is that government is always somewhat behind the curve. But the more exponentially powerful technology becomes at shaping more and more consequences – controlling what billions of people believe, think and do – the less we can afford any errors. Technology has made us too powerful to be negligent. Technology is the new infrastructure for society. At a certain point, governments must step in to create the "guardrails" for this new infrastructure. Like in 1982, when AT&T controlled 90% of the nation's telephone market, it was necessary to break up that company. Like our utilities - the US devised a regulatory structure in which they are given a quasi-monopoly, but in return they must agree to a number of "duty of care" rules and regulations.

We now find ourselves in a similar situation with digital technologies. The digital platform companies have created the new digital infrastructure for the 21st century. So now we must begin the crucial process of crafting the rules, regulations and "digital licenses" that these companies must abide by in order to operate. To do this the right way, we can look to our successful past. The Environmental Protection Agency was created in 1970 to oversee and consolidate the watchdog function of protecting the environment. 1977 saw the creation of the Department of Energy because we recognize that the landscape and the technology around energy was becoming sufficiently complex that we needed a federal agency that focused on that portfolio.

We have reached a similar moment now with the digital technologies and the "attention economy." We need to create a watchdog Attention Economy Agency to oversee a new classification for these companies as "attention utilities." The Attention Economy Agency would play a regulatory and watchdog role for this new sector that is increasingly becoming central to every aspect of our economy, culture and society. This AEA also would facilitate other federal agencies engaging in a "digital update" and "harms audit" of how the new attention economy is impacting the legal and regulatory frameworks under its purview. The EPA and the DOE functioned in that way as well, when they were first created, helping other federal agencies to incorporate that perspective into their own portfolios.

For example, there are restrictions on violence and advertising for Saturday morning cartoons and other programming for children, resulting from laws like the Children's Television Act passed in 1990. Yet Google's YouTube/YouTubeKids violates these regulations and norms of decency on a regular basis. The Federal Communications Commission should examine how to apply existing law to the online digital platforms. Other federal agencies, as well as state governments, should do the same. The AEA would help facilitate this kind of re-examination and update. And this agency would make sure that the government does not fall too far behind in its need to keep up with the fast-changing digital technologies.

The Honorable Robin L. Kelly (D-IL)

1. *When discussing deception online, one thing in particular that concerns me is phishing schemes used to obtain individuals' personally identifiable information, such as credit cards and health data. This is of particular concern for vulnerable populations such as those for whom English is a second language, as well as seniors or other populations with lower tech literacy rates. What opportunities exist to provide consumers with the confidence that the website requesting their information is legitimate? Twitter has the blue check mark. Is there a way to provide an equally easy and identifiable verification of websites requesting PII?*

This question - how to protect vulnerable populations and their PII - illustrates exactly why we need privacy (and other ethical and humane aspects of technology) by design, not by requiring individuals make burdensome, heavily-researched choices in every moment. The world is getting more and more complicated. Everyone is busy. No one has time to research the basis of every supply chain or every button they push, especially when technology bombards them with more and more communication and choices. Users should be able to trust that technology has their best interests in mind – and have platforms proactively protect users. The default should be settings that we can trust.

Today's tech platforms are like a car that only goes 0 mph or 100 mph. When it gets into a metaphorical crash – mental health problems like anxiety or loneliness, or political problems like polarization – then, technology companies blame the driver. But it's not a driver issue, it's a design issue. Cars should be safe to drive at most speeds. Technology platforms should be safe and harm-minimizing for all of us, most of the time, by default.

As I wrote previously:

I believe in a world where the technology industry is remade in a manner that becomes a more empowering tool – something that serves humanity and life again. Where it is built around servicing our needs and strengthening the fabric of our society, not parasitically extracting value from the most vulnerable organs of society. Where technology strengthens our capacity to see multiple perspectives, nuance and complexity – where there are no black and white answers.

We need technology to aid us in these endeavors for our civilization to survive.

Chapter 2

Online Imposters and Disinformation*

Committee on Science, Space, and Technology

Thursday, September 26, 2019
House of Representatives,
Subcommittee on Investigations and Oversight,
Committee on Science, Space, and Technology,
Washington, D.C.

The Subcommittee met, pursuant to notice, at 2:01 p.m., in room 2318 of the Rayburn House Office Building, Hon. Mikie Sherrill [Chairwoman of the Subcommittee] presiding.

COMMITTEE ON SCIENCE, SPACE, AND TECHNOLOGY
SUBCOMMITTEE ON INVESTIGATIONS AND OVERSIGHT
U.S. HOUSE OF REPRESENTATIVES

HEARING CHARTER

Online Imposters and Disinformation
Thursday, September 26, 2019
2:00 p.m.
2318 Rayburn House Office Building

* This is an edited, reformatted and augmented version of Hearing before the Subcommittee on Investigations and Oversight of the Committee on Science, Space, and Technology, House of Representatives, Serial No. 116–47, dated September 26, 2019.

In: A Closer Look at Online Deception and Disinformation
Editor: Suzanne M. Williams
ISBN: 979-8-88697-310-5

PURPOSE

The purpose of the hearing is to explore the enabling technologies for disinformation online, including deep fakes, explore trends and emerging technology in the field, and consider research strategies that can help stem the tide of malicious inauthentic behavior.

WITNESSES

- **Dr. Siwei Lyu,** Director, Computer Vision and Machine Learning Lab, SUNY - Albany
- **Dr. Hany Farid**, Professor of Electrical Engineering & Computer Science and the School of Information, UC-Berkeley
- **Ms. Camille Francois,** Chief Innovation Officer, Graphika

KEY QUESTIONS

- How extensive is online disinformation and how does it affect Americans?
- What are some emerging expressions of online disinformation and online imposters?
- Why is social media so readily exploited for spreading disinformation?
- What are some of the technology and social solutions we have today to combat malicious online imposters, deep fakes and disinformation?
- What are the research and workforce needs associated with these challenges?

BACKGROUND

Researchers generally define *misinformation* as information that is false or misleading but promulgated with sincerity by a person who believes it is true. *Disinformation* is shared with the deliberate intent to deceive. Disinformation represents an intentional effort to shape or distort public perceptions around a particular issue through the dissemination of false information – or opinions or true information being delivered by a false messenger. Global governments and domestic agitators have long used disinformation in its many forms as a weapon against their adversaries. The problem has become far more pervasive in the past decade with the explosive growth of social media, which provides an opportunity to hostile actors to project disinformation directly into the popular discourse at little cost. The natural anonymity of the internet also makes it cheap and easy for bad actors to impersonate public figures or create fake personalities that don't exist in order to proliferate content.

The shape of disinformation is also changing because fake content and videos can now be created automatically through the use of artificial intelligence. AI programs can write convincing articles and blog posts that seem to be written by real humans, and AI can create fake videos featuring "people" who do not really exist. While audio has traditionally been the least advanced aspect of deep fake technology, recent breakthroughs have occurred that have substantially closed the gap between fake audio content and its parallel video content. AI achievements in this space are exploding, with new advances occurring every 2-3 months.

The phenomena of online imposters and disinformation are virtually inextricable. To the extent that all information, true or false, is received differently according to what messenger delivered it, perhaps all information proliferated by online imposters is disinformation. A relatively low percentage of what might be classified as "disinformation" online is counterfactual in the strictest sense of the word (e.g. "the Moon landing was faked"). A more frequent expression might be when a foreign-based troll or bot retweets or shares a political statement that itself would be either factually true or a matter of opinion (e.g. "Congressional Candidate X cares about family values"), but is revealed to be disingenuous/of false pretenses when the real author is revealed.

Online imposters and their activities can be classified into three baskets:

- **Digital astroturfing**, in which bots and trolls create multiple fake personalities to artificially boost an influence campaign, spread lies and/or enflame public discourse.
- **Digital imposters**, in which bad actors create bogus profiles for real public figures.[1]
- **Deep fakes**, in which bad actors manipulate a public figure's physical likeness to create highly-realistic videos and audio clips.

Recent Episodes

Malicious online imposters and disinformation intended to cause harm or artificially influence social discourse take a wide variety of expressions that diversifies every year:

Astroturfing during political content: On September 21, Twitter announced it was suspending 4,258 accounts operating from the UAE that were proliferating a coordinated disinformation campaign targeting Qatar and Yemen.[2]

Astroturfing during political conflict: In August 2019, Twitter announced that it had identified and taken down 200,000 accounts linked to the Chinese government that sought to present an artificial groundswell of public opposition to the pro-democracy campaign in Hong Kong.[3]

---

[1] https://www.vice.com/en_us/article/ae5m7z/meet-the-people-pretending-to-be-celebrities-on-social-media

[2] https://www.hongkongfp.com/2019/09/21/twitter-closes-thousands-fake-news-accounts-including-4302-chinese-accounts-targeting-hong-kong-protests/

[3] https://www.reuters.com/article/us-hongkong-protests-twitter/twitter-facebook-accuse-china-of-using-fake-accounts-to-undermine-hong-kong-protests-idUSKCN1V91NX

Twitter shared information about the accounts it had identified with Facebook, which was able to execute its own takedown of Facebook accounts.

Audio deep fakes: In August 2019, news media reported on the first known major incidence of an audio-only deep fake being used in a crime. Thieves used sophisticated voice-mimicking software to imitate a senior executive at a British energy company in order to convince a managing director to wire $240,000 to an account in Hungary.[4]

Political impersonation: The intelligence firm FireEye reported that Iranians posing as Americans set up fake social media accounts in 2018 to interfere in U.S. Congressional races. Some of the fake accounts impersonated the candidates themselves. The researchers found that the impersonators were a part of a broader campaign by Iranian actors, which included entire fake news websites and letters and op-eds in a handful of U.S. newspapers.[5]

Nonconsensual pornography: In June 2019, a programmer created an app called DeepNude which allowed users to create extremely realistic nude renderings from images of clothed women – allowing the subjects to be victims of revenge porn without ever having taken a nude photo. Paradoxically, revenge porn laws are unlikely to prohibit these renderings because the victim's actual nude image is not displayed, even while the forgeries can be difficult to detect.[6]

Synthetic political messaging with organic augmentation: In a February 2018 indictment, Special Counsel Robert Mueller described one effort by the Russian government to interfere with American political discourse by creating the @TEN_GOP Twitter handle to pose as the Tennessee Republican party.[7] The account eventually gathered more than 100,000 followers, but its content was received by a much larger audience as it was retweeted by several prominent figures with larger followings.[8] Twitter shut down the @TEN_GOP account in August 2017.

Political impersonation: In June 2018, a network of foreign actors created and promoted a fake Tweet from Senator Marco Rubio. The culprits did not make a fake account for Senator Rubio; rather, they Photoshopped one of his real tweets to change its content, then proliferated it as a screenshot across (non-Twitter) discussion forums. The tweet was not widely debunked in the media until the Atlantic Council's Digital Forensics Lab discovered it a year later.[9][10]

Fake reviews: A cottage industry dedicated to selling fake reviews on Amazon has developed in recent years. Vendors pay perpetrators to create profiles for "consumers" that seem authentic and then leave five-star reviews with detailed narrative descriptions. A project called ReviewMeta analyzed 203 million Amazon reviews and found 11.3% of them to be inauthentic. A similar

---

[4] https://www.washingtonpost.com/technology/2019/09/04/an-artificial-intelligence-first-voice-mimicking-software-reportedly-used-major-theft/

[5] https://www.rollcall.com/news/congress/iranians-may-used-influence-operations-2018-midterms

[6] https://www.vice.com/en_au/article/kzm59x/deepnude-app-creates-fake-nudes-of-any-woman

[7] https://www.documentcloud.org/documents/4380502-Indictment.html#document/p15/a404968 P. 15

[8] Including Eric Trump, Donald Trump Jr., Kellyanne Conway, and Roger Stone.

[9] https://medium.com/dfrlab/top-takes-suspected-russian-intelligence-operation-39212367d2f0

[10] https://twitter.com/marcorubio/status/1141468656603455488

project called Fakespot argues the figure is closer to 30%. Amazon sued over 1,000 sellers for buying reviews from 2015-2018, but it also claims the incidence of fake reviews is <1%.[11][12]

Digital astroturfing: In May 2018, a Facebook page called the "WalkAway Movement" was created, and #WalkAway began to trend on Twitter. The page described #WalkAway as a "grassroots movement" of Democrats fleeing the party – but in fact, it was an astroturf campaign conducted by US-based political trolls, amplified by Russian troll farms.[13] The Facebook page grew to 19,000 members in just one month. #Walkaway was the Number 1 most-used hashtag in overall use on Twitter by June 30. Not every account that retweeted #WalkAway was a bot, but participation from both bots and American citizens misrepresenting their identities was able to amplify an inauthentic campaign to artificially expand its reach.

Inauthentic representations of public figures: In the first hours after the Santa Fe High School shooting in May 2018, which left 10 dead, online hoaxers created fake Facebook accounts using the shooter's name and doctored photos that linked him to both 2016 Presidential candidates Trump and Clinton. One disinformation analyst noted it took less than 20 minutes for the first fake Facebook account to be created after the suspect's name was revealed.[14]

Acronyms and vocabulary

- **Bot** – an autonomous program that can "behave" like an authentic human user on social media. The more sophisticated algorithms the bot is following, the more realistic its behavior. Not all bots are malicious – e.g. the USGS Earthquake Notification Service is a bot.

- **Troll farm** – an organization of (human) internet users seeking to create conflict or promote inflammatory content online in some coordinated fashion.

- **Deep neural network** – a multi-layer set of algorithms, modeled loosely after the human brain, that uses sophisticated mathematical modeling to process data and information in complex ways, including recognizing patterns.

- **GAN** – generative adversarial network. A type of machine learning system. GAN is the technique most commonly associated with creating deep fakes, but is not the only method.

- **GPU** – graphical computing unit. An inexpensive, commercial available type of computing hardware that can be incorporated into a regular laptop or desktop computer in order make more sophisticated graphics, including deep fakes.

- **IP Address** – A unique numeric identifier assigned to every computer or smartphone. Most IP addresses are dynamic, i.e. change periodically, but the address will always include a signifier of the rough location of the device. Any user can search an IP address for its details

[11] https://thehustle.co/amazon-fake-reviews
[12] https://www.npr.org/2018/07/30/629800775/some-amazon-reviews-are-too-good-to-be-believed-theyre-paid-for
[13] https://arcdigital.media/pro-trump-russian-linked-twitter-accounts-are-posing-as-ex-democrats-in-new-astroturfed-movement-20359c1906d3
[14] Chris Sampson. https://twitter.com/TAPSTRIMEDIA/status/997541195114000384

to get a sense of its location (E.g. "U.S. House of Representatives") as well as which ISP (below) is serving the connected device. IP addresses can be concealed using a VPN (below), but VPNs must be purchased and requires some extra steps on the part of the user.

- **ISP** – internet service provider. The utilities that provide internet access but do not adjudicate platforms of content. E.g. Comcast, Verizon, AT&T.

- **Recommendation algorithm** – the automated capability that Youtube and other platforms use to guess what kind of new content a user might be interested viewing based on the content they have already explored. The results are used to suggest new videos to watch, highlight stories to read and otherwise make content more prominent to the user.

- **VPN** – virtual private network. A method of connecting to the internet that (1) conceals a device's IP address, and thus conceals its general geographic location; and (2) enhances privacy for the user by encrypting data that is transferred over WiFi.

Social media platforms' approach

Social media platforms, researchers and federal agencies use a variety of terms to describe the challenge of online imposters and disinformation:

- **Facebook**, which is also the parent company of Instagram and Whatsapp, uses the term "coordinated inauthentic behavior." This includes accounts run by humans impersonating real people; accounts for non-existent people, and users that promote content because they are paid to.

- **Twitter** focuses on "platform manipulation," defined as "using Twitter to engage in bulk, aggressive or deceptive activity that misleads others and/or disrupts their experience." This includes "inauthentic engagements" that attempt to make content appear more popular than it is and "coordinated activity, that attempts to artificially influence conversations through the use of multiple accounts, fake accounts, automation and/or scripting."[15]

- **YouTube**, owned by Google, has specific terms of use policies against *Impersonation* and *Spam, deceptive practices & scams*.[16] Under the latter category, Youtube names Voter Suppression (content aiming to mislead voters about the time, place, means or eligibility requirements for voting), incentivization spam (in which engagement metrics, such as likes and positive comments, are sold, and rep), posting of content that is autogenerated by computers in order to post it quickly, and repetitive/excessive posing of the same material in comments or videos. It also names "borderline content," which seeks to misinform users in harmful ways but does not violate the black letter of its community standards agreement.

The First Amendment does not restrict private companies from moderating content on their own. But social media companies lean heavily on Section 230 of the Communications Decency Act, which became law in the 1990s, to limit their responsibilities to adjudicate disinformation online.

---

[15] https://help.twitter.com/en/rules-and-policies/platform-manipulation
[16] https://support.google.com/youtube/answer/2801973?hl=en

Section 230 says that "no provider or user of an interactive computer service shall be treated as the publisher or speaker of any information provided by another information content provider."[17]

Since late 2016, the major platforms have taken steps in fits and starts to address the issues of disinformation. In December 2016, Facebook announced its Third Party Fact-Checking project to help identify and debunk content that is demonstrably false. Facebook has conducted several updates to its News Feed recommendation algorithm to demote various types of false content when it is identified. For example, an update in June 2019 was designed to "reduce the reach" of posts that make sensational and misleading health claims.[18] In September 2019, Facebook introduced a Deepfake Detection Challenge and committed $10 million to fund the project, which will partner with Microsoft, Massachusetts Institute of Technology (MIT), the University of California-Berkeley, Cornell Tech, Oxford, and others.

Twitter has established a policy of releasing all information about imposter accounts it identifies and removes after the takedown has been executed, including all data on content proliferated by the troll or bot. This practice better allows researchers and cybersecurity professionals to better understand the state of the art in adversarial operations. In January 2019, Twitter also brought back the "chronological timeline," allowing users to read tweets from users that they follow according to when they were written. In 2016 Twitter had reorganized users' feeds with a recommendation algorithm, which tended to highlight more controversial viral content.[19]

In January 2019, Youtube announced that while they would continue to host videos were identified for perpetuating falsehoods, its recommendation algorithms would no longer recommend the videos to users.[20]

Emerging Trends

Malicious actors who seek to misrepresent themselves or spread disinformation online are constantly evolving in their strategies as companies and "white hat" researchers grow more adept at combatting their previous approaches. Trends to anticipate on the five-year horizon:

- **Chinese-sponsored disinformation.**[21]
- **Instagram** will be a more frequent forum for disinformation via viral memes (e.g. photoshopped images) and digital astroturfing.[22] Instagram may be more vulnerable because unlike Facebook, it does not have a Real Name Policy.
- **For-profit disinformation** will expand. Social media manipulation is already a more frequent offering in the bundle of services offered by public affairs companies. More hired guns are likely to conduct activities that interfere with Democratic institutions.[23]

---

[17] https://www.law.cornell.edu/uscode/text/47/230

[18] https://www.socialmediatoday.com/news/facebook-updates-news-feed-algorithm-to-demote-misleading-health-claims/558100/

[19] https://www.engadget.com/2018/12/18/twitter-chronological-timeline-feature-latest-tweets/

[20] https://youtube.googleblog.com/2019/01/continuing-our-work-to-improve.html

[21] https://www.npr.org/2019/09/05/757803903/experts-warn-u-s-should-prepare-for-election-interference-from-china?fbclid=IwAR3R_8TPQRWy42ppPZkNXP_o2Vw9BTmfOg9bR4RrZwdaqa8ktIrl2tbqzkA

[22] https://issuu.com/nyusterncenterforbusinessandhumanri/docs/nyu_election_2020_report?fr=sY2QzYzI0MjMwMA

[23] ibid

- **Video deepfakes will grow more convincing**.
- Convincing **deepfake audio** renderings will be deployed with greater frequency.
- **Cyborg** accounts will be used to support digital astroturfing. These are accounts where the content is primarily created and posted by bots, but regular engagement from the (human) account owner makes the account's activity look more authentic and makes it harder for algorithms to identify the hallmarks of a bot.
- **Distributed operations.** The U.S. Cyber Command reportedly used offensive hacking to temporarily take down internet access for the Russian Internet Research Agency (IRA) on U.S. election day in November 2018. While this effort may have forestalled some of the activities the IRA had planned to carry out against American voters, Russia and other adversaries are likelier to disperse their activities across various operational centers in order to avoid single points of failure in the future.[24]

Strategies to detect online imposters

Current strategies to identify deceptive online content fall into two categories: passive forensic detection and active forensic detection.

Passive forensic detection is the process of vetting pieces of content one at a time to determine whether they are authentic. The idea is to identify discrete qualities about the video, tweet, Facebook group or meme that suggest it may be false, misleading or presented by an imposter. As an example, imagine watching a video of a politician that has already been posted on Facebook and looking for clues as to whether it is a deep fake: is the subject blinking normally? Is the format consistent with older (verified) videos of this politician? Tech companies can also run online context through algorithms that automatically "look for" the hallmarks of deception. For example, the GIF-hosting company Gfycat has trained artificial intelligence to spot some types of fraudulent videos as they are uploaded by scouring the internet for other (authentic) versions of the photo or video and running an automatic comparison.[25]

Active forensic detection is less widely utilized today. It seeks to build unique characteristics into digital content that can be used to proactively affirm that the content is authentic. The focus of these activities is to counter disinformation by identifying content that is real. For example, imagine a link to a video of a politician that is clearly marked as "verified content" because the content has already satisfied an active forensic detection review and has earned a digital signature of authenticity before being proliferated online. For example, a company called Factom uses blockchain technology to affirm the existence of a piece of data or a document at a certain time – assuring that a video was taken at a specific discrete time and that it was created by the specific camera attached to its digital signature.[26] An app called TruePic is designed to create a digital signature for visual content, so that information about a photo or video's true origin and metadata is made inextricable from the file itself.[27]

Research Needs

---

[24] Ibid pg 5

[25] https://www.wired.com/story/gfycat-artificial-intelligence-deepfakes/

[26] https://www.wired.com/story/the-blockchain-solution-to-our-deepfake-problems/

[27] https://truepic.com/technology/#controlled-capture

A new research field is emerging around combating of disinformation which we might call *digital information forensics*. Practitioners in the field will need to adopt a holistic perspective on disinformation tools and tactics in an effort to develop and implement technological strategies to counter them. But experts are concerned that digital forensics efforts are currently being limited by the absence of a well-developed digital forensics workforce, which would consist of researchers who could identify disinformation and understand evolving methods to develop and disseminate it. The expansion of the digital forensics workforce through academic and professional programs could be an important foundation for combating disinformation.

Federal agencies also have a role to play in supporting anti-disinformation research efforts. Perhaps the leading federal effort to combat deep fakes is Defense Advanced Research Projects Agency (DARPA) Media Forensics program (MediFor), which is focused on developing applied technologies to detect inauthentic content and improve the integrity of digital content.[28] DARPA recently launched a follow-on program called Semantic Forensics – SemaFor – which seeks to develop innovative semantic technologies for automatically analyzing multi-modal media assets (text, audio, image, video) to defend against large-scale, automated disinformation attacks.[29]

The National Institute of Standards and Technology (NIST) could have a significant impact by supporting more basic research in the field. One example of such research would be the creation of large, controlled, high-quality data sets for the academic sector to use in its research activities. NIST's ability to produce basic data under a broadly-acceptable standard could provide valuable support to researchers seeking applied solutions. The National Science Foundation (NSF) oversees a wealth of research related to cybersecurity and could serve as an important funding source for research on disinformation and online imposters.

---

[28] DARPA MediFor Program, https://www.darpa.mil/program/media-forensics.

[29] https://www.darpa.mil/news-events/semantic-forensics-proposers-day

Chairwoman SHERRILL. The hearing will now come to order. Good afternoon, and welcome to a hearing of the Investigations and Oversight Subcommittee. We're here today to discuss online impostors and disinformation. Researchers generally define misinformation as information that is false, but promulgated with sincerity by a person who believes it is true. Disinformation, on the other hand, is shared with the deliberate intent to deceive. It turns out that these days the concepts of disinformation and online impostors are almost one in the same. We all remember the classic scams and hoaxes from the early days of e-mail—a foreign prince needs help getting money out of the country. But today the more common brand of disinformation is not simply content that is plainly counterfactual, but that is being delivered by someone who is not who they say they are. We are seeing a surge in coordinated disinformation efforts, particularly around politicians, hot-button political issues, and democratic elections.

The 2016 cycle saw Russian troll farms interfering in the American discourse across Facebook, Twitter, and Instagram, trying to sway public opinion for their preferred candidate. But at the same time they were after something else much simpler—to create chaos. By driving a wedge into the social fissures in our society, sowing seeds of mistrust about our friends and neighbors, exploiting social discord, they think they might destabilize our democracy, and allow the oligarchy to look a little more attractive by comparison.

When I was a Russian Policy Officer in the Navy, I learned how central information warfare is in Russia's quest to dominate Western nations. And, unfortunately, modern technology makes information warfare a far easier proposition for antagonists—foreign or domestic. In fact, it's perhaps too easy today to proliferate convincing, harmful disinformation, build realistic renderings of people in videos, and impersonate others online. That's why the incidents of harmful episodes have exploded in the last few years. They range from fake reviewers misleading consumers on Amazon, to impersonating real political candidates, to fake pornography being created with the likenesses of real people. Earlier this year an alleged deep fake of the President of Gabon helped trigger an unsuccessful coup of the incumbent government. Deep fakes are particularly prone to being weaponized, as our very biology tells us that we can trust our eyes and our ears.

There are social science reasons why disinformation and online impostors are such a confounding challenge. Research has shown that online hoaxes spread 6 times as fast as true stories, for example. Maybe human nature just likes a good scandal, and confirmation bias shapes how we receive information every time we log on, or open an app. If we encounter a story, a video, or an influence campaign that seems a little less than authentic, we may still be inclined to believe it if the content supports the political narrative already playing in our own heads. Our digital antagonists, whether the intelligence service of a foreign adversary, or a lone wolf propagandist working from a laptop, know how to exploit all of this.

Our meeting today is the start of a conversation. Before we, as policymakers, can address the threat of fake news and online frauds, we have to understand how they operate, the tools we have today to address them, and where the next generation of bad actors is headed. We need to know where to commit more resources, in the way of innovation and education. Our distinguished witnesses in today's panel are experts in the technologies that can be used to detect deep fakes and disinformation, and I'm glad they're here to help us explore these important issues. We're especially thankful that all three of you are able to roll with the punches when we had to move the hearing due a change in the congressional schedule, so thank you all. I'd also like to thank my Republican counterparts who have been such great partners in this matter. He will be here shortly, but Mr. Gonzalez of Ohio is joining us today to inform his work on deep fakes, and I'm proud to be a co-sponsor of his bill, H.R. 4355, here he is, and I thank you for being here, Mr. Gonzalez.

[The prepared statement of Chairwoman Sherrill follows:]

Prepared Statement of Chairwoman Mikie Sherrill, Chairwoman, Subcommittee on Investigations and Oversight, Committee on Science, Space, and Technology, U.S. House of Representatives

Good morning and welcome to a hearing of the Investigations and Oversight Subcommittee.

We're here today to discuss online imposters and disinformation. Researchers generally define misinformation as information that is false but promulgated with sincerity by a person who believes it is true. Disinformation, on the other hand, is shared with the deliberate intent to deceive.

It turns out that these days, the concepts of disinformation and online imposters are almost one and the same. We all remember the classic scams and hoaxes from the early days of email - a Nigerian Prince needs help getting money out of the country! But today, the more common brand of disinformation is not simply content that is plainly counterfactual, but that it is being delivered by someone who is not who they say they are.

We are seeing a surge in coordinated disinformation efforts particularly around politicians, hotbutton political issues, and democratic elections. The 2016 election cycle saw Russian troll farms interfering in the American discourse across Facebook, Twitter, Instagram, YouTube and beyond, trying to sway public opinion for their preferred candidate. But at the same time, they were after something else much simpler: to create chaos. By driving a wedge into the social fissures in our society, sowing seeds of mistrust about our friends and neighbors, exploiting social discord, they think they might destabilize our democracy and allow the oligarchy to look a little more attractive by comparison. When I was a Russian policy officer in the Navy, I learned how central information warfare is in Russia's quest to dominate western nations. And unfortunately, modern technology makes information warfare a far easier proposition for our antagonists, foreign or domestic.

In fact, its perhaps too easy today to proliferate convincing, harmful disinformation, build realistic renderings of people in videos, and impersonate others online. That's why the incidence of harmful episodes has exploded in the last few years. They range from fake reviewers misleading consumers on Amazon, to impersonating real political candidates, to fake pornography being created with the likenesses of real people. Earlier this year, an alleged deepfake of the President of Gabon helped trigger an unsuccessful coup of the incumbent government. Deep fakes are particularly prone to being weaponized, as our very biology tells us that we can trust our eyes and ears.

There are social science reasons why disinformation and online imposters are such a confounding challenge: research has shown that online hoaxes spread six times as fast as true stories, for example. Maybe human nature just likes a good scandal. And confirmation bias shapes how we receive information every time we log on or open an app. If we encounter a story, a video or an influence campaign that seems a little less than authentic, we may still be inclined to believe it if the content supports the political narrative already playing in our own heads. Our digital antagonists, whether the intelligence service of a foreign adversary or a lone wolf propagandist working from a laptop, know how to exploit all of this.

Our meeting today is the start of a conversation. Before we as policymakers can address the threat of fake news and online frauds, we have to understand how they operate, the tools we have today to address them, and where the next generation of bad actors is headed. We need to know where to commit more resources in the way of innovation and education.

Our distinguished witnesses on today's panel are experts in the technologies that can be used to detect deep fakes and disinformation, and I'm glad they are here to help us explore these important issues. We are especially thankful that all three of you were able to roll with the punches when we had to move the hearing due to a change in the Congressional schedule.

I'd also like to thank my Republican counterparts who have been such great partners on this matter. Mr. Gonzalez of Ohio is joining us today to inform his work on deep fakes. I'm proud to be a cosponsor of his bill H.R. 4355, and I thank you for being here, Mr. Gonzalez.

Chairwoman SHERRILL. Unfortunately Ranking Member Norman could not be with us today, but we are happy to have the full Committee Ranking Member in his place, so the Chair now recognizes Mr. Lucas for an opening statement. Thank you, Mr. Lucas.

Mr. LUCAS. Thank you, Chairwoman Sherrill, for holding this hearing on the growing problem of disinformation on social media. We all know that photos these days can be digitally altered so easily that it's almost impossible to tell what's real and what's not. Now there's a growing problem where audio and video can be altered so convincingly that it can appear that someone has said or done something that never happened. These deep fakes can be produced more and more easily.

You know, there was once a rumor that I myself was a deep fake, just impersonating the real Frank Lucas. The good news, or, depending on your perspective, perhaps the bad news, is the technology hasn't come quite that far, and I'm the real deal. But once it's on the Internet, it never goes away. But deep fake technology is getting more and more sophisticated, and it's also getting easier to produce. As our witnesses will discuss today, the technology for generating deep fakes is improving at a rapid clip. Soon anyone with a decent computer, and access to training data, will be able to create increasingly convincing deep fakes that are difficult to detect and debunk. False and misleading content like this undermines public trust, and disrupts civil society. Unfortunately, the technology for generating deep fakes is developing at a speed and a scale that dwarfs the technology needed to detect and debunk deep fakes. We must help level the playing field.

This Committee took the first steps to do this yesterday by passing a bipartisan legislation aimed at improving research into the technology to detect deep fakes. I want to commend Representative Anthony Gonzalez for introducing this bill, and his leadership on the issue of technology and security. I often say that one of our most important jobs on the Science Committee is communicating to the American people the value of scientific research and development. Legislation and hearings like this are a great example of how the work we do here can benefit directly people across the country, and I look forward to hearing from our witnesses, and I yield back my time, Madam Chair.

[The prepared statement of Mr. Lucas follows:]

Prepared Statement of Ranking Member Frank Lucas, Committee on Science, Space, and Technology, U.S. House of Representatives

Thank you, Chairwoman Sherrill, for holding this hearing on the growing problem of disinformation on social media.

We all know that photos these days can be digitally altered so easily that it's all but impossible to tell what's real and what's not.

There's now a growing problem where audio and video can be altered so convincingly that it can appear that someone has said or done something that never happened. These deepfakes can be produced more and more easily.

You know, there was once a rumor that I MYSELF was a deepfake, just impersonating the real Frank Lucas. The good news-or maybe the bad news-is that technology hasn't come quite that far and I am the real deal.

But deepfake technology IS getting more sophisticated. And it's also getting easier to produce. As our witnesses will discuss today, the technology for generating deepfakes is improving at a rapid clip. Soon, anyone with a decent computer and access to training data will be able to create increasingly convincing deepfakes that are difficult to detect and debunk.

False and misleading content like this undermines public trust and disrupts civil society.

Unfortunately, the technology for generating deepfakes is developing at a speed and scale that dwarfs the technology needed to detect and debunk deepfakes. We must help level the playing field.

This Committee took the first step to do that yesterday by passing bipartisan legislation aimed at improving research into the technology to detect deepfakes.

I want to commend Representative Anthony Gonzalez for introducing this bill and for his leadership on the issue of technology and security.

I often say that one of our most important jobs on the Science Committee is communicating to the American people the value of scientific research and development. Legislation and hearings like this are a great example of how the work we do here can directly benefit people across the country.

I look forward to hearing from our witnesses, and I yield back my time.

Chairwoman SHERRILL. Well, thank you, Ranking Member Lucas. And we have an additional opening statement today from my colleague across the aisle, Representative Waltz of Florida. Unfortunately, Mr. Waltz could not make it to the hearing today, but considering his great interest in the issue, I allowed him to submit a video of his opening statement, so we'll now hear from Mr. Waltz.

Mr. WALTZ. Hello, everyone. I'm sorry I can't be in town for the hearing today, but I wanted to make sure to share my concerns about digital impostors. Everyone in this room relies on social media, video messages, and other digital technology to connect with our constituents. We listen to their concerns, we share information about our work in Congress. But deep fake technology, which can literally put words in our mouths, undermines public trust in any digital communication. Today's witnesses will paint a picture of just how sophisticated the technology has become for creating realistic images, videos, and personalities online.

Before I conclude my statement, I want to say a few words about our distinguished Subcommittee Chairwoman, Mikie Sherrill. I think we can all agree that Mikie is one of the most intelligent, accomplished, and persuasive Members of Congress. In fact, she's so persuasive that she convinced me, a Green Beret, to cheer on Navy football in this year's rivalry game. Thanks, Chairwoman Sherrill, for bringing attention to the problems of deep fake technology, and go Navy, beat Army.

Chairwoman SHERRILL. What a pleasure. As you all saw that— thank you so much for your work. That was obviously a deep fake. That is what we're looking at, and that is what we're discussing today. Thank you so— right? How nice is that? And, sadly, knowing how deep the commitment to our respective services' football is, I do know that that was not actually your sentiment, although it should be. So thank you, Mr. Waltz and Mr. Beyer, for your willingness to participate in our deep fake demonstration, and thank you to our distinguished witnesses, Dr. Lyu, for creating this video. I'll now recognize Mr. Beyer and Mr. Waltz for a few remarks.

Mr. Beyer?

Mr. BEYER. Yes. Thank you, Madam Chair, very much. Congressman Waltz and I really had fun making the deep fake video. You can see that it clearly was in jest. As an Army brat, I would never throw a Green Beret under the bus. But you also see how dangerous and misleading it could be. I'm sure we fooled a couple of people. For instance, what if I had said, instead of go Navy, go beat Army, I had said, it's time to impeach the President? Well, that would be viral everywhere. I mean, the things would be ringing off the hook, and the social media——

Mr. WALTZ. Please do not do that to my staff.

Mr. BEYER. No. And Mr. Waltz would be the first to know, so my friends might appreciate it, but I don't think he would at all, so obviously the potential for serious harms with these deep fakes is quite great on elections, international stage for diplomatic purposes, and even for our private lives. That's why we, as a country, need to take swift action and invest in the research and the tools for identifying and combating deep fakes, and create a national strategy immediately, especially for election integrity, and ahead of the 2020 presidential election.

The stakes are high. We've got to act now. We already know of Russia's intentional campaign to spread disinformation throughout the last one, and I don't even want to imagine what Russia, or China, or just private players, the havoc they could wreak on our elections and on our personal lives. So thank you very much to Mikie Sherrill and Frank Lucas for leading this effort. I yield back.

Chairwoman SHERRILL. Thank you very much. Mr. Waltz?

Mr. WALTZ. Thank you, Madam Chairwoman. And while I do certainly hold you in the highest regard that was not me. But, just to add to my colleagues, that's just an example, and a small example, of what a deep fake synthetic video can do. And we've seen this insidious capability. We're seeing, I think, the birth of it. But I certainly support my colleagues in how we can get our arms around this as a country. I think it's important to note that Mr. Beyer and I both consented to that video, but as, you know, putting words in the mouth of a U.S. Army Green Beret and cheering on for Navy is not the worst application of this technology, and it's certainly not difficult to imagine how our enemies or criminal groups can wreak havoc on governments, on elections, on businesses, on competitors, and the privacy of all Americans. So these videos, and this technology, have the potential to truly be a weapon for our adversaries. We know that advanced deep fake technology exists within China and Russia. We know that they have the capability, and that both countries have demonstrated a willingness to use asymmetric warfare capabilities. So, as the technology for generating deep fakes improves, we do risk falling behind on the detection front. That's why this hearing is so important, and I certainly commend you for calling it. It will help us examine solutions for both detecting and debunking the deep fakes of the future. And, you know, at the end of the day, I just have to say go Army, beat Navy. I yield back. [The prepared statement of Mr. Waltz follows:]

What you just saw was an example of a "deepfake," or synthetic video that can be generated thanks to advancements in artificial intelligence and machine learning.

As we have just seen, deepfakes have the ability to make people-myself included- appear as though they have said or done things that they have never said or done. And advancements in the underlying technology, as we will hear today, are making it much more difficult to distinguish an authentic recording from synthetic, deepfake impersonations.

Importantly, Mr. Beyer and I both consented to and participated in the creation of this deepfake. But a Green Beret cheering for Navy is not the worst application of the technology.

It's not difficult to imagine how deepfakes of nonconsenting individuals could be used to wreak havoc on governments, elections, business, and the privacy of individuals.

Deepfakes have the potential to be a weapon for our adversaries and we know that advanced deepfake technology exists in China and Russia and that both countries have asymmetric warfare capabilities.

As the technology for generating deepfakes improves, we risk falling behind on the detection front. That's why today's hearing is so important. It will help us examine solutions for detecting and debunking deepfakes of the future.

Thank you Chairwoman Sherrill and Ranking Member Norman for convening this important hearing.

Yield back.

Chairwoman SHERRILL. I don't know why I let you testify in my—no, thank you very much. Those were really sobering comments, and I appreciate you both for showing us a little bit of what we're contending with.

[The prepared statement of Chairwoman Johnson follows:]

Prepared Statement of Chairwoman Eddie Bernice Johnson, Chairwoman, Committee on Science, Space, and Technology, U.S. House of Representatives

Thank you Madam Chair, and I would like to join you in welcoming our witnesses this morning.

I'm glad we're holding this hearing today. It's worth acknowledging just how deeply the phenomenon of online disinformation affects most of our lives these days. As long as there's been news, there's been fake news. But the American people are far more connected than they used to be. And the new tools that enable fake images, misleading public discourse, even long passages of text are alarming in their sophistication. Maybe we all should have seen this coming, the explosion of disinformation that would accompany the information age.

I suspect my colleagues here in the House are already taking this matter seriously, because in a way, online imposters and twisted facts on the internet present a real and active threat to the way we do our own jobs. We all use social media to connect with our constituents and to hear about their concerns. My staff want to read the comments and the posts from the people in Dallas and hear what they have to say. If I am to believe that a large percentage of the comments on Twitter are coming from "bots" or some other source of disinformation, the waters get muddy very quickly.

We have to acknowledge the serious legacy of disinformation is in this country. In the late 1970s, I was working under President Carter as a Regional Director for the Department of Health. Around that time, the Soviet Union's KGB kicked off a campaign to plant the idea that the United States government invented HIV and AIDS at Fort Detrick. The KGB wrote bogus pamphlets and fake scientific research and distributed them at global conferences. It sold a complex narrative in which the United States military deliberately infected prisoners to create a public health crisis - biological warfare against our own people. The KGB's efforts were so pervasive that by 1992, 15% of Americans considered it "definitely or probably true" that the AIDS virus was created deliberately in a government laboratory. Decades later, a 2005 study found that a substantial percentage of the African American community believed that AIDS was developed as a form of genocide against black people.

How absolutely devastating such disinformation can be. It is clear that information warfare can have such profound, destructive effects. I think it is long past time to recognize how vulnerable we are to the next generation of hostile actors.

As Chairwoman Sherrill said, the first step in addressing a big problem is understanding it. Not every Member of this Committee, myself included, is well-versed in what a "deep neural network" is or how a "GAN" works. However, we have a sense already that the federal government is likely to need to create new tools that address this issue.

We also need to have a serious conversation about what we expect from the social media platforms that so many of us use every day. These companies have enjoyed a level of growth and success that is only possible in the United States. They were created in garages and dorm rooms, but they stand on the shoulders of giants like DARPA, which created the internet, and the National Science Foundation, which developed the backbone of computer networks that allowed the internet to blossom. The American consumer has been overwhelmingly faithful to social media over the past decade. We will need those companies to help combat disinformation. It can no longer be ignored.

I am pleased to welcome our witnesses today, and I'm also pleased that we had bipartisan agreement in yesterday's markup on a bill that would enable more research on deep fakes. These issues require a bold bipartisan response. I thank my colleagues on both sides of the aisle for working together to address these important issues. With that, I yield back.

[The prepared statement of Mr. Norman follows:]

Prepared Statement of Ralph Norman, Ranking Member, Subcommittee on Investigations and Oversight, Committee on Science, Space, and Technology, U.S. House of Representatives

Good Afternoon and thank you, Chairwoman Sherrill, for convening this important hearing.

We are here today to explore technologies that enable online disinformation. We'll look at trends and emerging technology in this field, and consider research strategies that can help to detect and combat sophisticated deceptions and so-called "deepfakes."

Disinformation is not new. It has been used throughout history to influence and mislead people.

What is new, however, is how modern technology can create more and more realistic deceptions. Not only that, but modern disinformation can be spread more widely and targeted to intended audiences.

Although media manipulation is nothing new, it has long been limited to altering photos. Altering video footage was traditionally reserved for Hollywood studios and those with access to advanced technological capabilities and financial resources.

But today, progress in artificial intelligence and machine learning have reduced these barriers and made it easier than ever to create digital forgeries.

In 1994, it cost $55 million to create convincing footage of Forrest Gump meeting JFK. Today, that technology is more sophisticated and widely available.

What's more, these fakes are growing more convincing and therefore more difficult to detect. A major concern is this: as deepfake technology becomes more accessible, the ability to generate deepfakes may outpace our ability to detect them.

Adding to the problem of sophisticated fakes is how easily they can spread. Global interconnectivity and social networking have democratized access to communication.

This means that almost anyone can publish almost anything and can distribute it at lightspeed across the globe.

As the internet and social media have expanded our access to information, technological advancements have also made it easier to push information to specific audiences.

Algorithms used by social media platforms are designed to engage users with content that is most likely to interest them. Bad actors can use this to better target disinformation.

For example, it is difficult to distinguish the techniques used in modern disinformation campaigns from those used in ordinary online marketing and advertising campaigns.

Deepfakes alone are making online disinformation more problematic. But when combined with novel means for distributing disinformation to ever more targeted audiences, the threat is even greater.

Fortunately, we are here today to discuss these new twists to an old problem and to consider how science and technology can combat these challenges.

I look forward to an engaging discussion with our distinguished panel of witnesses on how we can better address online disinformation.

Thank you again, Chairwoman Sherrill, for holding this important hearing, and thanks to our witnesses for being here today to help us develop solutions to this challenge. I look forward to hearing your testimony.

I yield back.

Chairwoman SHERRILL. At this time I would like to introduce our three witnesses.

First we have Dr. Siwei Lyu. Dr. Lyu is a Professor at the University of Albany's College of Engineering and Applied Sciences. He is an expert in machine learning, and media forensics. Next is Dr. Hany Farid. Dr. Farid is a Professor at the University of California Berkeley School of Electrical Engineering and Computer Science and the School of Information. Dr. Farid's research focuses on digital forensics, image analysis, and human perception. Last we have Ms. Camille Francois. Ms. Francois is the Chief Innovation Officer at Graphika, a company that uses artificial intelligence to analyze online communities and social networks.

As our witnesses should know, you will each have 5 minutes for your spoken testimony. Your written testimony will be included in the record for the hearing. When you all have completed your spoken testimony, we will begin with questions. Each Member will have 5 minutes to question the panel. And we'll start with you, Dr. Lyu.

Statement of Dr. Siwei Lyu, Professor, Department of Computer Science, Director of Computer Vision and Machine Learning Lab, State University of New York, Albany

Dr. LYU. Good afternoon, Chairwoman Sherrill, Ranking Member Lucas, and Members of the Committee. Thank you for inviting me today to discuss the emerging issue of deep fakes. You have just seen a deep fake video we created for this hearing, so let me first briefly describe how this video, and similar fake videos, are made. Making a deep fake video requires a source and a target. In this case, the source was Representative Beyer, and the target was Representative Waltz. Mr. Beyer's staff was kind enough to prepare a video of the Congressman for this project. While Mr. Waltz's office consented to this video demonstration, it is important to know that we didn't use any video from his office. Instead, we conducted an Internet search for about 30 minutes, and found one suitable minute-long YouTube video of Mr. Waltz, and that's our target video. The next step involves a software tool we developed, which used deep neural networks to create the fake video. It is important to note that our tool does not use a generative adversary network, or GAN.

It first trains the deep neural network models using the source and the target video. It then used the models to extract facial expressions in the source video of Mr. Beyer, and generate a video of Mr. Waltz with the same facial expressions. The audio track is from the original video of Mr. Beyer, and was not modified. The training and the production are performed on a computer equipped with a graphical processing unit, or GPU. The computer and the GPU can be purchased from Amazon for about $3,000. The overall training and production took about 8 hours, and were completely automated, after setting a few initial parameters.

So a similar process was also used to generate the fake videos that are being displayed on the screen right now. Although we do not distribute this particular software, true, similar software making deep fakes can be found on code-sharing platforms like GitHub, and are free for anyone to download and to use. With the abundance of online media we share, anyone is a potential target of a deep fake attack.

Currently there are active research developments to identify, contain, and obstruct deep fakes before they can inflict damages. The majority of such research is currently sponsored by DARPA (Defense Advanced Research Projects Agency), most notably the MediFor (Media Forensics) program. But it is also important that the Federal Government fund more research, through NSF (National Science Foundation), to combat deep fakes. As an emerging research area that does not fall squarely into existing AI (artificial intelligence) or cybersecurity programs, it may be wise to establish a new functional program at NSF dedicated to similar emerging technologies. It can serve as an initial catch-all for similar high-risk and high-impact research until either an existing program's mission is expanded, or a new dedicated program is established.

We should also examine the approaches we share software code and tools, especially those with potential negative impacts like deep fakes. Therefore, it may be wise to consider requiring NSF to conduct reviews of sponsored AI research and enforcing controls on the release of software codes or tools with dual use nature. This will help to reduce the potential misuses of such technologies.

Last, but not least, education on responsible research should be an intrinsic part of AI research. Investigators should be fully aware of the potential impact of the sponsored research, and provide corresponding trainings to the graduate students and post-docs working on the project. Again,

NSF could enforce such ethics training and best practices through a mandatory requirement to sponsored research projects. The creation of new cross-function NSF programs for emerging technologies, the introduction of controls on the release of NSF-funded AI research with potential dual use, and required ethics training for NSF-funded AI research will go far in defending against the emerging threat posted by deep fakes.

Thank you for having this hearing today, and giving me the opportunity to testify. I'm happy to answer any questions you may have. Thank you.

[The prepared statement of Dr. Lyu follows:]

Prepared Statement of Dr. Siwei Lyu

Backgrounds

Deepfakes are the most recent twist to the disconcerting problem of online disinformation. The term deepfake first emerged in late 2017 as the name of a Reddit account that began posting synthetic pornographic videos generated using an AI-based face-swapping algorithm. The term has subsequently become synonymous with three types of AI-generated impersonation videos.

1. Head puppetry entails synthesizing a video of a target person's head using a video of a source person's head, so the synthesized target appears to behave the same way as the source.

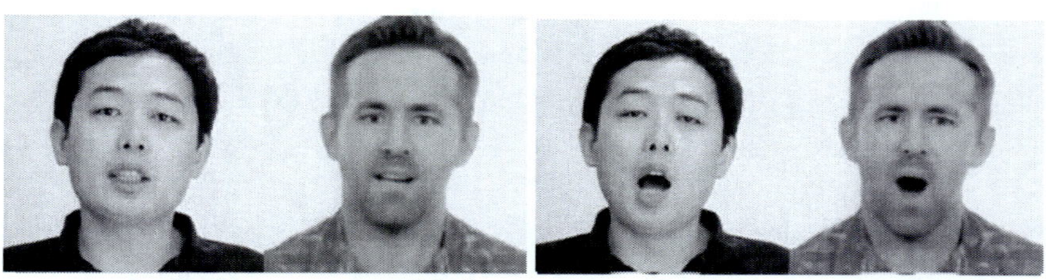

source (real) target (fake) source (real) target (fake)

2. Face swapping involves generating a video of the target with the faces replaced by synthesized faces of the source while keeping the same facial expressions.

3. Lip synching is to create a falsified video by only manipulating the lip region so that the target appears to speak something that s/he does not speak in reality.

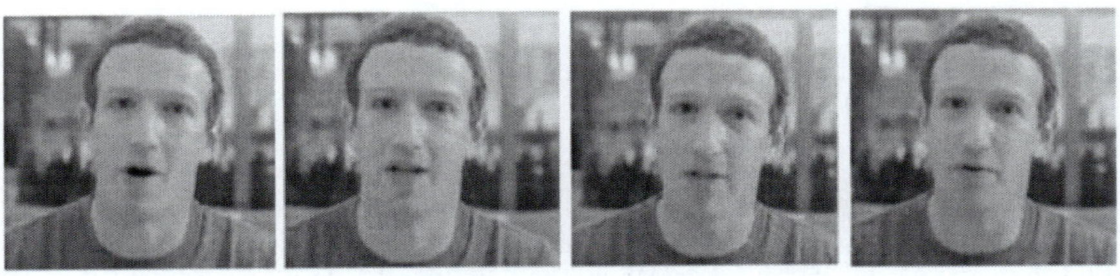

Source: Bill Posters and Daniel Howe. The Spectre Project.

Photos and videos have been doctored since their nascence. But there are three reasons why the current concerns over deepfakes and other AI-driven audio and visual media manipulations are justified. First, deepfakes can be made more easily, quickly, and with better quality — thanks to the rapid advancement of computer hardware and software technology, in particular those related to AI. Second, the capability to make deepfakes has been democratized through software tools that can be downloaded freely from online code sharing platforms.[30] Third, anyone with an online media presence is a potential target of a deepfake attack. A fake video showing a politician engaged in an inappropriate activity may be enough to sway an election if released close to voting day. A fake video of a falsified recording of a high-level executive commenting on his/her company's financial situation could potentially send the stock market awry. A fake video made by falsely implanting a woman's face in a pornographic video and shared on social-media platforms could tremendously traumatize the victim. The stakes are too high to ignore.

[30] e.g., FakeAPP (used to be on Reddit but now defunct), DeepfaceLab (https://github.com/iperov/DeepFaceLab), faceswap-GAN (https://github.com/shaoanlu/faceswap-GA), faceswap (https://github.com/deepfakes/faceswa), and more recently ZAO (https://apkproz.com/app/zao).

How Are Deepfakes Made?

Deepfakes are created with a type of AI technology commonly known as deep neural networks.[31] A deep neural network model learns to synthesize realistic faces through training, which involves exposing the model to a large number of face images of different people with varying expression, head poses, and lighting conditions. Once the model is properly trained, it is ready to be used to generate deepfakes. Specifically, a face detection method is first run on the input video to locate the target's faces. Then facial landmarks corresponding to distinct locations such as the tips of eyes, eyebrows, nose, mouth, and contour of the face are extracted. Using these landmarks, the detected faces are warped to the same size and in a standard configuration. The standardized faces are fed to the deep neural network model to synthesize a new set of faces of different identity, which are then warped back to match the target's head orientations in the input.

Current computer hardware and AI technology has made it much easier to create deepfakes: a computer that is used to run the generation algorithm with a special computing hardware known as graphical computing unit (GPU) can be readily purchased for an affordable price on Amazon.[32] The training videos for the targets can be easily downloaded from social-media platforms such as YouTube, Instagram, and Facebook in large volume and high quality. Convenient software tools have made the whole process automated barring the choice of a few parameters. As a result, a few good-quality, minute-long videos, a commodity computer with a GPU, and several hours of training are sufficient to generate deepfakes with decent visual quality.

How to Combat Deepfakes with Technology Development

While sophisticated deepfakes still take time and skill to produce, rough-and-ready fake videos may still cause harm. It is thus important to have effective technologies to identify, contain, and obstruct deepfakes before they can inflict

---

[31] GANs are only one type of deep neural network model for creating deepfakes. For example, the deepfake created for today's hearing did not use a GAN, but instead a different model known as the variational auto-encoders. This is important because any legislative or rule making effort to address deepfakes should not rely on a single tool. Instead Congress should attempt to future-proof regulation to cover the act instead of the tool.

[32] An example of computer configuration for this purpose includes an HP-Z800 workstation (~$1,000) equipped with an Nvidia2080Ti GPU (~$1,200) and other necessary peripherals. Cost effective and large-scale production can also be conducted usingcloud platforms such as Amazon AWS or Google Cloud Platform.

damage. This should be done by focusing on improving forensic capabilities and making it harder to train deepfakes using online videos.

Effective deepfake forensic detection methods look for traces of the synthesis process to differentiate deepfakes from real videos. For instance, synthesized faces are warped and processed to fit the target's head orientation, such operations leave traces that can be exploited to detect deepfakes. Another type of detection techniques involves examining physiological inconsistencies such as the lack of realistic eye blinking and heart beating. A third approach is to "use AI to fight AI", using another deep neural networks to detect deepfakes. State-of-the-art detection methods have shown promising accuracy on benchmark datasets, but their actual performance on real life deepfakes have yet to be tested.[33] Also, due to the complex nature of deepfakes, no single type of technology or specific method will be the silver bullet, and an effective solution may come as a combination of all these approaches.

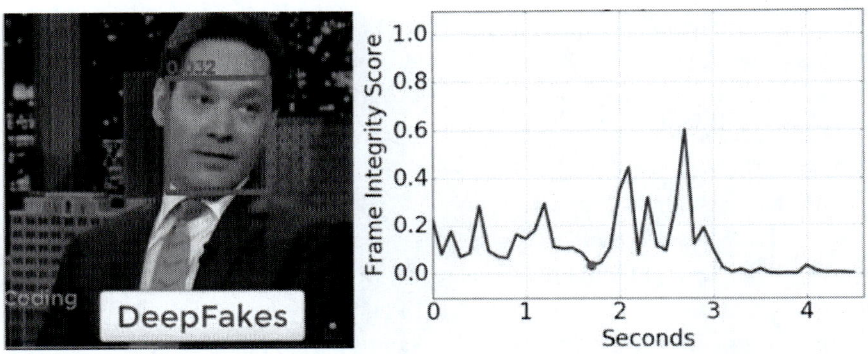

Detection results of a state-of-the-art deepfake detection method over a fake video on youtube.com. The lower integrity score (range in [0,1]) suggests a video frame more likely to be generated using deepfake algorithms.

In addition to deepfake forensics, there are also technologies to prevent the re-use of online images and videos as training data for the deep neural network generating deepfakes. This wouldinvolve inserting imperceptible "adversarial noise" into images and videos before they areuploaded to online social-media platforms. The adversarial noise correspond to subtle perturbations that human eyes cannot see nonetheless can disrupt a face detection algorithm and make it difficult to automate the training process. A

[33] One notable effort towards this goal is the upcoming *Deepfake Detection Challenge* (https://deepfakedetectionchallenge.ai)sponsored by Facebook, Microsoft and Partnership on AI, to advance the state-of-the-art deepfake detection capacities.

dedicated adversary could overcome adversarial noise by painstakingly selecting the target's face in every frame of a training video, but that requires 1,500 hand-marked selections for each 60 second training video.[34]

Perspectives

As the underlying technology continues to develop, the current barriers to making deepfakes will fall and their quality will keep improving. What is also evolving is the quintessential cat-and- mouse game experienced by all attacker-defender relationships, and malicious attackers seem to have an upper-hand — they can adjust the generation algorithm whenever a new detection method is made public. Currently, the majority of research on combating deepfakes is sponsored under DARPA.[35] But it is important that the federal government also fund more civilian research through NSF. One reason this has not yet happened is because the grant-making capabilities of NSF are focused around existing directorates that are not well equipped to support research into cross-functional emerging technologies. It may be wise to fund the establishment of a new Emerging Technologies Directorate at NSF, which can function as a catchall until either an existing directorate's mission is expanded or a new directorate is created. This would create a research home not just for deepfake forensics but also other emerging technologies.

The open-source model of disseminating research code is an enabling factor of the current deepfake problem and requires more scrutiny. The availability of easy-to-use and easy-to-access software tools has significantly lowered the technical threshold for an ordinary user to create deepfakes. A nation state with more manpower and computing resources can build upon them refined and customized versions to make more crafted deepfakes with higher level of realism and use them in a disinformation campaign. It may thus be wise to consider requiring NSF to conduct an ethics review of proposed grants around dual-use technology like deepfakes with mandatory controls on the release of the underlying technology into the proverbial wild.

---

[34] This is calculated based on a target video quality of 25 frames per second, which is the lowest frame rate for uploaded YouTubevideos. YouTube videos. The highest quality YouTube videos are uploaded at 60 frames per second, which would more than double the number of hand-marked selections for a 60 second video and the work to hand select faces.

[35] Most notably, the DARPA Media Forensics (MediFor) program (https://www.darpa.mil/program/media-forensics).

Last but not least, education on responsible research should be an intrinsic part to the current AI research. Deepfakes add just one more item to the long list of various ethical issues of AI algorithms, such as built-in biases and prejudice, violations of individual privacy and safety, and the lack of accountability and transparency. As academic or industrial researchers working in these areas, we should recognize the potential impact of our research on society, and take them seriously as part of our due responsibilities. We should also provide training to students and post-docs on such issues. These practices could, again, be enforced through requirements from NSF on funded AI research that make such training and compliance mandatory.

Conclusion

It is not an exaggeration to say that we are on the cusp of deepfakes being cheap, easy to produce, indistinguishable from real videos, and ready to cause real damages. We therefore need a comprehensive and robust solution to this problem. The situation calls for continuous investment and perhaps an escalated funding level from the federal government to this strategically important research area. The situation surrounding deepfakes may not turn out to be as severe as we are predicting now. But it is better safe than sorry.

Biographical Sketch

Dr. Siwei Lyu

Siwei Lyu is a Professor of Computer Science and the Director of Computer Vision and Machine Learning Lab at University at Albany, State University of New York. Dr. Lyu received his Ph.D. degree in Computer Science in 2005 from Dartmouth College and under the supervision of Prof. Hany Farid, and his M.S. degree in Computer Science in 2000 and B.S. degree in Information Science in 1997, both from Peking University, China. Dr. Lyu's research interests include digital media forensics, computer vision, and machine learning. He is the recipient of the National Science Foundation CAREER Award in 2010, IEEE Signal Processing Best Paper Award, and the Google Faculty Research Award in 2019 for his work on digital media forensics. He has published one book on digital media forensics and over 120 refereed journal and conference papers in relevant research fields.

Chairwoman SHERRILL. Thank you very much. Dr. Farid?

Statement of Dr. Hany Farid, Professor of Electrical Engineering and Computer Science and the School of Information, University of California, Berkeley

Dr. FARID. Chairwoman Sherrill, Ranking Member Lucas, and Members of the Committee, thanks for the opportunity to talk with you today on this important topic. Although disinformation is not new, what is new in the digital age is the sophistication with which fake content can be created, the democratization of access to sophisticated tools for manipulating content, and access to the Internet and social media, allowing for the delivery of disinformation with an unprecedented speed and reach.

The latest incarnation in creating fake audio, image, and video, so-called deep fakes, is being fueled by rapid advances in machine learning, and access to large amounts of data. Although there are several variations, the core machinery behind this technology is based on a combination of traditional techniques in computer vision and computer graphics, and more modern techniques from machine learning, namely deep neural networks. These technologies can, for example, from just hundreds of images of the Chairwoman, splice her likeness into a video sequence of someone else. Similar technologies can also be used to alter a video of the Chairwoman to make her mouth consistent with a new audio recording of her saying something that she never said. And, when paired with highly realistic voice synthesis technologies that can synthesize speech in a particular person's voice, these deep fakes can make a, for example, CEO announce that their profits are down, leading to global stock manipulation; a world leader announcing military action, leading to global conflict; or a Presidential candidate confessing complicity to a crime, leading to the disruption of an election.

The past 2 years have seen a remarkable increase in the quality and sophistication of these deep fakes. These technologies are not, however, just relegated to academic circles or Hollywood studios, but are freely available online, and have already been incorporated into commercial applications. The field of digital forensics is focused on developing technologies for detecting manipulated or synthesized audio, images, and video, and within this field there are two broad categories: Proactive and reactive techniques.

Proactive techniques work by using a specialized camera software to extract a digital signature from a recorded image or video. This digital signature can then be used in the future to determine if the content was manipulated from the time of recording. The benefit of this approach is that the technology is well-understood and developed. It's effective, and it is able to work at the scale of analyzing billions of uploads a day. The drawback is that it requires all of us to use specialized camera software, as opposed to the default camera app that we are all used to using, and it requires the collaboration of social media giants to incorporate these signatures and corresponding labels into their systems.

Notice that these proactive techniques tell us what is real, not what is fake. In contrast, reactive techniques are focused on telling us what is fake. These techniques work on the assumption that digital manipulation leaves behind certain statistical, geometric, or physical traces that, although not necessarily visually obvious, can be modeled and algorithmically detected. The benefit of these techniques is that they don't require any specialized hardware or software. The drawback is that, even despite advances in the field, there are no universal forensic techniques that can operate at the scale and speed needed to analyze billions of uploads a day.

So, where do we go from here? Four points. One, funding agencies should invest at least as much financial support to programs in digital forensics as they are in programs that are fueling advances that are leading to the creation of, for example, deep fakes. Two, researchers that are developing technologies that can be weaponized should give more thought to how they can put proper safeguards in place so that their technologies are not misused. Three, no matter how quickly forensic technology advances, it will be useless without the collaboration of the giants of the technology sector. The major technology companies, including Facebook, Google, YouTube, and Twitter, must more aggressively and proactively develop and deploy technologies to combat disinformation campaigns. And four, we should not ignore the non- technical component of the issue of disinformation, us—the users. We need to better educate the public on how to consume trusted information, and not spread disinformation.

I'll close with two final points. First, although there are serious issues of online privacy, moves by some of the technology giants to transform their platform to an end-to-end encrypted system will make it even more difficult to slow or stop the spread of disinformation. We should find a balance between privacy and security, and not sacrifice one for the other. And, last, I'd like to re- emphasize that disinformation is not new, and deep fakes is only the latest incarnation. We should not lose sight of the fact that more traditional human-generated disinformation campaigns are still highly effective, and we will undoubtedly be contending with yet another technological innovation a few years from now. In responding to deep fakes, therefore, we should consider the past, the present, and the future as we try to navigate the complex interplay of technology, policy, and regulation, and I'm sorry I'm 15 seconds over.

[The prepared statement of Dr. Farid follows:]

Prepared Statement of Dr. Hany Farid

Background

Rumors quickly spread in Trent, Italy that members of the Jewish community murdered a young boy and drained and drank his blood to celebrate Passover. Before long, the city's entire Jewish community is arrested and tortured, fifteen of which are found guilty and executed. The year was 1475.

Fast forward to 2018. Rumors quickly spread in Athimoor-Kaliyam, India that roving gangs are kidnapping children. Over a period of several months, nearly two dozen innocent people are dragged from their vehicles and killed. The rumors this time spread through WhatsApp instead of word of mouth. Disinformation is not new, nor are its deadly consequences. What is new, thanks to the internet and social media, is its reach and frequency. Today, disinformation propagates around the world at the speed of light.

From small- to large-scale fraud, to sowing civil unrest, interfering with democratic elections, and inciting violence, disinformation campaigns today are leading to dangerous and deadly outcomes.

Add to this phenomenon the ability to create increasingly more compelling and sophisticated fake videos of anybody saying and doing anything – popularly referred to as deep fakes – and the threat only increases. This is the landscape that awaits us in 2019 and beyond.

Creating Deep Fakes

Advances in machine learning and access to large and diverse data sets have led to computer systems that are able to synthesize images of people who don't exist, videos of people doing things they never did, and audio recordings of them saying things they never said. These deep fakes are a dangerous addition to an already volatile online world in which rumors, conspiracies, and disinformation spread often and quickly.

By providing millions of images of people to a machine-learning system, the system can learn to synthesize realistic images of people who don't exist. Similar technologies can, in live-stream videos, convert an adult face into a child's face, raising concerns that this technology will be used by child predators.

With just hundreds of images of someone, a machine-learning system can learn to insert them into a video. This face-swap deep fake can be highly entertaining, as in its use to insert Nic Cage into movies in which he never appeared. The same technology, however, can also be used to create non-consensual pornography or to impersonate a world leader. Similar technologies can also be used to alter a video to make a person's mouth consistent with a new audio recording of them saying something that they never said. When paired with highly realistic voice synthesis technologies that can synthesize speech in a particular person's voice, these lip-sync deep fakes can make a CEO announce that their profits are down, leading to global stock manipulation, a world-leader announce military action, leading to global conflict, or a presidential candidate confess complicity in a crime, leading to the disruption of an election.

What is perhaps most alarming about these deep-fake technologies is that they are not only in the hands of sophisticated Hollywood studios. Software to generate fake content is widely and freely available online, putting in the hands of many the ability to create increasingly compelling and sophisticated fakes. Coupled with the speed and reach of social media, convincing fake content can instantaneously reach millions.

How do we manage a digital landscape when it becomes increasingly more difficult to believe not just what we read, but also what we see and hear with our own eyes and ears? How do we manage a digital landscape where if anything can be fake, then everyone has plausible deniability to claim that any digital evidence is fake?

Detecting Deep Fakes

Despite efforts by digital forensic researchers, no current technology exists that can contend with the vast array of different types of deep fakes at a speed and accuracy that can be deployed at internet-scale.

There are several challenges that the digital forensic community is facing.

Deep fakes are relatively new and have developed in sophistication much faster than expected. There are significantly more researchers working to develop techniques for synthesizing increasingly more realistic audio, images, and video, than there are those of us trying to detect this content. This means that the nature and quality of deep fakes is developing at an unprecedented rate that is difficult to keep pace with. In addition, the scale and speed of the internet makes deploying effective technology incredibly challenging: Facebook, for examples, sees some one billion daily uploads and YouTube sees some 500 hundred hours of video uploaded every minute. The sheer amount of information uploaded everyday makes any filtering technology incredibly difficult.

There is, however, a family of technologies that could be considered for wide deployment. Control-capture technologies can authenticate content at the point of recording by extracting, at the time of recording, a unique digital signature from any recorded digital content, cryptographically signing this signature, and then placing it on a secure central server or a distributed immutable ledger like the blockchain.[36] This signature can then be compared to any version of the same content found online to determine if the content has been altered from the time of recording. Although this approach tackles disinformation differently than forensic techniques – by telling us what is real instead of what is fake – these technologies are available today and can operate at internet-scale.

We should be exploring the further development and deployment of both control-capture and forensic technologies.

The Future

Despite the challenges, I propose several calls to action.

---

[36] For full disclosure, I am a paid advisor to a company, Truepic that develops control- capture technology.

1) Funding agencies have to invest at least as much financial support to programs that seek to build systems to detect fake content as they do to programs in computer vision and computer graphics that are giving rise to the sophisticated synthesis technologies described above.
2) Researchers that are developing technologies that we now know can be weaponized should give more thought to how they can put proper safeguards in place so that their technologies are not misused.
3) No matter how quickly forensic technology advances, it will be useless without the collaboration of the giants of the technology sector. The major technology companies (including, Facebook, Google/YouTube, and Twitter) must more aggressively and proactively deploy technologies to combat disinformation campaigns, and more aggressively and consistently enforce their policies. For example, Facebook's terms of service state that users may not use their products to share anything that is "unlawful, misleading, discriminatory or fraudulent". This is a sensible policy — Facebook should enforce their rules.
4) Lastly, we should not ignore the non-technological component to the issue of disinformation: us the users. We need to educate the public on how to consume trusted information, we need to educate the public on how to be better digital citizens, and we need to educate the public on how not to fall victim to scams, fraud, and disinformation.

Conclusion

I will end where I began. Disinformation is not new. Deep fakes is only the latest incarnation. We should not lose sight of the fact that more traditional human-generated disinformation campaigns are still highly effective, and we will undoubtedly be contending with yet another technological innovation a few years from now. In responding to deep fakes, therefore, we should make every effort to consider the past, present and future as we try to navigate the complex interplay of technology, policy, regulation, and human nature.

Lastly, I would be remiss in not mentioning that although there are serious issues of online privacy, moves by some of the technology giants to transform their platform to an end-to-end encrypted system will only make the problem of disinformation worse. Such end-to-end encrypted systems will make it even more difficult to understand and slow or stop the spread of disinformation. We should make every effort to consider the balance between privacy and safety and how these can be best accomplished.

Biographical Sketch

Dr. Hany Farid, Ph.D.

Hany Farid is a Professor at the University of California, Berkeley with a joint appointment in Electrical Engineering Computer Science and the School of Information. His research focuses on digital forensics, image analysis, and human perception. He received his undergraduate degree in Computer Science and Applied Mathematics from the University of Rochester in 1989, his M.S. in Computer Science from SUNY Albany, and his Ph.D. in Computer Science from the University of Pennsylvania in 1997. Following a two-year post-doctoral fellowship in Brain and Cognitive Sciences at MIT, he joined the faculty at Dartmouth College in 1999 where he remained until 2019. He is the recipient of an Alfred P. Sloan Fellowship, a John Simon Guggenheim Fellowship, and is a Fellow of the National Academy of Inventors.

Chairwoman SHERRILL. Thank you very much. Ms. Francois?

Statement of Ms. Camille Francois, Chief Innovation Officer, Graphika

Ms. FRANCOIS. Chairwoman Sherrill, and Ranking Member Lucas, Members of the Committee, thank you for having me here today. We're here to discuss the growing issue of online imposters and disinformation. As you know, this problem is nuanced and complex. I've been looking at disinformation campaigns for many years, and I have seen great diversity in the types of actors, techniques, and impacts that those disinformation campaigns can have. I want to highlight that, while we tend to focus on fake content, the most sophisticated actors I have seen operate online actually tend to use authentic content weaponized against their targets. This is what I want to talk about a little bit more.

It's really hard to give a sense of the growing and global scale of the issue, but here are a few recent examples. Today a report by my colleagues over at the Oxford Internet Institute highlighted that more than 70 countries currently use computational propaganda techniques to manipulate public opinion online. Since October 2018, Twitter has disclosed information around more than 25,000 accounts associated with information operations in 10 different countries.

Twitter is one thing. On Facebook, over 40 million users have followed pages that Facebook has taken down for being involved in what they call coordinated inauthentic behavior. Those may seem like huge numbers, but, in fact, they represent a needle in a hay-stack, and the danger of this particular needle is its sharpness. Targeting specific communities at the right time, and with the right tactics, can have a catastrophic impact on society, or on an election. That impact remains very difficult to rigorously quantify. For instance, if you take a fake account, what matters is not just the number of followers it has, but who those followers are, how they have engaged with the campaign, and how they have engaged both online and offline. Similarly, for a piece of content, it's not often the payload that matters, but really the delivery system, and the targeted system.

We are finding more and more state and non-state actors producing disinformation. What keeps me awake at night on this issue is also the booming market of disinformation for hire. That means troll farms that one can rent, bot networks that one can purchase, for instance. These tools are increasingly attractive to domestic political actors, who also use them to manipulate American audiences online. I see that you discovered how easy it was to make a deep fake, and I encourage you to also discover how easy it is to buy a set of fake accounts online, or, frankly, to purchase a full blown disinformation campaign.

The good news here, if there is any, is that, as a society, and as a professional field, we've come a long way since 2016. These problems began long before 2016, but it really took the major Russian interference in the U.S. election to force us toward a collective reckoning. In 2016 the top platforms, law enforcement, and democratic institution sleepwalked through the Russian assault on American democratic processes. Those who raised the alarm were, at best, ignored. Today we're in a better place. We have rules, definition, and emerging processes to tackle these campaigns. Coordination between researchers, platforms, and public agencies have proven successful, for instance, in protecting the U.S. 2018 midterms from Russian disinformation efforts. Then, those actors worked hand in hand to detect, take down, and, to a certain extent, document the Russian attempts to deceive an manipulate voters.

We still have a long way to go, but the scale of the problem is staggering. Sophisticated state actors, and, again, a growing army of hired guns, are manipulating vast networks' interactions among billions of people on dozens of platforms, and in hundreds of countries. This manipulation is discoverable, but almost in a way that a submarine is discoverable under the ocean. What you really need is sophisticated sensors that must evolve as rapidly as the methods of evasion. That requires a serious investment in the development of analytic models, computational tools, and domain expertise on adversary trade crafts. We need better technology, but also more people able to develop and adopt rapidly evolving methods.

Accomplishing this also requires access to data, and that is currently the hardest conversation on this topic. The task at hand is to design a system that guarantees user security and privacy, while ensuring that the corps of scientists, researchers, and analysts can access the data they need to unlock the understanding of the threats, and harness innovative ways to tackle the issue. Today we're very far from having such a system in place. We critically need not just the data, but the community of scholars and practitioners to make sense of it. That emerging field of people dedicating to ensuring the integrity of online conversation needs support, funding, and a shared infrastructure.

[The prepared statement of Ms. Francois follows:]

Prepared Statement of Camille Francois, Chief Innovation Officer, Graphika, and Affiliate at the Berkman Klein Center for Internet & Society, and Ben Nimmo, Director of Investigations, Graphika

The threat represented by the proliferation of information operations designed to deceive andmanipulate users on social media demands a unified, forceful response by the whole of society.

The problem is nuanced and complex. There is enormous diversity in the types of actors, techniques, and impacts across the many campaigns our team has analyzed over the past few years.

To date, Facebook, Twitter, and Google alone have detected and taken down information operations emanating from at least 25 different countries, some of them designed to control domestic politics, others targeting geopolitical rivals. The countries named as points of origin for these operations, most of which were not directly attributed to state actors, include

Russia, Iran, Bangladesh, Venezuela, Spain, China, Saudi Arabia, Ecuador, United Arab Emirates, Egypt, Myanmar, Iraq, Ukraine, Israel, Thailand, the Philippines, Honduras, India, Indonesia, Pakistan, the United Kingdom, Romania, Moldova, Macedonia, and Kosovo.

Some of these operations were directly coordinated by state actors. The best known are Russia and Iran, but China,[37] Honduras, and others also belong on the list.[38] Campaigns in Spain[39] and India[40] were linked to political parties; others were run by shadowy marketing companies, mercenary firms that execute influence operations on behalf of their clients, as witnessed in Israel,[41] Egypt, and the United Arab Emirates.[42] Some appeared linked to individual media outlets, as in the case of Kremlin-sponsored outlet Sputnik,[43] small groups of activists, as in the United Kingdom,[44] or even to specific individuals with political agendas, as in the Philippines during the recent senatorial election.[45]

The global impact of deliberate manipulations of political conversations on social media is difficult to quantify, but a few data points can help us grasp orders of magnitude.[46] Since October 2018, Twitter has published 25,084 accounts associated with information operations in ten different countries and has confirmed that tens of thousands more low-grade spam accounts were also involved in similar behavior.[47] The full archive of information operation[48] posts shared by Twitter encompasses over 65 million tweets, spanning more than five years of posting.

Over the past two years, Facebook has announced taking down 12,085 accounts, pages, groups, and Instagram accounts for engaging in what it calls

---

[37] https://newsroom.fb.com/news/2019/08/removing-cib-china/.

[38] https://newsroom.fb.com/news/2019/07/removing-cib-thailand-russia-ukraine-honduras/.

[39] https://newsroom.fb.com/news/2019/09/removing-coordinated-inauthentic-behavior-in-spain/.

[40] https://newsroom.fb.com/news/2019/04/cib-and-spam-from-india-pakistan/.

[41] https://newsroom.fb.com/news/2019/05/removing-coordinated-inauthentic-behavior-from-israel/.

[42] https://newsroom.fb.com/news/2019/08/cib-uae-egypt-saudi-arabia/.

[43] https://newsroom.fb.com/news/2019/01/removing-cib-from-russia/.

[44] https://newsroom.fb.com/news/2019/03/removing-cib-uk-and-romania/.

[45] https://newsroom.fb.com/news/2019/03/cib-from-the-philippines/.

[46] These figures are based on the platforms' public announcements, made intermittently through their blog posts. As a result, they represent voluntary disclosures on incidents that have been investigated to date, and are therefore not fully representative of the scale of the problem.

[47] https://about.twitter.com/en_us/values/elections-integrity.html#data.

[48] For a searchable archive, see our efforts to make this data more available to the public on www.io-archive.org.

"coordinated inauthentic behavior." Just over 40 million other accounts followed one or more of these assets. The least-followed operation gathered under 1,000 followers, while the most followed, run by commercial companies in the United Arab Emirates and Egypt, gathered over 13 million.[49] Reach measured in number of followers here is a very imperfect proxy for impact, though: *who* those followers are and *how* they are engaged often matter more than *how many* they are.

For the individual user, 50 million tweets or 40 million followers are almost too many to visualize, but for the platforms themselves, with hundreds of millions of active users, they represent only a fraction of daily activity. For the operators, meanwhile, what matters most is often a small group of deliberately chosen targets: a protest community, a politically influential group, or even an individual journalist who might unwittingly spread the desired narratives and alter their behavior based on anything from an artificially boosted trend to the release of hacked[50] materials.[51] The impact of these operations, from ruined reputations, to gaming the journalistic agenda, to election dynamics, are very real. The increase in information operations since 2016, and the range of actors carrying them out, should be ample evidence of the effectiveness of these methods.

It is critical to understand that these types of operations long predate 2016. Iran's known operations targeted US audiences with fake social media profiles as early as 2013. Russia's Internet Research Agency began attacking domestic opposition on Russian-language channels asfar back as 2010 and further developed these methods in the 2014 Ukrainian conflict while ramping up US involvement in the same year. As early as 2012, the campaign of Mexican presidential challenger (and eventual president) Enrique Pena Nieto was accused of benefiting from large-scale amplification by Twitter bots (automated accounts), nicknamed Penabots. This problem has been with us for a while.

Unfortunately, it took until the Russian interference in the 2016 US election to force us toward a collective reckoning. In 2016, the major platforms, law enforcement, and democratic institutions sleepwalked through the Russian assault on US democratic processes, and those in the open- source community who raised the alarm were, at best, ignored. As just one example, Russian operators ran a Twitter account that claimed to be the unofficial outlet

[49] https://newsroom.fb.com/news/2019/08/cib-uae-egypt-saudi-arabia/.

[50] On hack-to-leaks operations, see our work on False Leaks at CYBERWARCON 2018: https://www.youtube.com/watch?v=P8iXN8j4gMk.

[51] https://www.nature.com/articles/d41586-019-02235-x.

of the Republican Party in Tennessee and registered it to a Russian mobile phone number, yet the account survived three complaints to Twitter from the actual Tennessee Republican Party.[52] Even when disinformation became a national security issue for American democracy, we collectively failed to properly recognize and address it. It's fair to say that back then, most platforms were unaware of the scale or seriousness of this type of activity, did not have applicable rules against it, and weren't actively looking to protect their users from it.

We've come a long way since then. The main platforms, but also investigative journalists, government actors, and a network of skilled researchers are now actively looking for, investigating, and coordinating to take down influence operations across a wide range of online environments. They have begun working with external researchers, both to expose more operations and to explain what they have found. These green shoots are promising and should be commended. But unfortunately, we are not the only ones making progress.

There are now more actors perpetrating information operations, and primary adversaries are better resourced and more sophisticated every day. Facebook confirmed in July 2018 that the Internet Research Agency's operators were taking ever more effective steps to mask their presence, including using internet phone numbers to register accounts and proxy servers in third countries to mask their origins. They also paid third parties to run ads on their behalf.[53] A separate Russian operation, exposed in June 2019 and suspected of being run by an intelligence service, went a step further by creating hundreds of blogs and social media accounts to post forged documents and divisive content and then abandoned most of the accounts after they had posted just once.[54] A government-linked operation in China used large numbers of hijacked and repurposed accounts to spread its message.[55] An operation emerging from Iraq used stolen official personal identification documents in an attempt to avoid systems in place to detect false accounts.[56] And as the mainstream platforms crack down on information operations, we also see operators invest in alternative and more marginalized platforms to run

---

[52] https://www.buzzfeednews.com/article/kevincollier/twitter-was-warned-repeatedly-about-this-fake- account-run#.tjENWBAQlv.

[53] https://newsroom.fb.com/news/2018/07/removing-bad-actors-on-facebook/.

[54] https://medium.com/dfrlab/top-takes-suspected-russian-intelligence-operation-39212367d2f0.

[55] https://www.aspi.org.au/report/tweeting-through-great-firewall.

[56] https://newsroom.fb.com/news/2019/09/removing-coordinated-inauthentic-behavior-from-iraq-and-ukraine.

operations in more permissive environments. We tend to focus on the major platforms, but as their efforts to combat bad actors become more effective, the problem is migrating to smaller platforms that lack the capabilities and, sometimes, the will to fight back. We have documented one Russian operation alone that worked across more than 30 different platforms to spread false narratives.

So how do we tackle this issue together? Disinformation and information operations present a multi-faceted problem requiring technical, methodological, and policy solutions borrowed from disciplines as diverse as cybersecurity, data science, and consumer protection and privacy law. We need to understand all vectors critical to a disinformation campaign's impact: Manipulative actors, deceptive behaviors, and harmful content. These three vectors are what we call the "ABC's of disinformation."[57] Content elements, like "deep fakes," get the most public attention, but their impact depends on more hidden but critical matters of how that content is being disseminated and who is hiding behind a campaign.

Science and technology have a crucial role to play in tackling this problem. The sheer volume of information on these platforms, and the speed with which it is shared, require new methods for campaign detection that can scale beyond our current capabilities. As our opponents become more effective at concealing their identities, we need to continuously innovate by creating forensic approaches that will be both accurate and difficult to undermine. And for us to make real, measurable progress on these fronts, we need to address the thorny but essential problem of data availability.

The task at hand is to design a system that guarantees user security and privacy while ensuring that academic researchers, cybersecurity professionals, and human rights investigators can access the data they need to unlock our understanding of these threats and harness innovative ways to tackle the issue. Today, we're very far from such a system.

Let me illustrate: The most well-understood campaign ever, for which the most data to date has been made available by all platforms, is the Russian campaign targeting the American public around the 2016 election. The trove of data released by US platforms and institutions has enabled superb academic

[57] See attached paper: Francois, Camille. "Actors, Behaviors, Content: A Disinformation ABC. Highlighting Three Vectors of Viral Deception to Guide Industry & Regulatory Responses," A working paper of the Transatlantic High Level Working Group on Content Moderation Online and Freedom of Expression: https://www.ivir.nl/twg/.

work by our colleagues.[58] The Graphika team, along with our colleagues at the Oxford Internet Institute, spent seven months investigating additional, non-public data on behalf of the Senate Intelligence Committee.[59]

Our confidence in the completeness of this picture is false. There remain critical data blind spots. For instance, while platforms released a trove of data regarding the Internet Research Agency's public posts on social media, little to nothing has been shared regarding the GRU's campaigns, when in reality the GRU is the better funded and more persistent actor. It is also inherently more threatening, given its advanced hacking capabilities and readiness to leak apparently compromising material. Similarly, we know that Russian operators used private messaging to target and cultivate relationships with activists, campaign staffers, and journalists, but there is no data available anywhere to indicate a sense of scale and no public records to learn from to determine how best to immunize future targets against these types of threats. Finally, we know that the Russian operators designed their messages to be inflammatory and sometimes overtly hateful: how many of these posts have been moderated by platforms long before anyone cared about Russian trolls? Are we missing a large chunk of content from the public record? We believe that these data blind spots undermine our preparation for the threats ahead. We can, and must, do better.

Data availability is a major part of the solution. Another is ensuring that a community of scholars and practitioners exists to leverage it. At present, the study of these kinds of information operations on social media is a nascent discipline. We need help to turn it into a comprehensive and cooperative field that brings together experts who span the social and data sciences under a common framework, and with common goals.

In summary, the emerging field of interdisciplinary scholars and practitioners dedicated to ensuring the integrity of online conversations needs support, funding, and shared infrastructure that allow effective and collaborative innovation. We need this field to keep maturing and growing, to

---

[58] See for instance: Stewart, Leo G., Ahmer Arif, and Kate Starbird. "Examining trolls and polarization with aretweet network." In Proc. ACM WSDM, Workshop on Misinformation and Misbehavior Mining on the Web. 2018. Boatwright, Brandon C., Darren L. Linvill, and Patrick L. Warren. "Troll factories: The internet research agency and state-sponsored agenda building." Resource Centre on Media Freedom in Europe (2018); Benkler, Yochai, Robert Faris, and Hal Roberts. Network propaganda: Manipulation, disinformation,and radicalization in American politics. Oxford University Press, 2018. (Chapter 8: *Are the Russians coming?*).

[59] Howard, Philip N., Bharath Ganesh, Dimitra Liotsiou, John Kelly, and Camille François. *The IRA, socialmedia and political polarization in the United States, 2012-2018*. University of Oxford, 2018.

blossom into a community of ethnographers, historians, data scientists, cognitive psychologists, computer scientists, political scientists, sociologists, and many others. The diversity of this community will enable us to address our biggest challenges with a variety of informative perspectives. In this way, we will continue to collaboratively build upon a robust set of interdisciplinary methods, scientific rigor, and shared ethical principles.

* * *

Chairwoman SHERRILL. Thank you, Ms. Francois. We'll have to get to the rest of it as we go through the questions, but thank you very much. At this point we'll begin our first round of questions, and I'm going to recognize myself for 5 minutes.

I'd just like to start with Dr. Farid and Dr. Lyu, because we read a lot about the potential for deep fakes to be used on political candidates, and we watched Dr. Lyu's very compelling example here in this room, so thank you for that brilliant demonstration. I hope my fellow Members of Congress who aren't in the room today will actually get a chance to see for themselves, and hear just how limitless the potential impacts of deep fakes can be.

Let's talk about some hard truths. On a scale of 1 to 10, what do you think are the chances of a convincing video deep fake of a political candidate, someone running for Congress, or President, or Governor, emerging during the 2020 election cycle, and why do you think that?

Dr. FARID. I'm going to save five, to minimize my chances of being wrong. I am—and for another reason too, that I think we shouldn't—despite the sophistication of deep fakes, we shouldn't overlook that traditional disinformation works really well, and it's easy, right? Teenagers in Macedonia were responsible for a lot of the disinformation campaigns we saw in 2016. So I think it's coming. I don't know whether it'll be in 2020, or 2022, or 2024, but largely because the cheap stuff still works, and it's going to work for a while. I think we'll eventually get out ahead of that, and then this will be the new front.

But I think it is just a matter of time. We've already seen nefarious uses of deep fakes for cases of fraud, and I think the bigger threat here is not going to be—the first threat I predict is not going to be an actual deep fake, but the plausible deniability argument, that a real video will come out, and somebody will be able to say, that's a deep fake. And that, in some ways, is the larger threat that I see coming down the road, is once anything can be faked, nothing is real anymore. And I think that's probably more likely to happen before the first real deep fake comes out.

Chairwoman SHERRILL. That's interesting. Dr. Lyu?

Dr. LYU. Yes. Thank you for the question. As, actually, I mentioned in the opening remarks, the technical capability of making high-quality deep fakes is already at the disposal of whoever wants to make it. As I mentioned, for the deep fake videos we made, we have a specially made software, but anybody can potentially also develop similar softwares based on the open-source software on the GitHub, and then they can just buy a computer for about, you know, a couple thousand dollars, and then run this for a couple hours. Everything is automatic. So this is really the reality that, you know, people, whoever want to make these kind of videos, they have that capacity.

However, the question whether we will see such a video in a coming election really—as Professor Farid mentioned, depends on a lot of other factors, especially, you know, deep fake is not the only approach for disinformation. So it is kind of difficult to come up with a precise number there, but the possibility is certainly substantial. Thank you.

Chairwoman SHERRILL. Thank you. And then, Ms. Francois, you have a lot of experience observing how trolls and bots behave when they identify a hoax they might want to spread. If a convincing deep fake of a politico emerges next year, what do you expect the bot and troll participation to look like in proliferating the video? In other words, will we see this sort of erupt all at once, or does it percolate in dark areas of the Internet for a short-period of time before it emerges? How does that work?

Ms. FRANCOIS. All of the above are possible. I will say that, if we are facing a sophisticated actor able to do a convincing deep fake, they will be able to do a convincing false amplification campaign, too.

Chairwoman SHERRILL. Thank you very much. And then, Dr. Farid, you said in your testimony that researchers working on technologies to detect disinformation should give more thought to proper safeguards so their work cannot be misused or weaponized. What kind of safeguards do you believe could be adopted voluntarily by the research community to protect against the spread of disinformation?

Dr. FARID. Good. So I think there's two things that can be done. So, first, you have to understand in computer science we have an open source culture, which means we publish work, and we put it out there. That's been the culture, and it's wonderful. It's a wonderful culture. But when that technology can be weaponized, maybe we should think about putting the data, and the code, and the GitHub repository, where anybody can download it, as Professor Lyu was saying. So that's number one, is just think about how you disseminate. We can still publish and not put the details of it out so that anybody can grab it, No. 1.

No. 2 is, there are mechanisms by which we can incorporate, into synthetic media, watermarks that will make it easier for us to identify that. That can become a standard. We can say academic publishers who are going to post code should incorporate into the result of their technology a distinct watermark. That is not bullet- proof, it's not that it can't be attacked, but it's at least a first line of defense. So those are the two obvious things that I can see.

Chairwoman SHERRILL. That was perfect timing. Thank you very much, I appreciate it. I would now like to recognize Mr. Lucas for 5 minutes.

Mr. LUCAS. Thank you, Madam Chair. Dr. Farid, following up on what the Chair was discussing, in your written statement you say that no matter how quickly forensic technology for detecting deep fakes develops, it'll be useless without the cooperation of the technology giants like Google and Facebook. How do we bring those people to the table to begin this collaboration?

Dr. FARID. Yes. So the bad news is they have been slow to respond, for decades, really. It's not just disinformation. This is the latest, from child sexual abuse, to terrorism, to conspiracy theories, to illegal drugs, illegal weapons. The technology sector has been very slow to respond. That's the bad news. The good news is I think a combination of pressure from here on Capitol Hill, from Brussels, from the UK, and from the public, and from advertisers, there is now an acknowledgement that we have a problem, step number one.

Step number two is, what are we going to do about it? And I still think we are very slow here, and what you should understand is we are fighting against business interests, right? The business model of Facebook, Google, YouTube, Twitter is data, it's content. Taking down content is bad for business. And so we have to find mechanisms and either through regulatory pressure, advertising pressure, public pressure, bring them to the table. I will say the good news is, in the last 6 months, at least the language coming out of the technology sector is encouraging. I don't know that there's a lot of action yet.

So I will give you an example. We all saw a few months ago an altered video of Speaker Pelosi. This was not a confusing video, we all knew it was fake, and yet Facebook gleefully let it on their platform. In fact, defended the decision to leave it on their platform, saying, we are not the arbiters of truth, OK? So we have two problems now. We have a policy problem, and we have a technology problem. I can help with the technology problem. I don't know what I can do about the policy problem, when you say, we are not the arbiters of truth. So I think we have to have a serious look at how to put more pressure on the technology sector, whether that's regulatory, or legislative, or advertising, or public pressure, and they have to start getting serious as to how their platforms are being weaponized to great effect in disrupting elections, and inciting violence, and sowing civil unrest. I don't think they've quite come to grips with that reality.

Mr. LUCAS. Well, when that moment comes, and inevitably it will, in your opinion, what will that collaboration look like? There's a government element, there's an academic element, there's a public-private partnership element.

Dr. FARID. Yes.

Mr. LUCAS. Can you just——

Dr. FARID. Sure.

Mr. LUCAS [continuing]. Daydream for a moment here with me?

Dr. FARID. So I think the good news is the Facebooks and the Googles of the world have started to reach out to academics, myself included, Professor Lyu included. We now receive research funding to help them develop technology. That's good. I think the role of the government is to coax them along with regulatory pressure. I think what we've noticed over the last 20 years of self-regulation is not working. I'd like it to work, but it doesn't work in this particular space.

So I think the role of the government can be through oversight, it can be regulatory, it can be through a cyber ethics panel that is convened to talk about the serious issues of how technology is being weaponized in society. But very much I think the academic/ industry model has to work, because most of the research that we are talking about is happening at the academic side of things, and obviously the industry has different incentives than we do in the academy, so I think there is room for everybody.

I'll also mention this is not bounded by U.S. borders. This is very much an international problem, so we should be looking across the pond to our friends in the UK, in the EU, and New Zealand, and Australia, and Canada, and bringing everybody on board because this is a problem for not just us, but for the whole world.

Mr. LUCAS. One last question. In your written testimony you suggest there's a non-technological component to solving the problem related to deep fakes and disinformation. Specifically, you wrote that we need to educate the public on how to consume trusted information, and how to be better digital citizens. What should this public education initiative——

Dr. FARID. Yes.

Mr. LUCAS [continuing]. Look like?

Dr. FARID. I'm always reluctant to say this, because I know how taxed our schools are in this country, but at some point this is an educational issue, starting from grade school on the way up. And, as an educator, I think this is our role. We have to have digital citizenry classes. Some of the European countries have done this. France is starting to do this, the UK is starting to do it. Public service announcements (PSAs) explaining to people how information can be trusted, what disinformation is, but we've got to start taking more seriously how we educate the next generation, and the current generation. And whether that's through the schools, through PSAs, through industry sponsored PSAs, you know, I think all of those are going to be needed.

Mr. LUCAS. And you would agree that our technology giant friends have a role in that education process?

Dr. FARID. They absolutely have a role. They made this mess, they need to help fix it.

Mr. LUCAS. Very concise. Thank you, Doctor. I yield back, Madam Chair.

Chairwoman SHERRILL. Thank you, Mr. Lucas. And now, Ms. Wexton, I recognize you for 5 minutes.

Ms. WEXTON. Thank you, Madam Chair, and thank you to the panelists for appearing today. I want to speak a little bit about the explosive growth that the major social platforms have experienced over the past few years, because I'm worried that these companies are more focused on growth, and getting more users, than they are about essential oversight and user support functions. And, in fact, as has been noted, they disclaim responsibility for any information that goes out onto the web by the users. And, in fact, it seems to me that they have a disincentive to purge suspicious, or fake, or bot accounts.

You know, I have here an article from July of last year, where Twitter's stock price went down by about eight and a half percent after they purged, over the course of two months, 70 million suspicious accounts. Now, don't feel too bad for Twitter, because their stock price went up 75 percent over that six month period, but, you know, by being socially responsible, or by being responsible, it hurt their bottom line.

Now, the platforms are incredibly powerful. We have already seen the power that they have here in the capitol, not just because of the lobbyists and everything, but because we all use them. We all have those platforms on our phones, and on our various devices. And, Dr. Farid, you spoke a little bit about how the basic features of the technology and the business model at social media companies kind of help exacerbate the proliferation of disinformation.

Can you explain, from a business perspective, what benefit a bot account or a fake account might represent for a social media company?

Dr. FARID. Sure. So, first of all, I think you're absolutely right that growth has been priority No. 1. And because the metrics of Silicon Valley are number of users, number of minutes online, it's because that's what eventually leads to advertising dollars. What we have to understand is that Silicon Valley, for better or worse, today is driven by ad revenue, and ad revenue is optimized by having more engagement, OK? So fake account, real account, don't care. Fake like, real like, fake tweet, doesn't matter, right, because at the end of the day, you get to report big numbers to the advertisers who are going to pay more money. Whether 50 percent of those accounts are fake or not, who's to know?

So that's the underlying poison, if you will, of Silicon Valley, I think, and is the reason why the system is entirely frictionless, by design. There's no friction to creating an account on Twitter, or on Facebook, or on YouTube, because they want that to be easy. They want bots to be able to create these things because that is what elevates the numbers. And I think this is sort of our core problem that we have here.

Ms. WEXTON. So, related to that, why would social media companies allow, or even encourage, their recommendation algorithms to——

Dr. FARID. Good.

Ms. WEXTON [continuing]. Put people, you know, to direct users to——

Dr. FARID. Good.

Ms. WEXTON [continuing]. Suggested videos, or things like that, that are sensational, or even false? Why would they do that?

Dr. FARID. The metric on YouTube is engagement, how long do you stay on the platform? And so what the algorithms learn is that, if I show you a video that is conspiratorial, or outrageous, you are more likely to click on it and watch it. If you are more likely to click or watch, you're going to stay on the platform longer, right? So the algorithms are not trying to radicalize you. What they are trying to do is to keep you on the platform for as long as possible. And it turns out, in the same way that people will eat candy all day long instead of broccoli, people will watch crazy videos all day long instead of PBS. I don't think this is surprising. And so the underlying algorithms, what they are being optimized for, in part, is exactly this.

And we have been studying the nature of these conspiracy videos for over a year now, and I will tell you that, despite claims to the contrary, there is a rabbit-hole effect, that once you start watching the slightly crazy conspiratorial videos, you will get more and more and more of that because you are more likely to click, you are more likely to view, they're going to get more data, and they're going to sell more advertising. That's the underlying business model, is how long do you stay on my platform? And, in that regard, the quality of the information is utterly unimportant to the platforms. It is what keeps you there.

Ms. WEXTON. So maybe we should all have more cats and kittens, and less conspiracy?

Dr. FARID. I'm all for cat videos.

Ms. WEXTON. So, switching gears a little bit, yesterday this Committee—we marked up a bill, it was Congressman Gonzalez's bill, that would expand research into technologies to help us better identify deep fake videos. And I had an amendment which was made in order, and approved by the Committee, to help increase education to help people identify deep fake videos, and so I was encouraged to hear you talk about that. So I would inquire of the panel, do you have any advice on what the most important elements of a public education campaign on deep fake videos should be?

Dr. FARID. Again, you know, I am reluctant to put this on our public schools. I think they are overtaxed, and overworked, and underfunded. But at the end of the day, this is sort of where it belongs. And I think if we can do this, not as an unfunded mandate, but actually give them the resources to create courses of digital citizenry, of how you are a better digital citizen, how you can trust information and not trust information.

I'll point out too, though, by the way, it's not just the young people. The senior citizens among us are more likely to share fake news than the young people, so this is across the spectrum. So I'm more—this—for me, the education level is more about the next 20, 30, 40 years than necessarily today. So I think a combination of PSAs, about returning to trusted sources, and about educating kids not just, by the way, about trusted information, but how to be a better digital citizen, how to interact with each other. The vitriol that we see online is absolutely horrific, and the things that we accept online we would never accept in a room like this, and I think we have to start teaching the next generation that this is not a way that we interact with each other. We need a more civil discourse.

Chairwoman SHERRILL. Thank you, Dr. Farid. And I'd now like to recognize Mr. Biggs for 5 minutes.

Mr. BIGGS. Thank you, Madam Chair, and I appreciate each of the witnesses for being here. It's a very, very interesting hearing, and appreciate the Chair for convening this hearing.

So one of the main things I'm worried about is the de facto gray area between misinformation and disinformation, despite the seemingly clear definitional difference between these concepts. While disinformation may be defined in terms of the malicious intent on the part of the sender, such intent, as we've seen today, can at times be very difficult to identify. And then, on top of that, we need to make sure the gatekeepers, themselves trying to police content, are objective. Objective enough to identify potential misinformation, and able to do so as expeditiously as possible.

It seems to me that, even if we have the technological anti- disinformation tools that we've learned about in this discussion, and that we anticipate seeing developed over time, human judgment will always be a key component of any anti-deep fakes effort, and human judgment can, of course, be fallible. In short, the difficulties and nuances of the battle pile up the deeper we delve into this topic. Maybe that's why I find it so interesting to hear what you all have to say today.

But I want to just get back to something, and I would say I feel like we've been doing what I would call an endogenous look, and that is what's the technology here? And you mentioned it, Dr. Farid, in item four on page four of your recommendations in your written report, but it really gets to what I think is a real-world problem I'd like all of you to respond to, and the last questioner just kind of touched on it a bit as well. What do you tell a 13- or 14-year-old that you're trying to warn of potential disinformation, misinformation? How do you do it as a parent, as a grandparent, as someone who cares for, loves, an individual. I mean, that really becomes a part of the equation as much as anything else on the technological side.

Dr. LYU. Well, thank you for asking the question, because the nature of my work, I usually show a lot of fake videos to my 12-year- old daughter, and she actually grow the habit of distrust for any video I showed to her. So I think this may be a very effective way to actually tell them—to show them that the existence of fake videos will make them aware that those are something they should be careful about.

Ms. FRANCOIS. I can take the question on, you know, what goes beyond technology, and I want to talk about one specific example. I think, when you look at the most sophisticated campaigns that have leveraged disinformation, and we're talking about actors who are willingly doing this, there's still a lot that we don't know. So, back to the Russian example, for instance, which is largely seen as the best-documented campaign, right, on which the platforms have shared a lot of data. I have myself worked with the Senate Select Intelligence Committee to document what happened. There are still essential pieces of that campaign that we know nothing about, and on which there's no data, in the eye of the public, to really understand how that technology was leveraged to manipulate audiences, direct messages, and how the Russians used to target deliberately specific journalists to feed them sources. We don't know anything about the scale of how much of that was going on.

Similarly, what the GRU was doing, alongside the IRA, is something that there's zero available data on. So I would go back to those important and large-scale campaigns that we know have really disrupted society and interrogate, where are our blind spots? How can we do better? How can we produce this data so that we actually are able to fully understand those tactics? And then, of course, to build the tools to detect it, but also to train people to understand it, and to build defense.

Mr. BIGGS. Thank you. Dr. Farid? What are you going to tell your kid?

Dr. FARID. I, fortunately, don't have kids, so I don't have to struggle with this problem.

Mr. BIGGS. They're a blessing and a curse.

Dr. FARID. I think this is difficult, because the fact is this generation is growing up on social media——

Mr. BIGGS. Yes.

Dr. FARID [continuing]. And they are not reading The Washington Post, and The New York Times, and MSNBC, and Fox News. They think about information very differently. And I can tell you what I tell my students, which is, do not confuse information with knowledge. Those are very different things. And I think there is this tendency that it's online, therefore it must be true. And so my job as an educator is to make you critically think about what you are reading. And I don't know how to do that on a sort of day-to- day basis, but I do that every day with my students, which is critical reasoning. And with critical reasoning, I think everything comes.

And, if I may, I wanted to touch one—because I think you made a good point about the—sort of the nuance between mis- and disinformation, and we should acknowledge that there are going to be difficult calls. There is going to be content online that falls into this gray area that it's not clear what it is, but there is black and white things out there, and we should start dealing with that right now, and then we'll deal with that gray area when we need to, but let's not get confounded with that gray area, and not deal with the real clear cut harmful content.

Mr. BIGGS. Right. So information's not knowledge. I'd like to tell people in Congress, activity is not progress either, so, I mean, we——

Dr. FARID. We agree on that.

Chairwoman SHERRILL. Thank you, Mr. Biggs. And next I would like to recognize Mr. Beyer for 5 minutes.

Mr. BEYER. Madam Chair, thank you very much.

Dr.—Ms. Francois—so Dr. Lyu talked about funding more civilian research through the National Science Foundation, and setting up an emerging technologies directorate, and you spoke about this emerging field of interdisciplinary scholars, practitioners, that needed support, funding, and shared infrastructure. How best do you see us making that happen? Do we need congressional legislation? How big a budget does it have to be? Is it only NSF, or NIST (National Institutes of Standards and Technology), or——

Ms. FRANCOIS. That's a great question, thank you. I think it can be a whole of government effort, and I do think that a series of institutions have to get involved, because indeed, as I say, it's very interdisciplinary. I do think that regulation has to play a role too, not only to address those critical and complex questions, like the one of data access that I discussed.

I want to build on a point that Dr. Farid made about the algorithmic reinforcement, as an example. This is something that we know is impacting society. People watch one video, and seem to end up in a filter bubble of conspirational video. But, unfortunately, we have very little serious research on the matter. We are making those observations on a purely empirical basis out of, you know, people who let their computers run. We can't afford to be in the dark on the impact of technology on society like this. And in order to do serious scientific research on those impacts at scale, we need data, and we need the infrastructure to systematically measure and assess how this technology is impacting our society.

Mr. BEYER. Thank you very much. Dr. Farid, I was fascinated you talked about determining what's real, rather than what's fake, and specifically talking about the control capture technologies. We've had a number of Science Committee hearings on blockchain technology, which inevitably lead into quantum computing (QC) technology. Is blockchain, and ultimately QC, the right way to deal with this?

Dr. FARID. I think blockchain can play a role here. So the basic idea, for those who don't know, blockchain—basically all you have to know is that it's an immutable distributed ledger. So immutable, when you put information on there, it doesn't change. Distributed as it's not stored on one central server, but on millions of computers, so you don't have to rely on trust of one individual.

So one version of control capture is, at the point of capture, you extract that unique signature, cryptographically sign it, and you put that signature on the blockchain for public viewing of it, and public access to it. It's a very nice application of blockchain. I don't think it's critical to the solution. If you have a trusted central server, I think that would work well, but the reason why people like the blockchain is that I don't have to trust a Facebook, or an Apple, or a Microsoft, I can trust the globe. So I do see that as being part of the control capture environment, and being part of the solution of a universal standard that says, if you want your content to be trusted, take it with this control capture, and then we can trust that going down the line. I think we're eventually going to get there. I think it's just a matter of time.

Mr. BEYER. And, Dr. Lyu, how would you contrast watermarking technology with the blockchain, with the control capture? And is one better than the other, or do you need both, or——

Dr. LYU. I think these technologies are somehow complementary. So watermark is the content you actually embed into the image, and blockchains are ways to actually authenticate if the watermark is consistent with the original contents we invited into the signal. So they can work together. You can imagine that we have watermark also being part of the blockchain, uploaded to the remote distributed serer. So they can work hand in hand in this case. But watermarks can also work independently from a single capture control mechanism for authenticity of digital visual media.

Mr. BEYER. Thank you. And Ms.——

Dr. LYU. Thank you.

Mr. BEYER. Ms. Francois, again, you talked about how the big data players, the Facebooks and Twitters, obviously are a huge part of the potential problem—source material, and have to be part of the solution, and you mentioned regulation as one of the pieces of the NSF/NIST piece. Not that you can do it in 45 seconds, but anything that you guys can prepare to help our Energy and Commerce Committee, the committees in both houses, looking at how we manage the social media giants would be very, very appreciated. Because understanding how they've gone from basically unregulated unicorn game changers in our society, to how they can properly play within the rules, is going to be a really, really big challenge for us.

Ms. FRANCOIS. I think it's going to be a lot of moving pieces. It's a complex problem, as I said, and I do believe that there's a lot of different bodies of regulation that can be applied and brought to bear to tackle it. One that is often left out of the conversation that I just want to highlight here is consumer protection. Dr. Farid talked about how the advertisers are getting the fake clicks. This can be a consumer protection issue. So different bodies of regulation, from cyber security to consumer protection, to address a whole of the disinformation problem, plus serious pressure to ensure that the data that the field needs is being shared in a way that makes it—for people.

Mr. BEYER. Yes. Thank you very much, and I yield back.

Chairwoman SHERRILL. Thank you. Next I'd recognize Mr. Waltz for 5 minutes.

Mr. WALTZ. Thank you, Madam Chairwoman. Ms. Francois, going back to the disinformation campaigns that the Russians, the Iranians, and others have ongoing, the FBI and Department of Homeland Security have briefed us that they're confident, at least at this point in time, that active hacking into our election infrastructure has diminished, at least for now.

Although I, and other colleagues, have worked to ensure that critical infrastructure is secured going forward, and this Committee has done work on that as well, but I'm interested in the disinformation piece of it, are you seeing increasing evidence of our adversaries conducting disinformation against individuals, whether they're thought leaders, journalists, politicians? For example, I could foresee hawks on Iran policy, or Russia, or others being specifically targeted during an election in order to change that election outcome, and therefore change our policy and voices. Are you seeing an increase there? What types of techniques are you seeing, and where are you seeing it, aside from the United States?

One of the things that I've pushed is for us to share what we're gathering. For example, the Taiwanese elections, or other elections, for us to create a collaborative approach with our allies as well. This is a problem with the West, and I think with free speech and free thought, as much as it is with, you know, 2020 elections. And I'd welcome your thought.

And then second, sorry, what would you think the response would be if we took more of a deterrence measure? For example, sending the signal that the Iranians, the Russians, and other bad actors, they have their own processes, and they have their own concerns, and often these regimes are more concerned with their own survival than they are with anything else, and at least demonstrating that we have that capability to interfere as well. I know that may present a lot of moral and ethical questions of whether we should have that capability, and whether we should demonstrate we should use it, but we've certainly taken that approach with nuclear weapons. And so I'd welcome your thoughts there.

Ms. FRANCOIS. Thank you. I want to start by saying that part of it—yes, I am seeing an increase. Part of it is an increase, the other part is simply just a reckoning, as I said. Iran is a good example. We see a lot of disinformation campaigns originating from the Iranian state, who's a very prolific actor in that space.

Now, people often ask me, is Iran following the Russian model. In reality the first Iranian campaign to use social media to target U.S. audiences date back from 2013, where we were asleep at the wheel, and not looking for them. So, despite our reckoning with sort of the diversity of actors who have been engaged with these techniques to target us, there is also an increase in both their scale and their sophistication. This is a cat-and-mouse game, and so what we also see is, as we detect actors and their techniques, they increase the sophistication. They make it harder for us to do the forensics that we need in order to catch those campaigns as they unfold.

Thank you for raising the question of deterrence. I do think that this ultimately is a cyber policy issue too, and therefore the government has a role to play. In the case of the U.S. midterms in 2018, we saw U.S. Cyber Command target the Internet Research Agency in St. Petersburg in an act of this attempted cyber deterrence. So I do think that there is a governmental response too by putting this problem in the broader context of cyber issue and cyber conflict.

Mr. WALTZ. Thank you for raising that. I think it's important for my colleagues to note that was a policy change under this Administration that then allowed Cyber Command to take those kind of, what they call active defensive measures, and taking election security very seriously. I want to distinguish, though, between active defense and the potential, at least, and sending the signal that we have the potential for offense. And your thoughts there on the United States also participating in disinformation, or at least a deterrent capability?

At the end of the day I think we can only do so much in playing defense here. We can only counter so much of this cat-and-mouse game. We have to fundamentally change our adversaries' behavior, and put them at risk, and their regimes at risk, in my own view. But I'd welcome your thoughts in my remaining time.

Ms. FRANCOIS. Yes, I think the—8 minutes to answer this complex question on the dynamics of deterrence and resilience in cyberspace. I will say what immediately comes to mind is, of course, a question of escalation. How much of these dynamics contribute to escalation is something that is an unknown in this space.

So far I think that the approach of being much more aggressive in both catching these campaigns, deactivating them, and publicly claiming that we have found them, and this is what they look like, seems to be a welcome move in this area. I think by exposing what actors are doing, we are also contributing to raising the cost for them to engaging in these techniques.

Chairwoman SHERRILL. Well, that was well done——

Mr. WALTZ. Thank you.

Chairwoman SHERRILL [continuing]. Ms. Francois. Thank you.

Next I recognize Mr. Gonzalez for 5 minutes.

Mr. GONZALEZ. Thank you, Madam Chair, and thank you for being here, to our witnesses, and your work on this topic. A very important topic, and one that's a little bit new to Congress, but one that, alongside of Madam Chair, and others on this Committee, we've been excited to lead on, and I think we're making progress, unlike some other areas of Congress that I'm a part of.

So, that being said, Dr. Lyu, I want to start with you, and I really just want to understand kind of where we are in the technology, from the standpoint of cost. So if, call it 2 decades ago, I used the Forrest Gump example, yesterday. You know, Forrest Gump, if you've seen the movie, makes it looks like he's shaking hands with Presidents, and all kinds of things, and you can't tell the difference, except for you just know that there's no way that happened. Hollywood studio could've produced that, but it was costly back then, right, however much it costs. Today I think some numbers came out that you were citing that as, you know, roughly a couple thousand dollars. How quickly is the cost going down, to the point that this will be a weapon, if you will, that, you know, a 16-year-old sitting behind his computer could pull off?

Dr. LYU. I think this is basically, you know, we used to call this Moore's Law, where the computational power just got doubled every 18 months, and I think Moore's Law has already been broken with the coming of GPUs. The computational power that are at our hand is extremely higher than we have imagined before, and this trend is growing. So I will predict in the coming years it will become cheaper and easier, and also better to produce these kind of videos, and the computer hardware and algorithms will all get rapid improvements.

Mr. GONZALEZ. Yes.

Dr. LYU. So that's coming. I think it's a coming event. Thank you.

Mr. GONZALEZ. Thanks. And I actually think, you know, we talk a lot about great power competition in Iran, and China, and Russia, and I think that makes sense. I'm also maybe equally concerned about just a random person somewhere in society who has access to this, and can produce these videos without any problem, and the damage that that can cause. And I don't know that we've talked enough about that, frankly.

But switching to Ms. Francois, you talked about how you found 70 countries use computational propaganda techniques in your analysis. And obviously a lot of this is spread through the platforms, and I think you talked really well about just how you can go down rabbit holes in the engagement metrics, and things like that. What do you think, and Dr. Farid, I'd welcome your comments as well, what do the platforms themselves need to be doing differently? Because it strikes me that they're being somewhat, or I would say, I would argue grossly irresponsible with how they manage some of the content on their systems today.

Ms. FRANCOIS. That's a great question. I just want it precise that the 70 countries method comes from the Oxford Internet Institute report that was published today.

Mr. GONZALEZ. OK. Thank you.

Ms. FRANCOIS. For me, the platform's play here is actually quite simple, and I would say clearer roles, more aggressive action, more transparency.

Mr. GONZALEZ. Yes.

Ms. FRANCOIS. Let's start with clearer roles. Some platforms still don't have a rule that governments are not allowed to leverage their services in order to manipulate and deceive. And they will say they have rules that kind of go to this point, you know, tangentially, but there's still a lot of more clear rules that need to be established. To the second point, aggressive enforcement. There's still a lot of these campaigns that go under the radar, and that go undetected. They need to put the means to the table to make sure that they actually are able to catch, and detect, and take down as much of this activity as possible. My team, this week, published a large report on a spam campaign that was targeting Hong Kong protestors from Chinese accounts, and then they——

Mr. GONZALEZ. Yes.

Ms. FRANCOIS [continuing]. Had to take it down. There's more that they can do. Finally, transparency. It's very important that the platform continue, and increase, their degree of transparency in saying what they're seeing on their services, what they're taking down, and share the data back to the field.

Mr. GONZALEZ. Yes. I think that makes a lot of sense. My fear is, you know, we're going to do the best we can. I don't know that, one, this is intellectually difficult to figure out, as Congress, and it's also politically difficult, which, to me, puts it in that, like, Never Never Land, if it's going to take a while. So my hope is that the social medial platforms understand their responsibility, and come to the forefront with exactly what you said, because if not, I don't know that we're going to get it right, frankly.

But with my final question, I'll throw just the word mental health, and the platforms themselves, and misinformation. Any studies that you're aware of that are showing the impacts on mental health, in particular teenagers, with respect to what's going on on the platforms today? Anybody can answer that.

Ms. FRANCOIS. Again, I want to say that in this field we direly lack the data, infrastructure, and access to be able to do robust at-scale studies. So there is a variety of wonderful studies that are doing their best with small and more qualitative approaches, which are really, really important, but we're still direly lacking an important piece of doing rigorous research in this area.

Mr. GONZALEZ. Thank you. And I'll follow up with additional questions on how we can get that data, and be smarter about that in Congress. So, thank you, I yield back.

Mr. BEYER [presiding]. Thank you very much, sir. Dr. Farid, I understand you developed a seminal tool for Microsoft called PhotoDNA that detects and weeds out child pornography as it's posted online. Can you talk about how this tool works? Could this be used to address harmful memes and doctored images? And how do the social media companies respond to this?

Dr. FARID. So PhotoDNA was a technology that I developed in 2008–2009 in collaboration with Microsoft and the National Center for Missing and Exploited Children (NCMEC). Its goal was to find and remove the most horrific child sexual abuse material (CSAM) online. The basic idea is that the technology reaches into an image, extracts a robust digital signature that will allow us to identify that same piece of material when it is reuploaded. NCMEC is currently home to 80 million known child sexual abuse material, and so we can stop the proliferation and redistribution of that content. Last year alone, in one year, the National Center for Missing and Exploited Children's CyberTipline received 18 million reports of CSAM being distributed online. That's 2,000 an hour. 97, 98 percent of that material was found with PhotoDNA. It has been used for over a decade, and has been highly effective. Two more things. That same core technology can be used, for example, to find the Christchurch video, the Speaker Pelosi video, the memes that are known to be viral and dangerous. Once content is detected, the signature can be extracted, and we can stop the redistribution.

And to your question of how the technology companies respond, I think the answer is not well. They were asked in 2003 to do something about the global distribution of child sexual abuse material, and for 5 years they stalled, they did absolutely nothing. We're not talking about complicated issues here, gray areas. We are talking about 4-year-olds, 6-year-olds, 8-year-olds being violently raped, and the images and the videos of them, through these horrific acts, being distributed online. And the moral compass of Silicon Valley for the last decade has been so fundamentally broken they couldn't wrap their heads around their responsibility to do something about that.

That doesn't bode well, by the way, for going forward, so I think that history is really important, and we have to remember that they come begrudgingly to these issues, and so we have to coax them along the way.

Mr. BEYER. Thank you very much. So there—these images have digital signatures, even before we talk about the capture control technology——

Dr. FARID. Yes.

Mr. BEYER [continuing]. Or the watermark——

Dr. FARID. That's exactly right. These don't have to be captured with specific hardware. So what we do is, after the point of recording, we reach in and we find a distinct signature that will allow us to identify, with extremely high reliability, that same piece of content. And that can be child abuse material, it can be a bomb-making video, it can be a conspiracy video, it can be copyright infringement material. It can be anything.

Mr. BEYER. But it has to show up first——

Dr. FARID. That's right.

Mr. BEYER [continuing]. In the public space——

Dr. FARID. Yes.

Mr. BEYER [continuing]. At least once, and we have to know that it's there in order to capture this——

Dr. FARID. That's the drawback. But the good news is that technology works at scale. It works at the scale of a billion uploads to Facebook a day, and 500 hours of YouTube videos a minute. And that's a really hard engineering problem to tackle, but this technology actually works, unlike many of the other algorithms that have extremely high error rates, and would simply have too many mistakes.

Mr. BEYER. Thank you very much. Dr. Lyu, you talked about using AI to find AI, and that more deep neural networks are used to detect the fakes, but there's the sense that the good guys are always trying to catch up with the bad guys, you know, the cat-and- mouse. Is there any way around the cat-and-mouse nature of the problem? Which, by the way, we just saw before, it's got to be out there before you can tag it and chase it down.

Dr. LYU. That's a very good question. Actually, I think on this point, I'm more pessimistic because I don't think there's a way we can escape that, because that's the very nature of this kind of problem. Unlike other research areas, where the problem's fixed, we're basically dealing with a moving target. Whenever we have new detection or deterrent algorithms, the adversaries will always try to improve their algorithm to beat us. So I think, in the long run, this will be the situation that will keep going.

But I—that also emphasize Dr. Farid's point that we need more investment onto the side of detection and protection for the sake that, you know, we have a lot more resources put into making deep fakes for, you know, all kinds of reasons, but the investment in detection has not been catching up with that level. So that's part of my testimony, is encouraging the Federal Government to put more investment into this important area. Thank you.

Mr. BEYER. Ms. Francois?

Ms. FRANCOIS. Yes, if I may add a very simple metaphor here, I think we also have a leveling of the playing field issue. We're currently in a situation where there are a lot of cats, and very few mouses. We need to bring the resources to the table that correspond to the actual scale and gravity of the problem.

Mr. BEYER. OK. Great. Thank you very much. I now recognize the gentleman from Ohio, Mr. Gonzalez.

Mr. GONZALEZ. Thanks. Didn't know I was going to get a few extra seconds. So I just want to drill down on that data-sharing component. So you mentioned that we just need a better data-sharing infrastructure. Can you just take me as deep as you can on that? What do we need specifically? Just help me understand that.

Ms. FRANCOIS. Yes. There are many different aspects to what we need, and I think that the—both the infrastructure, people involved, and type of data depend on the type of usage. So, for instance, facilitating academic access to at-scale data on the effects of technology on society is ultimately a different issue than ensuring that cybersecurity professionals have access to the types of forensics that correspond to a high-scale manipulation campaign that enables them to build better detection tools. And so I think the first step in tackling this problem is recognizing the different aspects of it.

Mr. GONZALEZ. Got it.

Ms. FRANCOIS. Of course, the key component here is security and privacy, which here go hand in hand. What you don't want is to enable scenarios like Cambridge Analytica, where data abuses lead to more manipulation. Similarly, when we see disinformation campaigns, we often see a lot of real citizens who are caught into these nets, and they deserve the protection of their privacy.

If you go down sort of the first rabbit hole of ensuring that cybersecurity professionals have access to the type of data and associated forensics that they need in order to do this type of detection at scale, and to build the forensics tool we need at scale, there's still, as I said, a lot we can do. The platforms right now are sharing some of the data that they have on these types of campaigns, but in a completely haphazard way. So they're free to decide when they want to share, what they want to share, and in which format. Often the format, they're sharing them in are very inaccessible, so my team has worked to create a database that makes that accessible to researchers. That's one step we can take. And, again, and I'll wrap on that, because this can be a deep rabbit hole——

Mr. GONZALEZ. Yes.

Ms. FRANCOIS [continuing]. You pushed me down this way. Again, if we take the Russia example, for instance when we scope a collection around something that we consider to be of national security importance, we need to make sure we have the means to ensure that the picture we're looking at is comprehensive.

Mr. GONZALEZ. Right.

Ms. FRANCOIS. Our own false sense of security, in looking at the data, thinking that they represent the comprehensive picture of what happened, and was directed at us, is a problem in our preparations for election security.

Mr. GONZALEZ. Thank you. Dr. Farid, any additional thoughts on that?

Dr. FARID. Yes. I just wanted to mention, and I think Ms. Francois mentioned this, there is this tension between privacy and security, and you're seeing this particularly with Cambridge Analytica. And I will mention too that this is not, again, just a U.S. issue, this is a global issue. And with things like GDPR (General Data Protection Regulation), it has made data sharing extremely more complex for the technology sector.

Mr. GONZALEZ. Yes.

Dr. FARID. So, for example, we've been trying to work with the sector to build tools to find child predators online, and the thing we keep running up against is we can't share this stuff because of GDPR, we can't share it because of privacy. I think that's a little bit of a false choice, but there is a sensitivity there that we should be aware of.

Mr. GONZALEZ. Yes. That's fair. I agree with you. Certainly, I think what you highlight, which I agree with, is there are gray areas——

Dr. FARID. Yes.

Mr. GONZALEZ [continuing]. OK, but there also, like, big bright lines. Child pornography, let's get that off our platforms.

Dr. FARID. Yes, I agree. And feels to me like, if you share child pornography, you have lost the right to privacy. I don't think you have a right to privacy anymore once you've done that, I should have access to your account. So I think there's a little bit of a false narrative coming out here, but I still want to recognize that there are some sensitivities, particularly with the international standards. The Germans have very specific rules——

Mr. GONZALEZ. Yes.

Dr. FARID [continuing]. The Brits, the EU, et cetera.

Mr. GONZALEZ. So the last question, and this is maybe a bit of an oddball, so with the HN site that was ultimately brought down, I believe Cloudflare was their host, is that——

Dr. FARID. Yes.

Mr. GONZALEZ. So we talk a lot about the platforms themselves, right, but we don't always talk about the underlying infrastructure——

Dr. FARID. Yes.

Mr. GONZALEZ [continuing]. And maybe what responsibilities they have.

Dr. FARID. Yes.

Mr. GONZALEZ. Any thoughts on that? Should we be looking there as well?

Dr. FARID. You should. And it is complicated, because——

Mr. GONZALEZ. Yes.

Dr. FARID [continuing]. When you go to a Cloudflare—as the CEO came out and said, I woke up 1 day, and I thought, I don't like these guys, and I'm going to kick them off my platform. That is dangerous.

Mr. GONZALEZ. That's very——

Dr. FARID. Yes. But Ms. Francois said it very well. Clear rules, enforce the rules, transparency. We have to have due process. So define the rules, enforce them consistently, and tell me what you're doing. I can fix this problem for the CEO of Cloudflare. Just tell me what the rules are. So—but I don't think they get a bye just because they're the underlying hardware of the Internet. I think they should be held to exactly the same standards, and they should be held to exactly the same standards of defining, enforcing, and transparency.

And, by the way, I'll also add that cloud services are going to be extremely difficult. So, for example, we've made progress with YouTube on eliminating terror content, but now they're just moving to Google Drive, and Google is saying, well, Google Drive is a cloud service, so it's outside of this platform. So I do think we have to start looking at those core infrastructures.

Mr. GONZALEZ. OK. I appreciate your perspective. Frankly, I don't know what I net out on it, I just know it's something that I think we should be looking at——

Dr. FARID. I agree.

Mr. GONZALEZ [continuing]. And weighing, so thank you.

Mr. BEYER. Thank you. Dr. Lyu, you know, Ms. Francois just talked about a level playing field, you know, that, the bad guys have a lot more tools and resources than the good guys.

Dr. LYU. Right.

Mr. BEYER. We talked a lot about the perils of deep fakes, but are there any constructive applications?

Dr. LYU. Actually——

Mr. BEYER [continuing]. Where we want to use deep fakes in a good way?

Dr. LYU. Yes, indeed. Actually, the technology behind deep fake, as I mentioned in my opening remark, is of dual use. So there's a beneficial side of using this technology. For instance, the movie industry can use that, reduce their costs. There are also ways to actually make sure a message can be broadcast to multilinguistic groups without, you know, regenerating the media in different languages. It is also possible to use this technology to protect privacy. For instance, for people like whistleblowers, or, you know, victims in violent crime. If they don't want to expose their identity, it's possible to use this technology, replacing the face, but leaving the facial expression intact there.

The negative effect of deep fake, this kind of technology, you get a lot of spotlight, but there's also this dual use that we should also be aware of. Thank you very much.

Mr. BEYER. Thank you. Ms. Francois, are there any good bots?

Ms. FRANCOIS. Yes. They're really fun. One of them systematically tweets out every edit to Wikipedia that is made from the Congress Internet infrastructure. In general what I'm trying to say is there are good bots. Some of them are fun and creative, and I think they do serve the public interest. I do not think that there are good reasons to use an army of bots in order to do coordinated amplification of content. I think when you are trying to manipulate the behavior to make it look like a broader number of people are in support of your content than actually is the case, I do not see any particularly good use of that.

Mr. BEYER. I want to send you one of my daughter's bots. She has a perfectly normal Twitter account, and then she has the Twitter bot account, where she leverages off of her linguistics background, and I cannot make heads nor tails of what it does. But perhaps——

Ms. FRANCOIS [continuing]. Can look at it.

Mr. BEYER [continuing]. You can. Yes, it's——

Ms. FRANCOIS. OK.

Mr. BEYER. She says it's OK. Dr. Farid, you talked—it would be a mistake for the tech giants to transform their system from end-to-end encrypted systems that would make the problem only worse. Can you walk us through that?

Dr. FARID. Sure, and I'm glad you asked the question. So let's talk about what end-to-end encryption is. So the idea is I type a message on my phone, it gets encrypted, and sent over the wire. Even if it's a Facebook service, Facebook cannot read the message. Under a lawful warrant, you cannot read the message. Nobody can read the message until the receiver receives it, and then they decrypt. So that's called an end-to-end encryption. Everything in the middle is completely invisible. WhatsApp, for example, owned by Facebook, is end-to-end encrypted, and it is why, by the way, WhatsApp has been implicated in horrific violence in Sri Lanka, in the Philippines, in Myanmar, in India. It has been linked with election tampering in Brazil, in India, and other parts of the world, because nobody knows what's going on on the platform.

So last year, you heard me say, 18 million reports to the National Center for Child Sexual Abuse Material, more than half of those came from Facebook Messenger, currently unencrypted. If they encrypt, guess what happens? Ten million images of child sexual abuse material, I can no longer see. This is a false pitting of privacy over security, and it's completely unnecessary. We can run PhotoDNA, the technology that I described earlier, on the client so that, when you type the message and attach an image, we can extract that signature. That signature is privacy preserving, so even if I hand it to you, you won't be able to reconstruct the image, and I can send that hash, that signature, along with the encrypted message, over wire, pull the hash off, compare it to a database, and then stop the transmission.

And I will mention, by the way, when Facebook tells you that this is all about privacy, is that on WhatsApp, their service, if somebody sends you a link, and that link is malware, it's dangerous to you, it will be highlighted in the message. How are they doing that? They are reading your message. Why? For security purposes. Can we please agree that protecting you from malware is at least as important as protecting 4-year-olds and 6-year-olds and 8- year-olds from physical sexual abuse?

We have the technology to do this, and the rush to end-to-end encryption, which, by the way, I think is a head fake. They're using Cambridge Analytica to give them plausible deniability on all the other issues that we have been trying to get them—progress on, from child sexual abuse, to terrorism, to conspiracies, to disinformation. If they end-to-end encrypt, we will lose the ability to know what's going on on their platforms, and you have heard very eloquently from my colleague that this will be a disaster. You should not let them do this without putting the right safeguards in place.

Mr. BEYER. So you were just making a powerful argument now for national and international level banning end-to-end encryption?

Dr. FARID. I wouldn't go that far. We want end-to-end encryption for banking, for finance. There are places where it is the right thing to do, but there are other places where we have to simply think about the balance. So, for example, in my solution I didn't say don't do end-to-end encryption. I said put the safeguards in place so that if somebody's transmitting harmful content, I can know about it.

I have mixed feelings about the end-to-end encryption, but I think, if you want to do it, and we should think seriously about that, you can still put the safeguards in place.

Mr. BEYER. And blockchain is not end-to-end encryption?

Dr. FARID. No, it is not.

Mr. BEYER. But it gets close?

Dr. FARID. These are sort of somewhat orthogonal separate issues, right? What we are talking about is a controlled platform saying that—everything that comes through us, we will no longer be able to see. That is super convenient for the Facebooks of the world, who don't want to be held accountable for the horrible things happening on their platforms, and I think that's the core issue here.

Mr. BEYER. Great, thanks. Anything else? All right. I think Mr. Gonzalez and I are done and thank you very much. It's a very, very interesting mission, and don't be discouraged that there weren't more Members here, because everyone's in their office watching this, and have their own questions. So thank you very much for being here, and thanks for your witness stuff. And the record will remain open for 2 weeks for additional statements from the Members, and, additionally, we may have questions of you to answer in writing. So thank you very much.

Dr. FARID. OK.

Mr. BEYER. You're excused, and the hearing is adjourned.

Dr. FARID. Thank you.

[Whereupon, at 3:26 p.m., the Subcommittee was adjourned.]

Appendix: Additional Material for the Record

Actors, Behaviors, Content: A Disinformation ABC Highlighting Three Vectors of Viral Deception to Guide Industry & Regulatory Responses*

Camille François
Graphika and Berkman Klein Center for Internet & Society at Harvard University[60]
September 20, 2019

Introduction

As the historic phenomenon of propaganda[61] unfolds today in a variety of social-media manifestations, a plethora of terms has emerged to describe its different forms and their implications for society: "fake news," online disinformation, online misinformation, viral deception, etc.[62] The speed and scale at which disinformation is now able to spread online has led to mounting pressure on regulators around the globe to address the phenomenon, yet its multifaceted nature makes it a difficult problem to regulate. Effective remedies must take into account the different vectors of contemporary disinformation and consider the multiplicity of stakeholders, tradeoffs in

---

* One in a series: *A working paper of the Transatlantic High Level Working Group on Content Moderation Online and Freedom of Expression*. Read about the TWG: https://www.ivir.nl/twg/.

[60] Camille François works on cyber conflict and digital rights online. She is Chief Innovation Officer of Graphika, where she leads the company's work to detect and mitigate disinformation, media manipulation and harassment in partnership with major technology platforms, human rights groups and universities around the world. She also is an affiliate of Harvard University's Berkman Klein Center for Internet & Society. An earlier version of this paper was presented as thesecond meeting of the Transatlantic Working Group on Content Moderation Online and Freedom of Expression, in Santa Monica, Calif., on May 9-12, 2019. The author thanks her colleagues in the working group for their engagement with this work during the sessions. Their feedback and encouragement greatly benefited this final paper.

[61] See for instance: Tworek, Heidi JS. *News from Germany: The Competition to Control World Communications, 1900– 1945*. Harvard University Press, 2019.

[62] For a thoughtful typology of the different aspects of the phenomenon, see for instance Claire Wardle and Hossein Derakhshan's "Information Disorder" framework: https://rm.coe.int/information-disorder-toward-an-interdisciplinary-framework-for-researc/168076277c.

different approaches, disciplines, and regulatory bodies able to meaningfully contribute to responses.

Major technology platforms have invested in better responses to disinformation, notably by adapting their community guidelines or terms of service. Observed through the lens of platform enforcement, "disinformation" breaks down into a number of different violations manifest on different products which are enforced by distinct teams. This points to a key concern with regard to the current industry responses to viral deception: while disinformation actors exploit the whole information ecosystem in campaigns that leverage different products and platforms, technology companies' responses are mostly siloed within individual platforms (if not siloed by individual products!).

This concise "ABC" framework doesn't aim to propose one definition or framework to rule them all, but rather seeks to lay out three key vectors characteristic of viral deception[63] in order to guide regulatory and industry remedies. Manipulative actors, deceptive behaviors, harmful content: each vector presents different characteristics, difficulties, and implications. Unfortunately, they are also often intertwined in disinformation campaigns, suggesting that effective and long-term approaches will need to address these different vectors with appropriate remedies.

This "ABC" also seeks to reconcile approaches throughout applicable disciplines (e.g., cybersecurity, consumer protection, content moderation) and stakeholders. While the public debate in the U.S. has been largely concerned with actors (who is a Russian troll online?), the technology industry has invested in better regulating behavior (which accounts engage in coordinated and inauthentic behavior?) while governments have been most preoccupied with content (what is acceptable to post on social media?).

"A" is for Manipulative Actors

> *"On the Internet, nobody knows you're a ~~dog~~ Russian military operative."*[64]

[63] Viral deception here is used as an umbrella term for the multiple facets of contemporary disinformation online, see Jamieson, Kathleen Hall. *Cyberwar: How Russian Hackers and Trolls Helped Elect a President What We Don't, Can't, and Do Know*. Oxford University Press, 2018.

[64] I hope readers will forgive this 2019 edit to the famous cartoon published by Peter Steiner in the *New Yorker* on July 1993.

The Russian disinformation campaign targeting the U.S. 2016 presidential election[65] has brought to the public's attention how keen certain government actors were to leverage social media to manipulate and influence audiences at home and abroad by engaging in information operations. It has also painfully brought to light the lack of government and industry preparedness and proactivity in the face of these threats. The cybersecurity sector, which bears the brunt of detecting these threat actors and preventing their nefarious activities, had been most focused on protecting physical networks and not enough on detecting those actors on social media networks. Facebook's April 2017 white paper on the issue of information operations (which also marks the first in-depth acknowledgement of this problem by a large technology platform) makes this point clearly and acknowledges that the Facebook cybersecurity team had to expand its scope to appropriately respond to this threat: "We have had to expand our security focus from traditional abusive behavior, such as account hacking, malware, spam and financial scams, to include more subtle and insidious forms of misuse, including attempts to manipulate civic discourse and deceive people."[66]

Manipulative actors, by definition, engage knowingly and with clear intent in viral deception campaigns. Their campaigns are covert, designed to obfuscate the identity and intent of the actor orchestrating them. Throughout the technology industry, detection and enforcement of this vector of viral deception campaigns rely on the cat-and-mouse game of a) identifying threat actors willing and able to covertly manipulate public discourse and b) keeping those actors from leveraging social media to do so,[67] as they refine their strategies to evade detection.

Because this detection practice has its roots in the cybersecurity realm, terms of service and community guidelines do not always address these issues, or provide a clear basis to support detection and enforcement efforts against manipulative actors. Precedents in this area include platform rules laying out specific actors who are prevented from using the services (e.g., Foreign

[65] See the Mueller Report: https://www.justice.gov/storage/report.pdf.

[66] Jen Weedon, William Nuland and Alex Stamos, "Information Operations and Facebook", v.1: https://fbnewsroomus.files.wordpress.com/2017/04/facebook-and-information-operations-v1.pdf.

[67] For an example of a takedown solely motivated by the actor behind the content, see Facebook's "The IRA Has NoPlace on Facebook" post on April 3, 2018: "We removed this latest set of Pages and accounts solely because they were controlled by the IRA — not based on the content." https://newsroom.fb.com/news/2018/04/authenticity-matters/.

Terrorist Organizations[68]), but it is worth noting that no major platform to date has included language in its terms of service explicitly prohibiting governments from covertly using its services to conduct influence campaigns.[69] Setting an industry precedent, in August 2019, following investigations disclosing that Chinese State- controlled media leveraged Twitter advertising to promote content critical of pro-democracy protests in Hong Kong, Twitter announced that it would no longer allow "State-controlled media" to use its advertising products.[70] The state-controlled media entities can continue to remain "organic users" (meaning normal and/or verified accounts on the Twitter platform), but their ability to use ads to reach users who are not already following them is now restricted. In doing so, Twitter will likely face difficulty determining which entities are "taxpayer funded entities" and "independent public broadcasters" allowed to use the advertising services vs. "state-controlled media (...) financially or editorially controlled by the state" prohibited from doing so. States have also used a variety of techniques to conceal their direct involvement in seemingly independent online media properties: the Kremlin-controlled Baltnews network71 and the Iranian-controlled IUVM72 network are good illustrations.

Note that this problem has little to do with "banning" anonymity or pseudonymity online: both serve important purposes in protecting vulnerable

---

[68] See for instance Microsoft's "*Approach to Terrorist Content*" statement (published May 20, 2016), which notes that "there is no universally accepted definition of terrorist content" and that Microsoft relies on organizations listed in the Consolidated United Nations Security Council Sanctions List to define and take action against terrorist content posted on its platforms: https://blogs.microsoft.com/on-the-issues/2016/05/20/microsofts-approach-terrorist-content- online/.

[69] There are, however, multiple policies that indirectly cover aspects of these campaigns. An example with Google Ads' "Misrepresentation Policy": https://support.google.com/ ads policy/answer/6020955?hl=en.

[70] In 2017, Twitter had similarly banned Russian State-controlled media Russia Today and Sputnik from using their advertising products (https://blog.twitter.com/en_us/topics/company/2017/Announcement-RT-and-Sputnik- Advertising.html). The August 2019 policy extends this ad-hoc remediation done in the wake of the investigation regarding the Kremlin's election interference efforts on social media to all of "state-controlled" media: https://blog.twitter.com/en_us/topics/company/2019/advertising_policies_on_state_media .html.

[71] See the Aug. 29, 2019 BuzzFeed investigation, "This Is How Russian Propaganda Actually Works in the 21st Century": https://www.buzzfeednews.com/article/holgerroonemaa/russia-propaganda-baltics-baltnews.

[72] See for instance DFRLab's "In Depth: Iranian Propaganda Network Goes Down," March 26, 2019, https://medium.com/dfrlab/takedown-details-of-the-iranian-propaganda-network-d1fad32fdf30.

voices and enabling them to participate in critical conversations.[73] Banning anonymity/pseudonymity would prevent such participation while doing little to prevent sophisticated and well-funded actors from exploiting this vector. The deceptive actors we are concerned with here are well-funded military and intelligence apparatus or campaign apparatus, not "somebody sitting on their bed that weighs 400 pounds," as President Trump famously characterized the anonymous troll. Clint Watts describes these figures as "Advanced Persistent Manipulators,"[74] a moniker that stresses the parallels and overlaps between the actors engaged in information operations[75] and hacking:[76]

> Similar to the challenge APT[77] actors have posed to information and cyber security professionals, social media companies now face malign actors that can be labeled as Advanced Persistent Manipulators (APMs) on their platforms. These APMs pursue their targets and seek their objectives persistently and will not be stopped by account shutdowns and platform timeouts. They have sufficient resources and talent to sustain their campaigns, and the most sophisticated and troublesome ones can create or acquire the most sophisticated technology.[78]

Since 2017, we have seen multiple examples of viral deception campaigns whose *primary* vector is a deceptive actor. Notable examples include false persona "Guccifer 2.0"[79] used by the GRU, falseidentities tying back to the

---

[73] For an examination of how manipulative actors use "pseudoanonymity" to "impersonate marginalized, underrepresented, and vulnerable groups to either malign, disrupt or exaggerate their cause," see Friedberg and Donovan's piece in the MIT JODS: https:// .mitpress.mit.edu/pub/2gnso48a.

[74] Clint Watts, "Advanced Persistent Manipulators", Feb. 12, 2019: https://securingdemocracy.gmfus.org/advanced-persistent-manipulators-part-one-the-threat-to-the-social-media-industry/.

[75] For a global inventory of actors organized for social media manipulation, see: Bradshaw, Samantha, and Philip Howard. "Troops, trolls and troublemakers: A global inventory of organized social media manipulation." (2017).

[76] See also "False Leaks: A Look at Recent Information Operations Designed To Disseminate Hacked Material," Camille Francois, *CYBERWARCON* 2018. Video: https://www.youtube.com/watch?v=P8iXN8j4gMk.

[77] APT here refers to Advanced Persistent Threat, a term commonly used in the threat intelligence industry to describe State-sponsored and state-affiliated groups engaged in hacking operations. See: https://en.wikipedia.org/wiki/Advanced_persistent_threat.

[78] Clint Watts, "Advanced Persistent Manipulators," Feb. 12, 2019: https://securingdemocracy.gmfus.org/advanced-persistent-manipulators-part-one-the-threat-to-the-social-media-industry/.

[79] Guccifer is a social media persona who claimed to be the hacker who hacked the Democratic National Committee in 2016, and who used this deceptive identity to engage WikiLeaks

Islamic Republic of Iran Broadcasting and operating on multiple platforms,[80] and Facebook's December 2018 takedown of accounts in Bangladesh that were found to be misrepresenting their true identity and attempting to mislead voters ahead of the elections.[81]

Governments also have a role to play in detecting and mitigating harms caused by manipulative actors online, although defining the contours of government action in this space remains a largely unexplored policy question. Around the U.S. 2018 midterms elections, for instance, the U.S. government led actions to detect and share relevant information on manipulative actors with the technology sector[82] and to disrupt and deter these actors from engaging in information operations.[83]

"B" is for Deceptive Behavior

"On the Internet, nobody knows you're a ~~dog~~ bot army."

Deceptive behavior is a fundamental vector of disinformation campaigns: it encompasses the variety of techniques viral deception actors may use to enhance and exaggerate the reach, virality and impact of their campaigns. Those techniques run from automated tools (e.g., bot armies used to amplify the reach and effect of a message) to manual trickery (e.g., paid engagement, troll farms). At the end of the day, deceptive behaviors have a clear goal: to

---

and the media. The account was in reality operated by Russian military intelligence: https://en.wikipedia.org/wiki/Guccifer_2.0.

80 See for instance Google's Kent Walker update on action taken against IRIB and broader State-Sponsored activity on Google's products: https://blog.google/technology/safety-security/update-state-sponsored-activity/.

81 https://newsroom.fb.com/news/2018/12/take-down-in-bangladesh/.

82 See for instance reporting by the Associated Press, "Facebook blocks 115 accounts ahead of US midterm elections", Nov. 6, 2018, https://www.apnews.com/19aabf8ba7b6466b859f4d0afd9e59be. The AP reports: "Facebook acted after being tipped off Sunday by U.S. law enforcement officials. Authorities notified the company about recently discovered online activity "they believe may be linked to foreign entities."

83 See Ellen Nakashima's reporting in the Washington Post, "U.S. Cyber Command operation disrupted Internet access of Russian troll factory on day of 2018 midterms", Feb, 26, 2019, https://www.washingtonpost.com/world/national-security/us-cyber-command-operation-disrupted-internet-access-of-russian-troll-factory-on-day-of-2018-midterms/2019/02/26/1827fc9e-36d6-11e9-af5b-b51b7ff322e9_story.html.

enable a small number of actors to have the *perceived impact* that a greater number of actors would have if the campaign were organic.[84]

Interestingly, while there are significant differences in the various disinformation definitions and terms of service applicable to the issue among technology companies, the focus on *deceptive behavior* appears to be a clear convergence point throughout the technology industry.

Google's definition of disinformation, as laid out in its February 2019 White Paper on "How Google Fights Disinformation," points to those deceptive behaviors as a core vector of how disinformation affects Google's platforms:

> We refer to [...] deliberate efforts to deceive and mislead using the speed, scale, andtechnologies of the open web as "disinformation.[85]

In Facebook's case, deceptive behavior is mostly defined through the "Coordinated Inauthentic Behavior"[86] policy, which has led to numerous takedowns since it was implemented in 2018.[87] While Facebook has shared records and data points regarding the content and accounts taken down for their participation in "coordinated and inauthentic behavior," enforcement in this realm remains opaque throughout the major technology companies.

While the detection and mitigation techniques in this area can be similar to spam detection, an area generally opaque for the public and regulators and not subject to much public scrutiny, the free speech implications of taking down content and social media accounts (especially political content during election cycles) justify much higher scrutiny of these practices. Relevant questions to technology platforms in this area include:

- Applicable rules: Which are the applicable policies set forth by the platform to address deceptive behaviors on their products?
- Enforcement: What enforcement options are available to the platforms to take action against accounts and content that violate the

[84] I am borrowing here from a definition my colleagues and I have used to frame detection techniques. See Francois, Barash, Kelly: https://osf.io/aj9yz/.

[85] "How Google Fights Disinformation," Feb. 2019, available at: https://storage.googleapis.com/gweb-uniblog-publish-prod/documents/How_Google_Fights_Disinfor mation.pdf.

[86] See "Coordinated Inauthentic Behavior Explained," https://newsroom.fb.com/news/2018/12/inside-feed-coordinated-inauthentic-behavior/.

[87] A blog post entitled "Removing Bad Actors on Facebook", from July 2018, seems to be the first public reference to "coordinated and inauthentic behavior": https://newsroom.fb.com/news/2018/07/removing-bad-actors-on-facebook/.

rules on deceptive behavior? Platforms generally acknowledge a range of options from content demotion to account suspension, although those enforcement options are rarely spelled out for users or made clear for users affected.

- Detection and prioritization: Which teams are effectively in charge of detecting deceptive behaviors, how much of this detection relies on machine learning classifiers (and which ones?), and how does prioritization of potential issues and focus areas work at the platform level?
- Transparency: How will affected users (including good faith actors mistakenly engaging in deceptive behaviors, consumers of information spread by deceptive behavior, bad faith actors seeking to best understand what telltale signs trigger enforcement, etc.) be notified when action is taken against content or accounts? Can those decisions be appealed, and if so, how? Will the platform share transparency metrics regarding its enforcement of rules relative to distortive behavior, both at the annual and the aggregate level (through the existing mechanism of Transparency Reports) and through press releases published when enforcement happens?
- Product vulnerabilities and changes: When deceptive behaviors exploit vulnerabilities in platforms and products, what changes are made to address them?[88]

The industry's lack of proactivity in tackling some of these campaigns and growing public anxiety about disinformation have led regulators to craft frameworks to specifically address deceptive behavior. California's "Bot Law," for instance, is a clear attempt to regulate deceptive behavior onsocial media:

> It shall be unlawful for any person to use a bot to communicate or interact with another person in California online, with the intent to mislead the other person about its artificial identity for the purpose of knowingly deceiving the person about the content of the communication in order to incentivize a purchase or sale of goods or services in a commercial

[88] An example of a product change directly motivated by a platform's need to tackle distortive behaviors on its products can be found in the January 2019 YouTube announcement: "'To that end, we'll begin reducing recommendations of borderline content and content that could misinform users in harmful ways": https://youtube.googleblog.com/2019/01/continuing-our-work-to-improve.html.

> transaction or to influence a vote in an election. A person using a bot shall not be liable under this section if the person discloses that it is a bot. The disclosure required by this section shall be clear, conspicuous, and reasonably designed to inform persons with whom the bot communicates or interacts that it is a bot.[89]

The "Manipulative Actor" and "Deceptive Behavior" vectors are particularly challenging to address through effective regulatory frameworks because of the dramatic asymmetry of information between the platforms targeted by these campaigns and the rest of the world. While open-source investigation techniques and a few available tools allow others to scrutinize online activity for campaigns run by a manipulative actor or using deceptive techniques, it is undeniable that platforms have much more visibility into those issues than external researchers and stakeholders. Some platforms' community standards or terms of service either indirectly prevent the type of external research that may lead to detecting and exposing distortive behaviors (e.g., when existing and important safeguards also prevent researchers from collecting the data they'd need to analyze distortive behaviors) or directly seek to prevent it (e.g., with rules explicitly preventing the use of data in order to perform detection of deceptive behavior).

Finally, some of the platforms' own systems may actually enhance those deceptive behaviors by disinformation actors: algorithmic reinforcement is a core concern in this area.[90] While anecdotal evidence suggests machine learning based recommendations systems may easily be gamed into promoting campaigns "boosted" by adversarial distortive behavior, the difficulties discussed above with regard to external research have prevented more systematic examinations of these issues throughout the various platforms.

"C" is for Harmful Content

"On the Internet, nobody knows you're a ~~dog~~ deepfake."

Finally, it is sometimes the case that the content of posts and messages justifies classifying a campaign as an instance of viral deception. Content is the most

[89] https://leginfo.legislature.ca.gov/faces/billTextClient.xhtml?bill_id=201720180SB1001.

[90] See for instance former YouTube engineer Guillaume Chaslot's project regarding algorithmic reinforcement of fringe and harmful views on YouTube: https://algotransparency.org/methodology.html.

visible vector of the three: while it is difficult for an observer to attribute messages to a manipulative actor or to observe behavioral patterns across a campaign, every user can see and form an opinion on the content of social media posts. This is likely why regulators have focused on content aspects when regulating disinformation.

This vector calls for detection and enforcement strategies in the realm of content moderation.[91] Unfortunately, regulatory and legal frameworks often struggle to properly define categories of "harmful content" they seek to regulate (see ongoing debates about the definitions of "violent extremism," "hate speech," "terrorist content," etc.) or to properly take into account that a lot of the speech they consider to be "harmful" is protected under human rights law. Governments' appetite to regulate viral deception through the content lens risk further eroding protections to freedom of expression online.

The intersection of harmful content and disinformation campaigns can manifest in several ways:

- Entire categories of content can be deemed "harmful" because they belong to the realm of viral deception, e.g., health misinformation.[92]

Technology platforms have so far mostly proposed to address the categories of content deemed most "harmful" for their disinformation nature by adding context for users alongside the content, such as "flags" or "fact-checking" content. Some platforms though have taken a more radical route by banning entire categories of disinformation content from their services.

Photo-sharing platform Pinterest, for instance, takes action against harmful medical information shared on its platform. Its "Health Misinformation" policy reads:

> Pinterest's misinformation policy prohibits things like promotion of false cures for terminal or chronic illnesses and anti-vaccination advice. Because

[91] For an in-depth discussion of the various issues plaguing the content moderation industry, see Roberts, Sarah T. *Behind the Screen: Content Moderation in the Shadows of Social Media*. Yale University Press, 2019. or Gillespie, Tarleton. *Custodians of the Internet: Platforms, content moderation, and the hidden decisions that shape social media*. Yale University Press, 2018.

[92] This is a good place for a quick reminder of the differences between misinformation and disinformation. Dictionary.com, which made "misinformation" the word of the year in 2018, defines it as "false information that is spread, regardless of whether there is intent to mislead." It describes disinformation as "deliberately misleading or biased information; manipulated narrative or facts; propaganda".

of this, you're not allowed to save content that includes advice where there may be immediate and detrimental effects on a Pinner's health or on public safety.[93]

- The content of a campaign itself (not its diffusion mechanism) can be manipulated to deceive users and therefore belong to the realm of "disinformation" (e.g., use of manipulated media on the range from "deepfakes" to "cheap fakes"[94]).
- "Harmful content" can be promoted by deceptive actors or by campaigns leveraging distortive behaviors (e.g., "troll farms amplifying harassment campaigns").

It should indeed be noted that viral deception campaigns whose primary vector is a deceptive actor or distortive behavior can participate in amplifying other types of harmful content categories, such as hate speech, harassment, and violent extremism.

Conclusion and Recommendations

Viral deception campaigns spread across platforms and through three core vectors: manipulative actors (A), deceptive behavior (B) and harmful content (C). As such, they represent a complex and multifaceted problem for policy makers and regulators to address. This "ABC" framework therefore offers a few modest recommendations for policy makers and regulators navigating this maze:

- Each dimension matters. Regulatory efforts focused on viral deception tend to exaggerate the role of harmful content: balanced approaches will consider how manipulative actors (both foreign and domestic) and deceptive behaviors contribute to the problem.
- Each dimension comes with its own set of challenges, tradeoffs, and policy implications. Specific disciplines may be necessary and/or best suited to address each of them. For instance, cybersecurity (and threat intelligence in particular) is a core component of how manipulative

---

[93] https://help.pinterest.com/en/article/health-misinformation.

[94] See Britt Paris and Joan Donovan, "Deep Fakes and Cheap Fakes", published Sept. 18th 2019 by the Data & Society Research Institute, https://datasociety.net/output/deepfakes-and-cheap-fakes/.

actors get detected; how the resulting signals get shared across the industry and with the relevant parties (researchers, public institutions) is a key policy question. Consumer protection frameworks (and stakeholders) may be ideally situated to help regulate deceptive behavior issues. Policies and regulatory frameworks that center around one type of remedy only (such as content takedowns) are insufficient.

- On a final (and related) note, Manipulative Actors (A) and Deceptive Behaviors (B) are dimensions on which the information asymmetry between the technology platforms on which this activity unfolds and the rest of the stakeholders in the debate is immense. How to ensure that the public, media, and policy stakeholders are able to meaningfully analyze both the issues and potential impacts of remedies in place is a fundamental question in this space.

Appendix: Examples of Disinformation Campaigns Spanning the Three Vectors

- A Disinformation Campaign in the Philippines (Facebook)

On March 28, 2019, Facebook removed 200 pages, groups and accounts engaged in "coordinated inauthentic behavior" on Facebook and Instagram in the Philippines. Facebook's press release[95] highlights the manipulative actor along with the deceptive behavior elements of the campaign [next page]:

> We're taking down these Pages and accounts based on their behavior, not the content they posted. In this case, the people behind this activity coordinated with one another and used fake accounts to misrepresent themselves, and that was the basis for our action.

Follow-up analysis highlights that the content taken down by Facebook in this campaign did contain "harmful content," notably in the form of hate speech and manipulated media (Photoshopped images of politicians in wheelchairs enticing viewers to question the health of candidates).[96]

---

[95] https://newsroom.fb.com/news/2019/03/cib-from-the-philippines/.

[96] https://medium.com/graphika-team/archives-facebook-finds-coordinated-and-inauthentic-behavior-in-the-philippines-suspends-a-set-d02f41f527df.

- The Russian Internet Research Agency's "Columbia Chemical" Campaign (Twitter)

On September 11, 2014, a set of seemingly uncoordinated Twitter accounts engaged in disseminating news of a chemical incident and toxic fumes in the city of St. Mary Parish in Louisiana. Along with the social media campaign, videos of the "incident" were uploaded and officials and media were contacted by available channels with an alarming messaging – "Take shelter!" – and links to a dedicated website.[97]

It wasn't long until officials realized that the campaign, with its false images of the incident and alarming messages, constituted harmful content – "a hoax," as it was initially described. It was later made clear that the accounts used to spread the content were coordinated to give the impression of a mounting local panic, using distortive behavior to create the illusion of a spontaneous wave of local panic.

It took a few more years for the major technology platforms and the U.S. Government to provide a final attribution on those accounts, confirming that the Internet Research Agency troll farm in Saint Petersburg was indeed the actor operating the accounts.[98]

---

[97] www.columbiachemical.com. Adrian Chen's 2015 account in The New York Times Magazine is the first public account of this campaign: https://www.nytimes.com/2015/06/07/magazine/the-agency.html.

[98] See for instance the reports commissioned by the Senate Select Intelligence Committee regarding the IRA's online activity targeting the USA: https://comprop.oii.ox.ac.uk/research/ira-political-polarization/.

Index

D

E

I

J

L

M

R

S

U

V

W

Y